Studies in Rhetorics and Feminisms

Series Editors, Cheryl Glenn and Shirley Wilson Logan

Claiming the Bicycle

Women, Rhetoric, and Technology in Nineteenth-Century America

Sarah Hallenbeck

Southern Illinois University Press
Carbondale

Portions of chapter 4 were previously published as Sarah Hallenbeck, "Riding Out of Bounds: Women Bicyclists' Embodied Medical Authority in the Nineteenth-Century Popular Magazine," *Rhetoric Review* 29.4 (2011): 327–45. Reprinted by permission of Taylor and Francis LLC (http://www.tandfonline.com).

Portions of chapter 4 and the conclusion were previously published as Sarah Hallenbeck, "User Agency, Technical Communication, and the Nineteenth-Century Woman Bicyclist," *Technical Communication Quarterly* 21.4 (2012): 290–306.

Printed in the United States of America

19 18 17 16 4 3 2 1

Cover illustration: © Mystic Seaport, Newberry Coll., #1980.41.870

Library of Congress Cataloging-in-Publication Data

Hallenbeck, Sarah, author.

Claiming the bicycle : women, rhetoric, and technology in nineteenth-century America / Sarah Hallenbeck.

pages cm. — (Studies in rhetorics and feminisms)

Summary: "'Claiming the Bicycle' considers how American women encouraged one another to adopt a new technology—the bicycle—adapt it to their own purposes, and use it to transform cultural assumptions about femininity and gender difference." — Provided by publisher.

Includes bibliographical references and index.

ISBN 978-0-8093-3444-5 (paperback)

ISBN 978-0-8093-3445-2 (e-book)

1. Cycling for women—United States—History—19th century. 2. Feminism—United States—History—19th century. 3. Cycling—Social aspects—United States—History—19th century. 4. Rhetoric—Social aspects—United States—History—19th century. I. Title.

GV1057.H35 2016

796.6082—dc23 2015020845

Printed on recycled paper. ♲

The paper used in this publication meets the minimum requirements of American National Standard for Information Sciences—Permanence of Paper for Printed Library Materials, ANSI Z39.48-1992. ∞

To my mother, Rosemary Hallenbeck

Contents

List of Illustrations ix

Preface
Considering Women, Rhetoric, and Technology xi

Acknowledgments xxvii

Introduction
Regendering of the Bicycle during the 1880s 1

Chapter One
Women Riders and the Invention of the Modern Bicycle 33

Chapter Two
Popular Magazines and the Rise of the "Bicycle Girl" 68

Chapter Three
Women's Written Instructions for Change 101

Chapter Four
Women Bicyclists' Embodied Medical Authority 132

Conclusion
Toward a Technofeminist Rhetorical Agency 167

Notes 179

Works Cited 183

Index 197

Illustrations

Columbia bicycle advertisement, 1885 9

Columbia bicycle and tricycle advertisement, 1885 13

Damascus Ladies' Model D, 1897 25

Damascus Gentlemen's Model A, 1897 26

Damascus wooden handlebars, 1897 27

Margaret Hobbs Lawson's "bicycle garment," 1893 47

Eliza Voorhis's cycling skirt, 1897 49

Misses' cycling trousers, September 1895 51

Sager saddle advertisement, April 1896 55

Naly and Jones patent illustration, 1893 56

Mary Hicks's umbrella attachment, 1896 63

"The New Woman—Wash Day" 71

Will Bradley's Overman Wheel Company advertising poster 76

Victor-Victoria Overman Wheel Company advertisement, April 1896 77

Woman positioning a bicycle for maintenance 125

Margaret Gast's racing card 161

Preface

Considering Women, Rhetoric, and Technology

On a hot June day in 1894, a crowd numbering in the hundreds gathered in downtown Boston to witness the start of a remarkable journey: a solo round-the-world bicycle trip, to be undertaken by the unlikeliest of adventurers. Annie Kopchovsky was a young immigrant, a Jewish wife and mother of three, who had attempted bicycling just three times before she rode her forty-three-pound machine out of the city that day. Yet she offered a compelling explanation for her decision to leave Boston: she claimed that she was undertaking her journey in response to a wager between two wealthy gentlemen about whether any woman living could circumnavigate the world aboard a bicycle. According to Kopchovsky, the gentlemen agreed that in addition to riding successfully around the world, the rider would need to earn $5,000 above her traveling expenses in order to claim a $10,000 reward for her efforts ("New Woman on a Tour"). For this reason, Kopchovsky began selling advertising space on her body soon after she embarked from Boston; the Londonderry Lithia Spring Water Company in Londonderry, New Hampshire, even gave her $100 to change her name. Annie "Londonderry," as she quickly became known, also financed her travels by giving riding demonstrations, speaking publicly in small towns across the American West, and authoring and selling a booklet entitled *The New Woman on Tour*. After many fits and starts, she completed her journey in fifteen months and returned home to live out her years with her family.

Remarkably, there is no record of the wager Londonderry described or evidence that she actually collected any money after her feat. As a result, journalist Peter Zheutlin has speculated that she manufactured the backstory as a justification for her adventure away from home—a way to make a statement and to escape the drudgery of family life while gaining publicity and profit (8). In an article published in the *New York World* upon her return, Londonderry described herself as a journalist and dubbed herself "Nellie

Bly Junior," after the most famous "girl stunt-reporter" of the day (qtd. in Zheutlin 165).[1] Londonderry's desire to gain recognition by offering the world the story of her adventures may have motivated her decision to undertake her round-the-world bicycle trip.

If this is the case, Londonderry's framing of the trip specifically as a *bicycle* journey—with women's mental and physical abilities dramatically at stake, for the whole world to see—could scarcely have been better calculated to capture the attention of late nineteenth-century Americans.[2] Londonderry left Boston just at the start of what her contemporaries often described as a national "bicycle craze." Americans of nearly every walk of life celebrated the promise of the new Safety bicycle[3]—so named because of its short height relative to the precariously high-wheeled Ordinary of the previous decade—for riders' unprecedented health, recreation, and mobility. In western towns and especially in eastern cities, bicycle schools and rinks were opening their doors to riders of even middling means. By the time Londonderry returned home in 1895, bicycle factories were remaining open around the clock to meet consumer demands for Safeties (Hubert 696), and competing industries as diverse as suit makers and piano manufacturers were lamenting the impact on their own businesses of the bicycle's coming (Dodge 120). Among the most eager disciples of the popular new activity were women, whose efforts to participate remained especially controversial even though by 1896, one in every three bicycles sold was purchased by a woman (Dodge 42).[4] Within this context, Londonderry's bicycle journey served as a particularly powerful rhetorical act—a defiant enactment of feminine strength and independence, perfectly calculated to capture the interests of Americans already enamored with her machine of choice.

Importantly, the sudden popularity of bicycling among late nineteenth-century American women—and Londonderry's bicycle journey more specifically—coincided with the culmination of decades of public debate regarding the "Woman Question," an umbrella term used to refer to a wide array of smaller questions related to women's proper social role in a rapidly changing world. In Europe and North America alike, doctors, educators, writers, and other commentators weighed in on women's biological and intellectual capabilities, asking several questions: In what ways are women biologically suited to their role in the domestic sphere, and how ought their biology to guide their educational, recreational, and occupational choices? How might women's departure from the home affect their children, husbands, and communities?

How might it affect their health and fertility? Such questions shaped public opinion about issues ranging from women's suffrage to coeducation to marriage rights to women's physical activity. Whereas social conservatives tapped into long-standing anxieties about women's fragile health by worrying that women's departure from the domestic realm would render both their biological ruin and societal destruction, progressives pointed to the emergence of a modern feminine figure, the "New Woman," whose physical and intellectual vitality would be a boon to modern society. By titling her pamphlet *The New Woman on Tour*, Londonderry was linking herself explicitly to the Woman Question debate; by undertaking her journey aboard a bicycle—a technology that promoted both mobility away from home and family and potentially strenuous physical exercise—she was strengthening the links between this debate and the popular new machine.

Londonderry's story, which has recently been taken up enthusiastically by authors, artists, and filmmakers,[5] offers a particularly fascinating example of the ways in which late nineteenth-century women attended to the bicycle as a meaning-making object as well as a means of locomotion. Yet the young mother from Boston was scarcely alone in her efforts to enlist the new machine in embodying and promoting New Womanhood. Countless other women across the country also contributed to the sense that, as Susan B. Anthony famously put it in an 1896 interview, "the bicycle has done more for the emancipation of women than anything else in the world" (Bly 9). Whether riding on long tours or doing local errands, these women embodied new identities and arguments about women's potentiality, making visible a wider range of performances of femininity than had been available in the preceding decades. Notably, they also wrote prolifically about the bicycle, authoring texts ranging from short stories to instructional manuals to patent applications for accessories related to bicycling. In their writings, they often situated the new machine as an object directly engaged with the Woman Question and used it to construct and advance new narratives about women's lives, capacities, and interests. This book takes up these women's varied rhetorical activities, tracing their collective role in bringing about important changes to the gender order in turn-of-the-century America.

A central concern of *Claiming the Bicycle* involves demonstrating that women bicyclists like Londonderry not only *drew from* the bicycle in constructing new identities and arguments for and about themselves but also exerted, through their writing and inventions, influence over the material and social development of the new technology. The bicycle club members, short story and travel writers, inventors, technical writers of advice and instructions, doctors, medical commentators, and racing competitors I consider in this book represent the wide range of women who, through various forms of engagement with the "bicycle craze" of the 1890s, "regendered" the new machine, influencing its uptake by late nineteenth-century Americans and even guiding its development into the physical form and social meanings that we know today. Acting outside of official processes of design, marketing, and distribution, these rhetors nevertheless made their marks both on the material form of the Safety bicycle and on Americans' conceptions of who might ride, under what conditions, and for what specific purposes. Here I situate *Claiming the Bicycle* at the intersections of feminist rhetorical studies, rhetorical agency, and technical communication, demonstrating how the book contributes to ongoing conversations among scholars interested in these distinct but overlapping areas of study.

Scholarly Conversations

Feminist Rhetorical Historiography

Significantly, *Claiming the Bicycle* speaks to a rich and diverse community of feminist scholars in rhetorical historiography who have considered American women's rhetorical activities during the nineteenth century, when issues as varied as abolition and dress reform, together with increased literacy and an expanding print culture, enabled women to exercise their voices as perhaps never before. Scholars have done much to describe nineteenth-century women's individual and collective religious and activist activities (Karlyn Kohrs Campbell, Patricia Bizzell, Carol Mattingly, and Jacqueline Jones Royster, for instance), their professional work (Susan Wells and Carolyn Skinner), and their contributions to rhetorical education (Catherine Hobbs, Jessica Enoch, and David Gold). However, as Gail Lippincott has noted, "the communication strategies of women engaged in scientific or technological activities have been largely overlooked" (45). *Claiming the Bicycle* looks to fill this gap by detailing nineteenth-century women's contributions to the cultural and material development of one technology and, in the process, complicating dominant assumptions about women's historic lack of access to or participation in technological innovation.

Additionally, *Claiming the Bicycle* offers a methodological contribution to feminist rhetorical historiography more broadly, extending the focus of previous scholarship on *collective* rhetorical activity—such as the activities of discrete clubs and organizations—to include what I describe as "collected" rhetorical activities: the highly varied, broadly distributed rhetorical activities of women who are not part of a discrete organization or collective and whose individual actions are not significant in themselves, but whose loosely coordinated efforts nevertheless generate rhetorical effects through their repetition and visibility. Such activities are of particular use in recovering the rhetorical activities of women, whose presence in powerful, culturally sanctioned public organizations has been limited and whose influence has, as a result, been difficult to trace. For instance, individual women technical writers were not often employed by bicycle manufacturers,[6] but they nonetheless published advice for proper bicycling posture, apparel, and mechanical tasks in popular venues. Because this advice was repeated and heeded by riders in locations far distant from their own, it generated a fairly consistent rhetoric of bodily deportment that influenced the public perception of women's bicycling, thus contributing almost imperceptibly to larger discourses about women's natural abilities and proclivities. As a result, this rhetoric of bodily deportment constituted a "collected" rhetorical activity—a fairly stable and coherent mechanism by which the advice of individual women was spread, amplified, and even contested. In general, such collected rhetorical activities are an underexplored form of what Jacqueline Jones Royster and Gesa Kirsch have described recently as "social circulation"—a means by which scholars can better understand "the social networks in which women connect and interact with others and use language with intention," thereby accounting more fully for "how ideas resonate, divide, and are expressed via new genres and new media" (101).

Yet *Claiming the Bicycle* does not just seek to recover the deliberate efforts of women rhetors to transform gender relations or to influence the development of a new technology. Rather, this book heeds Jessica Enoch's 2011 Octalog call for more scholarship that "interrogates the rhetorical work that goes into creating and disturbing gendered distinctions" (Agnew 115), joining a growing body of feminist rhetorical research that examines how material rhetorics—including rhetorics of time, space, objects, and other conditions of materiality—function both to naturalize and to transform gender relations. As Jordynn Jack has argued, feminist rhetoricians might benefit from examining how all of these rhetorics operate together "as an integrated system" (288) rather than in isolation from one another. *Claiming the Bicycle* takes up this project on a large scale, considering the inter-animation of gendered-and-gendering material elements, ranging from bicycle seats to bloomers to short stories, and situating them alongside the actual movements of women through space and time. Whereas most other work in this area has investigated the means by which gender differences are sustained, this book considers the means by which they are transformed through shifts in the material networks that women inhabit. In this case, I examine both the role of the bicycle, as an object, in transforming gender relations and the ways in which its use was encouraged and mediated by women themselves—through their inventive, creative, and instructional writing as well as through their own embodied performances. This book, then, provides one methodological model for feminist rhetoricians hoping to undertake similar projects investigating moments of transformation in the dominant gender order of a particular historical moment.

Rhetorical Agency

Additionally, in conceiving of late nineteenth-century American women's bicycling as a widely distributed or "collected" rhetorical activity, *Claiming the Bicycle* engages with recent scholarship that theorizes rhetorical agency. Following scholarly efforts to relocate agency outside the possession of the individual deliberating rhetor, the book demonstrates how women bicyclists harnessed rhetorical agency by engaging successfully, in various ways, with the broad and shifting array of other elements within the material-rhetorical networks in which they were enmeshed: patenting procedures, publishing opportunities within popular and professional venues, crowded racetracks, and bicycle clubs, for instance. Like the postmodern subjects about whom Carl Herndl and Adela Licona have written, late nineteenth-century bicyclists became rhetorical agents by occupying "the agentive intersection of the semiotic and the material through a rhetorical performance" (141), and they became visible through the visible "collected" repetition of performances at particular intersections.

Importantly, the book follows Dorothy Winsor, S. Scott Graham, and others in demonstrating that rhetorical agency ought to be understood not as acts of *resistance against* larger ideological or institutional structures, but as shaped by and partially dependent on these structures (Winsor 412)—as working within structures in order to "enlist [. . .] other forces into their own program of action" (419). Because, as Winsor notes, "[a]gency is made stronger by creating longer, stronger networks of people, objects, facts, institutions, and whatever else can be useful" (419), such alliances are necessary and productive ways of producing social change from within institutional structures. Though Winsor suggests that a model of agency contingent on alliances within existing networks is particularly useful for contemporary organizational contexts, such as the engineering firms about which she writes, she considers the possibility that this model applies to the workings of agency outside of organizations as well. *Claiming the Bicycle* substantiates this suggestion, demonstrating how women bicyclists dispersed in space and interests, acting outside of organizational contexts, are similarly both constrained and enabled by the material-rhetorical alliances afforded by the networks that surround them.

However, although rhetorical agency cannot be characterized solely as resistance against a larger ideological structure, *Claiming the Bicycle* indicates that it cannot be adequately described as working wholly within that structure either. Like the breastfeeding mothers Amy Koerber has considered, women bicyclists' rhetorical acts function, individually, "to disrupt the sense of this grid" ("Rhetorical Agency" 98) or structure. Significantly, as Koerber notes, "it is not only literate practices but also physical actions and ways of using the body" that are agential in this way and that "become integral to understanding how individuals resist the authority of powerful institutional discourses" ("Rhetorical Agency" 100). Undertaking an act previously considered physically dangerous or nearly impossible, Koerber suggests, constitutes such a system disruption, as such acts fall outside of the grid of possibility that constitutes cultural expectations. For instance, Koerber offers examples of women breastfeeding publicly or while pregnant as rhetorical acts that violated popular and medical perceptions of a woman's bodily capabilities and proprieties. In this book, similar embodied acts, such as women's bicycle racing, both are afforded by the material-rhetorical networks in which they emerge (such as racetracks, roadways, racing organizations, and newspaper accounts) and extend the "sense of the grid" on which appropriate feminine behavior is located. Though such individual acts are not often socially transformative in themselves, they "collect" over time to produce social change, or as Koerber notes, they often "hav[e] implications that extend beyond the individual events or acts they describe" ("Rhetorical Agency" 98).

If the impact of collected rhetoric is contingent on the visibility and legibility of many widely distributed individual rhetorical acts—and on an equally distributed audience's shared interpretation and recognition of their relatedness—than each individual rhetor must align herself with other elements of the network in which she operates. Similarly to the way the radioactive substance used for a PET scan causes particular parts of the brain to become visible within a much larger, messier network of activity, this book highlights these alliances within other elements in the network and demonstrates how their interventions impacted that network. Far from asserting the significance of any one rhetor, the book considers how each rhetorical effort both emerged from and reverberated within the larger network. And far from arguing that these rhetors were wholly aware of the collected impact of their individual actions, *Claiming the Bicycle* maintains that agents themselves are, as Marilyn Cooper has suggested, "very often not aware of their intentions . . . [and] do not directly cause changes" (421). In general, *Claiming the Bicycle* describes the means by which the rhetorical actions of individual bicycling women became collected and legible and thus helped contribute to the social and technological change that Susan B. Anthony and so many others celebrated in the 1890s and 1900s.

Cultural Studies in Technical Communication

In articulating the role that women bicyclists played in the cultural and material development of the Safety bicycle, *Claiming the Bicycle* also participates in a substantial tradition of cultural studies research in technical communication that situates technical writing practices within their cultural and historical contexts (see, for instance, Bernadette Longo, Elizabeth Tebeaux, Miles Kimball, and J. Blake Scott). Such work demonstrates the extent to which technical writing is not simply a neutral or transparent reflection of reality, as many assume, but an important site for reproducing, transforming, and challenging the dominant values and power relations of the contexts from which it emerges. As Bernadette Longo has suggested, technical communication "works to (de)stabilize knowledge and practice within [the] institutional and societal systems" by which it is shaped and serves a simultaneously shaping role (x). That is, materials such as user documentation, reports, and standard operating procedures influence the embodied practices and assemblages of bodies, spaces, times, and objects that become possible and that circumscribe technology users' rhetorical agency. For example, an instructional manual about bicycling could facilitate an individual nineteenth-century woman's ability to change a bicycle tire independently of a male chaperone, which would in turn allow her to undertake a long-distance bicycle trip by herself. During her trip, she might encounter families who see, for the first time, a woman physically capable of riding one hundred miles without compromising her health permanently, as many doctors asserted she might do. In this way, rhetorical agency works through rhetorical-material assemblages that are mediated, in large part, through technical communication—and that *simultaneously implicate* both the author (of the manual or report) and the user (the bicyclist). By demonstrating these complex processes in action, *Claiming the Bicycle* substantiates the notion that technical communication operates as an agent of cultural change in both historical and contemporary contexts.

Additionally, this book contributes to scholarship that expands the definition of technical communication to include a far broader range of activity, occurring not only within the contemporary organizations that have often been the focus of scholarly attention but also "in the gaps between" (Kimball 68) these discrete entities. Miles Kimball argues that such "gaps" are worthy of study because they help technical communicators "better understand the relationship between technology, discourse, and people's lives" (84)—and thus understand the cultural implications of their own work more broadly. Similarly, Johndan Johnson-Eilola has called for technical communicators to look beyond localized problem-solving skills that focus on the immediate issues at hand within organizations, toward "systems thinking" (186), a term he borrows from Robert Reich in order to emphasize the need to identify "larger issues in the system," including "how the problem develops and in what contexts it is considered a problem" (186). *Claiming the Bicycle* enacts such a broad approach, blurring the boundaries between what has been traditionally considered technical communication and what lies beyond in order to better capture the "larger issues" that influenced the bicycle's development. In addition to instructional manuals, advice columns, and patent applications, the book considers the role that popular commentary articles, travel narratives, and even short stories played in acclimating new users to the bicycle and vice versa. In general, examining such cultural artifacts as user-authored technical communication helps us develop a more nuanced understanding of how technology becomes integrated into the fabric of a particular cultural moment—an important project for feminist scholars who are interested in considering technology as a site for contesting, complicating, or otherwise impacting dominant constructions of gender.

In pursuing broader definitions of technical communication and the locations in which it originates, the book necessarily also contributes to scholarship that troubles clear, artificial distinctions between "users" and "producers" of technology. Following Robert R. Johnson, who argues that technical communicators have often assumed that technology users are "mere tool users"—"idiots" (44)—who passively use the tools they are provided, this study demonstrates the blurriness of lines between users and producers of both technology and technical communication. Women who invented bicycling garments and accoutrements, for instance, did so because of problems they encountered as users of the bicycle; the designs they developed emerged from their experience and were refined by fellow users—some of whom, in turn, authored advice columns in which they shared their recommendations for riding apparel with countless other users. One might go so far as to argue that the collected effort of these women contributed as significantly to the uptake of the bicycle by women as did the initial invention of the Safety machine. These "users-as-citizens," as Johnson might describe them, were thus scarcely passive recipients of the bicycle, but "active responsible members of the technological community" (61) whose contributions become visible when we expand our understanding of technical communication beyond the confines of the organization.

Theoretical Underpinnings and Methodology

In highlighting the role that women—as users of the new technology—played in shaping the terms of the bicycle's use, *Claiming the Bicycle* seeks to trouble the commonplace narrative that new technologies emerge as a matter of course, succeeding because they offer acontextual "improvements" over previous technologies. Rather, as historians and sociologists of technology have long argued, new technologies emerge in specific historical and rhetorical contexts, and their social value is negotiated among their users—such as bicycling women—as much as among designers and manufacturers.[7] The bicycle could, after all, have emerged in the 1890s very differently—as a specifically masculine mode of recreation resembling the high wheelers of the previous decade, for example, or as a child's toy. Given the condition of the roads in late nineteenth-century America and the pride that earlier riders of the masculine high-wheeled Ordinary bicycle took in their machine, it could have failed altogether. However, through the collective efforts of many stakeholders, including women as well as engineers, advertisers, and manufacturers, and through the influence of material rhetorics as well as human rhetors, the bicycle emerged in the precise form it did in the 1890s: as a two-wheeled machine celebrated for its broad accessibility, safety, and comfort and noted for its transformative effect on women's lives.

In order to trace the varied, widely distributed rhetorical activities that contributed to the development of the bicycle in the 1890s, *Claiming the Bicycle* combines the theoretical insights of actor-network theory (ANT) and cultural-historical activity theory (CHAT). The book situates women bicyclists' rhetorical actions within the networks of diverse, constantly shifting human and material elements that characterize both theories, following sociologist Bruno Latour in attending to the agency of nonhuman elements alongside that of humans. In the case of the bicycle, the book argues, objects such as roadways, bloomers, bicycle seats, and handbooks influenced both the uses to which the bicycle was put in the 1880s and 1890s and the geographic location, class, and sex of those who might ride. Whereas ANT is helpful for considering the crucial role of unstable alliances in composing a network, CHAT usefully attends to networks as locations for activities that require more stability and longevity: the socialization of people through activity. As Paul Prior et al. note, CHAT traces the socialization of people through "concrete interactions that are simultaneously improvised locally and mediated by historically provided tools and practices" (17); in the case of women bicyclists, riders were socialized into new gender norms through their activities, which were in turn enacted through material networks. Thus, in CHAT's configuration, gender socialization emerges from historically situated contexts of activity. By tracing out these contexts and attending to the performances they enabled, *Claiming the Bicycle* works to materialize the mechanisms for producing shifts in gender norms.

In reconstructing from archival materials the material-rhetorical networks in which bicycling emerged in the late nineteenth century, I have drawn from a wide variety of sources, including both traditional print sources, such as newspapers, magazines, and handbooks, and other types of sources that allowed me to catch a glimpse of women bicyclists in action, including clothing patterns, actual used apparel, and photographs. Additionally, I sought in my research to balance nationally distributed materials with broad readerships—such as popular magazines and newspaper articles in syndication—with hobbyist publications shared among bicyclists and with locally held archives for bicycle clubs and bicyclists. Finally, although women's bicycling is best documented in larger, mostly eastern cities, I sought a wide geographic distribution of materials, representing the activities of women in different areas of the country. Because the culture of bicycling differed slightly in Canada and Europe from that in the United States, I drew from materials from those areas only sparingly, when I had evidence that American women had access to them.

It is important to note that the material-rhetorical network that this book sketches out—one that takes into account gender, technology, and both embodied and textual practices—is necessarily a fragmented one. Because the efforts of women technology users to promote or describe a mundane, inexpensive, recreational technology have likely seemed trivial to archivists, historians, and even women themselves, the elements that might compose such a network—such as records remaining for women's bicycle clubs or unpublished personal accounts of individuals' bicycle outings—have often been discarded or only partially and arbitrarily preserved. As a result, I have taken some license in tracing out networks from surviving materials to exercise the "critical imagination" that Jacqueline Jones Royster and Gesa Kirsch call for in *Feminist Rhetorical Practices*. As they put it, such a strategy involves "seeing the noticed and the unnoticed, rethinking what is there and not there, and speculating about what could be there instead" (20). By linking seemingly disparate artifacts together and filling in the network as completely as possible, *Claiming the Bicycle* accounts for the collected impact of women's rhetorical practices.

As feminist sociologist Judy Wajcman has noted, "[T]he construction of technologies is . . . a moving, relational process achieved in daily social interactions" (*Technofeminism* 39). Wajcman points out that "[w]hilst the technology is made into a physical object during production, the symbolic meanings attached to it are continually being negotiated and reinvented" (*Technofeminism* 47). This constant change, I argue, is achieved through the varied rhetorical activities of overlapping groups of cultural commentators, technical communicators, and users. As Wajcman and others have suggested, such ongoing rhetorical activities ensure that "the possibility always exists for a technology and its effects to be otherwise" (*Technofeminism* 107). Whereas Wajcman isolates users' embodied interactions with technology—their *use*—as the primary means by which this possibility might be realized, *Claiming the Bicycle* considers use alongside a broader range of related rhetorical actions—written, spoken, and embodied—in order to offer a fuller account of the relationship between technology and social change.

The book's introduction, "Regendering of the Bicycle during the 1880s," demonstrates how women's embodied performances as tricyclists during that decade destabilized the physical network of spaces for riding that the male high-wheel riders of the day had established for themselves, leading to new demands for design innovation among both women and men. Previously, male riders had sustained their commitment to the dangerous, high-wheeled Ordinary machine by centering their activities within the relatively closed space of the all-male bicycle club. However, the appearance of women on the peripheries of this space shifted the range of purposes and audiences to which riders saw their machines as suited, so that both the tricycle and the high wheeler appeared inadequate in comparison with the Safety bicycle, resembling the machine we ride today. Through both their verbal articulations of desire for an alternate machine and their embodied enactments of the new purposes to which such a machine might be suited, the introduction demonstrates how women riders transformed the bicycle club from a space for acts of bravado and masculine solidarity to one for courtship and shared experience between the sexes—and how, in the process, they helped ensure the ascendance of a new machine, the Safety bicycle.

Chapter 1, "Women Riders and the Invention of the Modern Bicycle," further elaborates the active role that women played in ensuring the ascendance of the Safety bicycle as a technology of choice over the Ordinary. In this chapter, I argue that women contributed to the Safety's popularity not only by riding an already complete technological object but also by modifying that object through their own inventions and innovations intended to adapt the machine and its female rider to one another. At a time when few US patents were credited to women, women bicyclists generated at least nineteen patents for tools and accoutrements related to the Safety machine, including the bicycle umbrella, a bicycle lock, and numerous bicycle garments. These innovations and other, unpatented adjustments ensured that the new machine became suitable for touring and practical transportation—both purposes that encouraged women and men to enjoy the bicycle together. By examining patents and product discussions in trade catalogs and popular magazines, I demonstrate how early women bicyclists' rhetorical and material ingenuity enabled the spread of the sport among an initially skeptical group of female riders, hence promoting both the Safety bicycle and the altered gender relations it facilitated among its users.

Chapter 2, "Popular Magazines and the Rise of the 'Bicycle Girl,'" builds on the work of chapter 1, moving from the material changes that early women bicyclists initiated as inventors to the efforts of popular magazine writers to accomplish a rhetorical and symbolic regendering of the new machine. In their fiction, travel narratives, and reflective commentary pieces about bicycling, women writers drew from the material resources of the new "popular" magazine to combat prejudices about women bicyclists among larger, more far-flung audiences than ever before. These writers associated the bicycle with new patterns of courtship and new ways of embodying one's femininity. Widely distributed, inexpensive, and filled with an unprecedented number of images and advertisements, the popular magazine provided an effective vehicle for promoting not only women's bicycling in general but also a distinctly modern model of heterosexual desire, courtship, and domesticity to which the bicycle was not an impediment but an asset. Women writers played an important role both in fleshing out this model and in adding depth and nuance to the "bicycle girl" featured in advertisements and song.

Whereas chapter 2 examines how popular magazine writers wrote the bicycle into modern domestic and courtship narratives, chapter 3, "Women's Written Instructions for Change," deals with women bicycle enthusiasts' efforts to expand the uses to which the machine might be put beyond those imagined within popular magazines. Within user-authored instructional manuals and articles, as well as in newsletters circulated within women's bicycle clubs, women riders sought to complicate models for using the new technology that positioned female riders solely as companions to male riders or as homemakers in need of temporary relief from their natural duties. These authors capitalized on the widespread enthusiasm for bicycling that the popular magazines had helped authorize, constituting a diverse but united public of wheelwomen uniquely positioned to disprove cultural commonplaces about women's lack of physical stamina and mental acuity. Using varying rhetorical strategies that included both narrative and directive approaches, authors ranging from little-known bicyclist Maria E. Ward to Woman's Christian Temperance Union president Frances Willard used instructional materials as a means of promoting a "rhetoric of deportment" among women bicyclists that situated the bicycle as a vehicle for societal transformation.

Chapter 4, "Women Bicyclists' Embodied Medical Authority," suggests that bicycling served as a rhetorical resource for women seeking to influence professional medical discourse about women's bodies. Many popular writers interested in women's health drew from their embodied experiences aboard the bicycle to complicate cultural commonplaces about women's physical frailty. These writers sought to reclaim medical authority for women by grounding their claims in their own observations and felt experiences, rather than in older evolutionary metaphors that had dominated nineteenth-century approaches to women's health. Together with women bicycle racers and endurance riders, who demonstrated with their bodies that the "New Woman" was not subject to the apparent biological limitations of her foremothers, these rhetors show how the cumulative force of firsthand embodied performance and observations can serve as a powerful rhetorical resource for combating medically or scientifically authorized cultural commonplaces.

Finally, the book's conclusion, "Toward a Techofeminist Rhetorical Agency," explores contemporary analogues to the case studies described in the previous chapters, offering a sense of how teachers and students of rhetoric might understand their responsibilities and capacities to hone their skills in the service of desired social and technological change. In general, *Claiming the Bicycle* considers technology users' agency to participate—through both their direct, bodily interactions with the technology and their extra-organizational technical communication—in the ongoing negotiation of rhetoric, gender, and technology.

Acknowledgments

This project could never have been possible without the support and encouragement of Jordynn Jack, who helped me see how bicycling women really were part of the history of rhetoric, whether they wrote publicly about their experiences or not. I am very fortunate also to have benefited from the steady encouragement and insightful feedback of Jane Danielewicz, who allowed me space to develop my own questions but insisted that I articulate them in comprehensible ways. Dan Anderson pointed me in the right direction on more than one occasion, making this a more robust project both theoretically and practically. Beverly Taylor, Jeanne Moskal, and Jane Thrailkill took my ideas seriously before they even made it to the page.

Through the combined efforts of many, I was afforded the time and resources to locate and study the rich archival materials from which I draw in *Claiming the Bicycle*. The librarians at the Hagley Library in Wilmington, Delaware; the Connecticut Historical Society; the Hartford History Center at the Hartford Public Library; the Smithsonian Institution; the Indiana State Library; and the District of Columbia Public Library in Washington, DC, all directed me to invaluable rare books, trade catalogs, photographs, and manuscript materials. My trips to these archives were funded, in part, through financial assistance from the University of North Carolina at Chapel Hill and Duke University. When I could not travel to archives, I was fortunate to have access to materials through the superb interlibrary loan services at UNC–Chapel Hill, UNC Wilmington, and Duke. Finally, a generous summer research stipend from UNC Wilmington's College of Arts and Sciences allowed me uninterrupted time to complete the manuscript.

The project also benefited immeasurably from feedback from a wide range of readers. Over glasses of wine and plenty of delicious food, in person and over Skype, my writing group has never failed to make time for me and my bicycling women. Risa Applegarth, Heather Branstetter, Erin Branch, and Chelsea Redeker-Milbourne have been with this project from the start, listening carefully, reading generously, and providing invaluable suggestions on every chapter. Stephanie Morgan, Lindsay Rose-Russell, David Gold, and Michelle Smith have also contributed their sound advice at different stages, as have my excellent colleagues at Duke's Thompson Writing Program and here at UNC Wilmington. Diana Rancourt has offered an invaluable outsider's perspective along many a long run, and I remain convinced that our early morning workouts helped me to better understand the lived experiences of my research subjects. I am very thankful for Kristine Priddy's helpful assistance, Jessica Enoch's thoughtful and encouraging review of the manuscript, and the critical attention that series editors Cheryl Glenn and Shirley Wilson Logan offered it during its final stages.

Finally, I would like to thank my family for their tireless support in all my endeavors. My mother, Rosemary Hallenbeck, has supported this project both as a travel partner to archives and as a childcare provider, gently encouraging me to continue this project when I wanted to lay it aside. My father, Ralph Hallenbeck, has always been a model of tenacity and attention to detail, and my son, Rhys Emery, never fails to help me see the forest for the trees. Last of all, my deepest gratitude goes to my husband, Glenn Emery, for his unflagging faith in the value of this project and in the capacity of its writer to finish it.

Claiming the Bicycle

Introduction

Regendering of the Bicycle during the 1880s

I hear a sharp ring on the frosty way,
And I catch the gleam of a cycle bright,
Just a glimpse of a form in Quaker gray,
And then, the dear boy! he is out of sight.
Ah, out and away, ere the sun is high,
While the early clouds are all rose and pearl,
And the air like a wine that is bright and dry;
And I'm—only a girl.

I think of the hollows where leaves lie dead;
Of the gaunt trees' shadows against the sky;
Of the cool, clear stretch of blue overhead,
And the low, lush meadows he rattles by.
I look on the road with its dusty track,
Where the wind-gusts meet to whistle and whirl;
And—yes! I may look for his coming back,
For I'm only a girl.

I may watch and wait all day for the ring
Of his pretty plaything's glistening steel;
And, dressed in my gayest, may sit and sing
Over my work till I hear the wheel.
Then I shall see the eyes o' my lad,
And he a cheek and a drooping curl;
And—well, yes—perhaps—I'm a little glad
That I'm only a girl.

Published in the January 1885 issue of *Outing* magazine, Ruth Hall's poem "Only a Girl" offers a valuable glimpse into women's ambivalent role in the growing American cycling movement of the 1880s. Hall's speaker is "only a girl" dressed in her "gayest" as she sits at home awaiting the return of her beau from a bicycle ride. She betrays some longing as she imagines the scenes he might encounter on his tour—the blue sky, lush meadows, and dusty road—though in the end she claims she is "a little glad" to have been left behind. The sense in which the bicycle—at that time a high-wheeled machine requiring the rider to balance up to five feet above the ground—was a highly *masculine* object is strong, as evidenced by the speaker's assurance that her status as "only a girl" automatically disqualifies her from joining in on the ride.

Yet the very presence of a female writer in *Outing*, penning a poem about cycling with some imagination about what a ride might entail, betrays the instability of the bicycle's assumed masculinity during the mid-1880s. With the exception of a few exhibition riders, the high-wheeled bicycle, or Ordinary,[1] remained inaccessible to most women. By the mid-1880s, however, a different machine was beginning to draw many women out of their homes and into the streets alongside their husbands: the tricycle. In the March 1885 issue of *Outing*—just two months after "Only a Girl" was published, Minna Caroline Smith offered a contrasting picture of the status of women as cyclists, predicting that "within ten years there will be thousands of women riding in the United States where there are now scores" ("The Tricycle for American Women" 424). Whereas Hall had located her speaker and her beau solidly within the "separate spheres" of the nineteenth century, Smith emphasized the new mobility of the tricyclist alongside her beau, even going so far as to assert that "[s]ensible youths choose the society of the maiden who is equal to a reasonable amount of exertion in out-of-door pleasures, and the girl whose strength is small misses many invitations to sea and shore" (423). The expansion of the tricycle's popularity by the mid-1880s—and the responses it garnered, such as Smith's—helped initiate a powerful shift not only in the culture of bicycling but also in the sorts of activities in which "respectable" women and men might engage together, the mobility and independence of women of the middle and upper classes, and even the ways in which women might understand the capabilities of their bodies and minds.

This shift, of course, was gradual, and it did not end with Smith's image of easy companionship between tricyclist and Ordinary rider, or even with her prediction that "a large number of the . . . 'blessed busy women who support themselves'" would "adopt the tricycle for daily service" ("The Tricycle for American Women" 423). Neither did it occur seamlessly, simply through women and men purchasing ready-made machines and putting them to use. Rather, this shift occurred in fits and starts over the course of the next decade, through the tacit, widely dispersed collaboration of engineers, advertisers, commentators like Smith, and users themselves. Likewise, such a tremendous cultural shift involved not only the two aforementioned machines but also a constantly expanding array of other objects without which the two machines' utility would have been severely compromised: improved, expanded roadways; road maps; bicycle clubhouses; instructional manuals; and alternative models of bicycles that afforded different types of riding for different audiences. Chief among these alternatives to the Ordinary and the tricycle was the Safety bicycle, so called because of its safety relative to the harrowing Ordinary. This bicycle model eventually pushed the Ordinary and the tricycle out of the market, greatly expanding the range of people—geographically and financially—to whom the popular new activity was available. If the Ordinary had been decidedly *masculine* and the tricycle substantially *feminine* in its orientation as an object, the Safety defied gender categorization, materializing instead a new gender order in which men and women could share similar—though not identical—experiences.

This chapter traces the means by which the Safety and the gender relations it materialized gained a foothold in America, highlighting the role that women tricyclists during the late 1880s played in bringing about this change. Though not every American woman tricyclist consciously sought to transform the gender order through deliberate rhetorical action, collectively their embodied and discursive performances aboard the machine enabled this work. From Caroline Minna Smith's plea for women to take up tricycling in 1885 to the physical entry of bicycle clubmen's wives, daughters, and friends into club and road spaces previously deemed masculine, a wide range of women's activities helped—performatively and discursively—transform both the culture and the material form of the bicycle.

As Carl Herndl and Adela Licona have argued, rhetorical agency "is contingent on a matrix of material and social conditions," operating as a "diffuse and shifting . . . social location and opportunity into and out of which rhetors. . . . move" (133). In the case of the bicycle culture of the 1880s, women riders came to occupy such a location by attending to the opportunities present within the existing material network and then by expanding that network—and with it their own agency. That is, as women rode their tricycles in greater numbers during the late 1880s, new material conditions emerged: improved roads lobbied for by the powerful League of American Wheelmen, for instance, to accommodate tours of ladies and gentlemen together; genteel bicycle clubhouses where riders of both sexes could enjoy social gatherings such as dances and performances; and a new array of alternative machines, such as marine bicycles, tandem bicycles, and Safeties. The expanded network, in turn, afforded women more opportunities to exercise agency as cyclists—to impact cycling culture, the design of machines, and the gender order materialized through their performances.

As Nathan Stormer notes, "[B]odies and languages are configured into orders of things and of discourses" within "different performative regimes" (261). Within this configuration, the gap between language and objects collapses, and objects gain the potential to become discursive in their articulations with other objects. As Stormer explains, such articulations—networks—of rhetorical objects and discourses are produced historically, constantly shifting and gaining and losing discursivity. If we understand gender as produced through performances that articulate objects into discourse—such as a male cyclist riding an Ordinary bicycle on rough roads and performing a particular, historically produced form of masculinity—we see the necessity of attending to the shifting material networks that constituted bicycle culture in the 1880s. The appearance of the tricycle that Smith celebrated in 1885 becomes evidence not only of a historical occurrence but also of a shifting network, of expanding opportunities for women to exercise agency, and of the social instability of the Ordinary as the bicycle of choice. This chapter examines the network's components in four stages: the Ordinary bicycle era of the early 1880s, the increasing visibility of the tricycle within the bicycle scene in the mid-1880s, the incompatibility between the Ordinary and the Tricycle, and emergence of the Safety following women's expanded participation in bicycle culture. The chapter concludes with a brief look at the 1890s bicycle craze.

The Small and Stable Network of the Masculine High-Wheeled Bicycle

When Mark Twain first learned to ride the Ordinary in the mid-1880s, he described his experience humorously in terms that emphasized both his wonderment and his initial ineptitude:

> You hop along behind it on your right foot, resting the other on the mounting peg, and grasping the tiller with your hands. At the word, you rise on the peg, stiffen your left leg, hang your other one around in the air in a general and indefinite way, lean your stomach against the rear of the saddle, and then fall off, maybe on one side, maybe on the other; but you fall off. You get up and do it again; and once more, and several times. (79)

Twain's frequent falling was hardly an exception, and it might not have been an exaggeration: the Ordinary allowed riders to get atop the often five-foot-tall bicycle only once the machine was actually moving. The bicycle had no mechanism for resting the feet once the rider was mounted, since it had no gears. If the pedals did not move, the wheel did not move either. Complicating matters further, the Ordinary rider had to lean backward while going down hills to prevent the machine from tipping forward and causing a "header," a phenomenon that occurred all too often on the increasingly neglected, heavily rutted roads that spanned America in the years of railroad dominance.

Nonetheless, these challenges did not deter young, urban, middle- and upper-class American men from attempting to ride the Ordinary. On the contrary, the difficulty and exertion of riding the Ordinary constituted its primary appeal. As historian Anthony Rotundo has noted, during the late nineteenth century, many middle-class young men found themselves settling increasingly into sedentary professions but yearning to regain contact with their "bestial" or "primal" impulses, which they saw as indicative of a lost manly character (143). They understood themselves as beset by a host of vague modern maladies, including "neurasthenia," nervous debility stemming from the increased intellectualism of America's "urban brain workers." Fearful of feminization and overcivilization, these young men sought opportunities to enact, through their physical performances, a strong and emphatic masculinity to strengthen their bodies, fortify their minds, and herald the spirit of the times (Haller and Haller 8). The high-wheeled bicycle offered just such an opportunity, providing what science and technology studies scholar Nelly Oudshoorn describes as a "gender script" for its users, in which a product's design requires of its users a range of performances, competencies, and actions in line with gender norms (10). That is, the difficulty and danger of riding the high-wheeled bicycle affirmed the sort of masculinity that late nineteenth-century men sought; over time and repeated use, their individual performances reinforced for them a certain bodily "habitus," or as philosopher Pierre Bourdieu defines it, a certain way of relating to the world that is "particular but constant" and also "immediately present" (142) within a given world order. Struggling to learn to ride the Ordinary, demonstrating one's skill or speed aboard it, and—in Twain's case—exaggerating one's travails with good humor were all attractive to young male riders in the 1880s. In a network that was relatively small and contained, these sorts of masculine performances not only affirmed the gender order that left Ruth Hall's speaker longing for her cyclist beau's return home but also helped establish the prominence of the high-wheeled Ordinary's material design.

Almost immediately after pioneer bicycle manufacturer Albert Pope set up business in the late 1870s, young men began to flock to the Ordinary, particularly in urban areas of the Northeast. In 1880, for instance, a *Boston Globe* reporter commented that "[t]he steeds of steel may be found reposing in the entries of all the principal dormitories" (qtd. in Herlihy, *Bicycle* 196) of Harvard College. An 1881 article in the *Washington, DC, Evening Star* boasted that the number of riders in the city was increasing exponentially, from a mere 7 to 150 in under two years, with hundreds more projected to take up the new activity in the space of eighteen months ("The Original Seven" 2). But perhaps the biggest avenue for advancing the high-wheeled bicycle in its earliest years was the bicycle clubs that began forming in the late 1870s, spurred by the founding of a national organization, the League of American Wheelmen, in 1880. In his 1879 book, *The American Bicycler*, well-known league cofounder Charles Pratt urged:

> Wherever there are six or more gentlemen who ride the bicycle, and are enthusiastic in its use (but not professionals), living near enough together, and are either already companions or likely to be companionable to each other, it is desirable that they should form a club. (166)

Club membership, Pratt advised, would allow riders "good fellowship, companionship for spins, social standing in the bicycling community, special stimulus to interest, and incentives to excellence in riding," as well as "opportunities for comparison of experience and of opinions, for obtaining information, and for associated or disciplined riding on interesting occasions" (Pratt 165–66). Such invocations were attractive to young men and club life proliferated: by 1883, there were more than a thousand clubmen riding in New England and around five hundred riders in the New York City area alone ("The 1883 Meet Again" 176).

With high membership dues and stringent character requirements,[2] organized rides and races, uniforms, and social events, club life helped strengthen and stabilize the network surrounding the Ordinary bicycle. Club membership encouraged riders across the country to think of riding as a certain type of activity (masculine, modern), undertaken by certain members of society (respectable, professional class) within certain contexts (racetracks, club rides, tours). Members lobbied for better roads, as the railroad era had left America's roads in disrepair, but they did not emphasize the need for practical transportation to work. Collectively, as articulated in League of American Wheelmen publications and local newsletters, they understood the bicycle as a uniquely modern and manly recreational device, suitable for gentlemen of a certain age and class interested in racing, stunts, parades, and acts of endurance. The bicycle club, then, functioned to homogenize bicycle culture in America, to stabilize both the Ordinary bicycle and the model of masculinity that it represented.

Central to this model of masculinity was a pride in the difficulty and danger of learning to ride. Throughout the club scrapbook of the Washington, DC, based Capital Bicycle Club, for instance, are photographs and reports of riders attempting difficult technical feats aboard their bicycles, such as climbing the apparently legendary "stand pipe" hill, "undoubtedly the steepest hill in the immediate vicinity of the city, [with a] great number of loose stones [to make] it all the worse." They played games of "follow my leader," in which clubmen would follow one another along a predetermined course containing technically challenging sections of road described in great detail in the club scrapbook. For instance, according to a club newsletter, the 1886 birthday run for club president H. S. Owen featured "a most ingenious combination of obstructions" including "a gully about six feet deep, having steep sloping sides and a narrow bottom, which would just receive a wheel" (Capital Bicycle Club ser. 2, box 4). Such declarations, which often emphasize the difficulty of the terrain, reveal the centrality of stunts and challenges to the performance of masculinity that club life encouraged.

Importantly, the notion of bicycling that emerged from this figuring was distinct from our contemporary notions not only in that it involved a far smaller and more homogenous group of people or that it centered on the Ordinary, an object we now consider to be obsolete. As Wiebe Bijker and Trevor Pinch have suggested, the bicyclists of the day saw what we might understand as *design problems* or inadequacies—such as the height of the wheel or the inability of the rider to mount it without moving—as desirable features, even assets, and as a result, they were slow to innovate designs. Intended initially to cushion riders from the vibrations of the ground and to increase the racing speed of the machine, the high front wheel was a badge of honor for riders; in its 1884 bylaws, for instance, the Capital Bicycle Club even reported the average height of its members' wheels, alongside their average age (twenty-three) and height (five feet, ten inches) (Capital Bicycle Club ser. 2, box 4, 2). Whereas today's parents watch anxiously as their little children learn to ride, assuming the bicycle should be safe, nineteenth-century enthusiasts of the Ordinary bicycle celebrated their lack of safety, understanding themselves as engaged in a challenging and daring activity. Club riders and designers did not see the difficulty of mounting and maintaining the machine as problematic or unsafe because they envisioned its worth as encapsulated in its speed, danger, and durability rather than its safety. Members of the Capital Bicycle Club commented approvingly of riders who fell, even scrapbooking pictures of particularly spectacular falls.

This attitude toward the Ordinary bicycle as an instrument of speed and physical challenge, reproduced within the social context of the bicycle club, was further clarified in manufacturer trade catalogs and advertisements. For instance, one 1885 advertisement for the Pope Manufacturing Company's Columbia bicycle (fig. I.1) features a line of men riding along a waterfront, framed by racing records the Columbia model had earned at different distances.

In general, bicycling culture during the 1880s emerged within a fairly constrained network of actors and objects. Riders included mostly young, urban men of some means, whose membership in a national network of clubs contributed to the stability of this culture, with its focus on racing and stunts rather than practical endeavors, such as transportation to work; its concern with modern fellowship; and its adherence to the Ordinary as a bicycle design of choice. Bijker and Pinch have detailed the role that young men's desire for "macho riding" played in sustaining that design when other, safer, more accessible designs were available; they have argued that the Safety emerged only when the users demanded it for their own well-being. Although there is no doubt that as riders aged, they called for safer machines on which to avoid "headers," here I highlight the role that the discursive and embodied activities of female tricyclists played in promoting innovations in bicycle design. Additionally, I ground both male and female riders' activities within

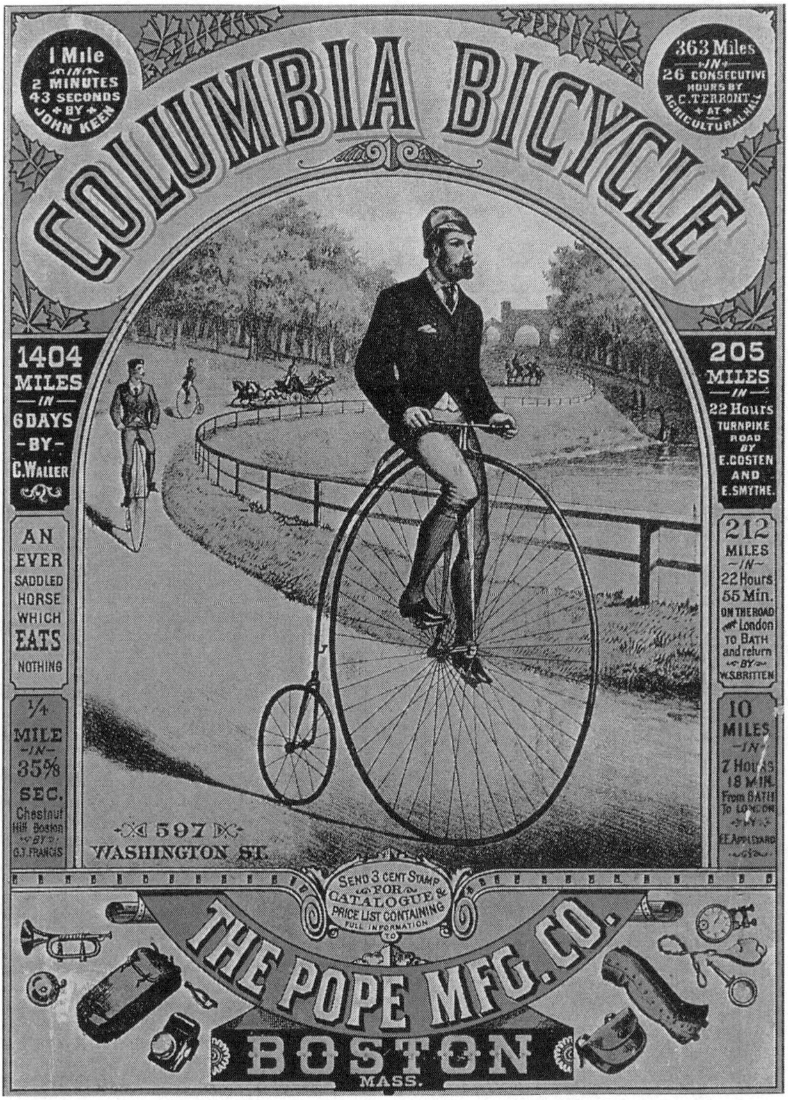

Figure I.1. Pope Manufacturing Company's Columbia bicycle advertisement with racing records, 1885. Reprinted from author's personal collection.

an expanding material network that participated in and encouraged a shifting set of design priorities. Gradually improving roadways, cyclist road maps, and even the advent of roadside motels and restaurants added to the range of contexts available to riders of both sexes, as did an expanding array of machines that included but were not limited to the tricycle.

The Genteel, Health-Bringing Tricycle and Bicycle Club Culture

During the summer of 1885, members of the Capital Bicycle Club enthusiastically documented a remarkable sight in their club newsletter. As they reported in a column preserved in the club scrapbook, "[A] young lady who has been riding a tricycle in the streets lately strengthens the belief that civilization has not yet discontinued its onward march." Throughout that summer, they continued to observe the rider, repeatedly linking her presence to societal advancement: "The beautiful Belva and her triumphant tricycle are still loose on the streets. The sight of a young lady riding a tricycle along Pennsylvania Avenue last week . . . gives additional assurances of the advance of civilization." Despite Minna Caroline Smith's assertions in *Outing* that tricycling had already gained popularity among women ("The Tricycle for American Women"), this early tricyclist appears to have been somewhat unusual on the streets of Washington, DC.

But by that fall, when several clubmen vacationed together in Martha's Vineyard, they discovered that "beautiful Belva" was not alone in her new interest. In a rather literary letter written back home to his fellow wheelmen, and included in the club scrapbook, one member noted that in Martha's Vineyard, "the girls . . . seem to engage in this sport as a golden opportunity to hand down to posterity faultless shapes and rounded forms which would otherwise, like Gray's 'Full many a rose,' be 'born to blush unseen'" (Capital Bicycle Club ser. 2, box 4). The tricycle, initially imported from Great Britain as an alternative to the Ordinary for racing (Herlihy, *Bicycle* 214), was reverberating subtly through the network of men's bicycle clubs. In doing so, it shifted clubmen's understanding of the activity to accommodate the possibility of feminine participation, albeit rare and peripheral to their own activities. In contrast to Ordinary machines, which they saw as mainly suited to demonstrations of agility and skill, these clubmen conceived of the tricycle primarily as a bringer of health to older men and, increasingly in the mid-1880s, to young women like Belva. Though some men did race tricycles, the three-wheeled vehicles had remained secondary to the high-wheeled Ordinary until the men began to conceive of the tricycle as a feminine machine.

As their compliments to Belva suggest, clubmen were particularly invested in the tricycle as a corrective to the physical weakness and poor health with which, allegedly, nineteenth-century American middle-class women were chronically afflicted. During the last decades of the nineteenth century, doctors scrambled to treat urban, middle- and upper-class women for perceived ailments, such as neurasthenia or "nerve wear," that they believed were brought on by causes as varied as the unique demands of modern urban life and excessive intellectual exertion associated with women's increasing access to higher education. Many physicians charged that advances in women's education and public activity were exhausting patients, sapping their sexual and reproductive abilities, and shortening their lives (Haller and Haller 33). Because they believed that "intellectual women" suffered for want of exercise, doctors prescribed various forms of calisthenics in mild doses. Within this context, male bicyclists' responses to "beautiful Belva" aboard her tricycle are hardly surprising, as these riders conceived of the new machine as a much-anticipated response to the modern "problem" of women's health. In doing so, they helped strengthen the association between the tricycle and femininity, understanding it tacitly a "women's machine" to complement their own "men's machine."

Although some male riders had taken up tricycling and had even had some success on the three-wheeled machine in races, American tricycle manufacturers began at mid-decade to shift their advertising focus to women, thus further establishing the gender of the tricycle. Some ads conveyed the commonplace that women ought to ride specifically to improve their health. In 1885, the Overman Wheel Company in Chicopee, Massachusetts, promised, "You Can Ride a Tricycle!" to a wide range of potential riders, including not only "the whole family" but also "doctors, lawyers, clergymen, ladies—young and old—and businessmen of all classes." The ad announced that all riders should "look out for changes" in their health:

> *No more medicine! No more headache! No sleepless nights!*
> *You will have muscles, appetite, self-reliance, a clear head,*
> *vigorous good humor.*
> *You can't be sick and ride a Tricycle. They don't go together.*

Although Overman's mention of ladies only among other groups of potential riders hints at a reluctance to feminize the machine too definitively, the ad's assertion that being sick and riding a tricycle "don't go together" indicates shifts in the network surrounding American bicycling culture: the tricycle's links to women and health were giving increasing visibility to a particular set of implied purposes for the machine. Additionally, the ad's bold announcement that "You Can Ride a Tricycle!" highlights another rhetorical distinction between the tricycle and the high-wheeled bicycle: whereas Ordinary enthusiasts like Twain celebrated the difficulty of learning to ride, the tricycle was marked for its ease of use—it was an accessible machine for all.

A Pope Manufacturing Company advertisement from the same year (fig. I.2), meanwhile, offers a stronger visual assertion of the tricycle's femininity alongside the masculine Ordinary, implicating both machines in a modern form of courtship that further demonstrates shifts under way in bicycle culture. Within this form of courtship, women and men could court away from home, and they could indulge more freely in shared hobbies, such as being outdoors. This image suggests an attitude of leisure among both riders, who appear to face one another in conversation even as they share in the exertion of riding their machines. And significantly, in place of the racing records framing the previous Ordinary rider, this ad includes a lengthy testimonial of the health benefits of riding. The shift illustrates the degree to which the emergence of female tricyclists had secured both new priorities and new contexts for riding.

If the tricycle seemed to materialize new attitudes about courtship and health among riders, it lacked its own tightly constrained context for use that the Ordinary enjoyed. Although the League of American Wheelmen made no explicit effort to exclude women from joining its ranks, it did not—as it had in appealing to male riders—encourage the formation of clubs. Rather, at both the national and local levels, clubmen saw the women aboard tricycles as fitting in only peripherally with the existing club scene. A few ladies' tricycle clubs did form, beginning with the Ladies' Tricycle Club of New York City in 1884. Though a club announcement in *Outing* listing ten members predicted that "judging from the interest and enthusiasm of its members, it bids fair to become in time quite a large and flourishing club" ("Our Monthly Record" 475), there are no further records of the club's doings in *Outing*. Based on frequency of advertisements alone, though, the number of female tricyclists was likely far fewer than the number of male Ordinary riders in the United States—both because of the smaller demand and because the tricycle exceeded the Ordinary in cost. An 1889 Overman catalog, for example, advertised the bicycle as costing between $122 and $134 "with delivery," whereas the tricycle cost $160 "crated and ready for delivery."

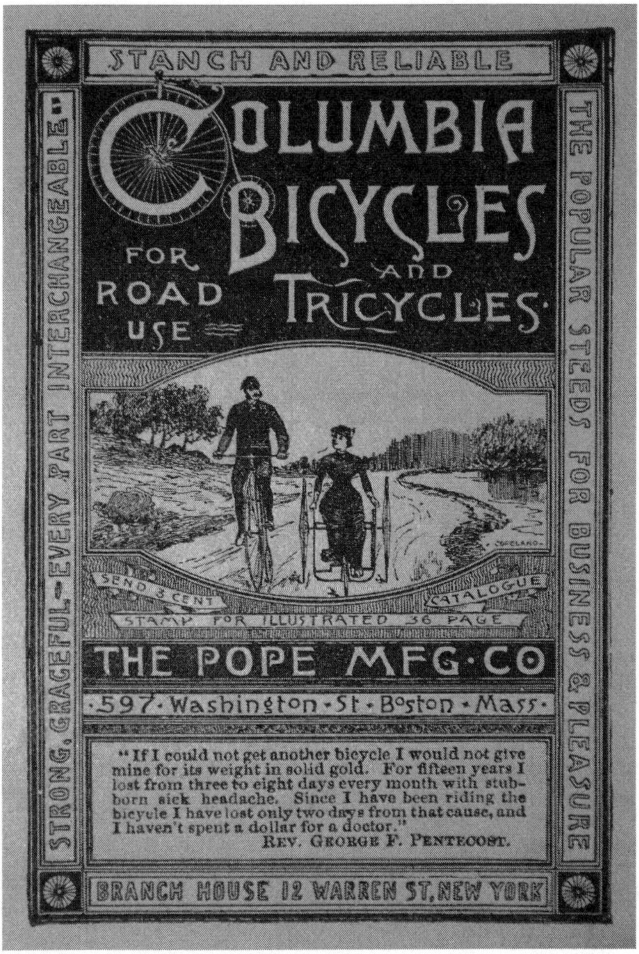

Figure I.2. Pope Manufacturing Company's Columbia bicycle and tricycle advertisement, 1885. Reprinted from author's personal collection.

As an object defined by its accessibility to riders and its promotion of courtship and health, the tricycle did not belong on difficult terrain suitable for stunt or endurance riding. And certainly the wider, lower-to-the-ground machine was relatively ill suited for many of the nation's notoriously poor roads, as the prospective tricycle rider would sit closer to the mud, dust, and debris; feel the vibrations of uneven ground more acutely; and require a clearer, wider path than the rider of the Ordinary. Overall, the material features of the tricycle offer a feminine gender script to complement the masculine script of the Ordinary; the two machines positioned male and female users differently in relation to a technology, attempting to permit different options for each while closing off others in design.

In the 1885 Pope advertisement featuring the cycling couple, the striking differences in the physical positioning of the two riders reinforce a sort of visual antithesis, rather than a continuum, between men and women, whereby the two machines visually maximize or even exaggerate the differences between the sexes. The Ordinary rider physically towers above the tricycle rider, who sits erect and refined between her wheels rather than above them, almost protected or encaged by the two wheels of her machine. The tricyclist need not straddle the machine, so she does not need to change her long skirts for riding; because her machine is neither fast nor versatile, her mobility remains limited, but she is able to take in the scenery with some ease. The Ordinary rider, in contrast, must—as Twain's commentary suggests—constantly attend to his machine in order to avoid falling. At the same time, the Ordinary rider can feel assured of his technical mastery in riding his vehicle, whereas the tricycle rider is repeatedly reminded that her machine is accessible to all, regardless of stamina or skill level. The two scripts limit the experience that riders of each sex can have, reinforcing gendered commonplaces about women's and men's separate "natures," as defined by their striking differences in stamina, skill, and relations to both technology and nature.

What was significant, however, was that women tricyclists gained at least limited access to the social and physical spaces of the bicycle club, and through their access they continued to shift the culture of club life. While club membership and many club activities remained the exclusive domain of men, the network surrounding clubs expanded to include club members' female guests, as well as a range of new activities focused on courtship and coed recreation. In the pages of an 1889 issue of *Outing*, for instance, a member of the Jersey City Athletic Club, Charles Meyers, described his club's efforts to appease the ladies who had assisted in the decoration of the club's lavish new clubhouse and now wanted access to the club itself. Clubmen allowed women to come to the club on Tuesday and Thursday afternoons, when they could ride sociable tricycles and play lawn games with their beaus, and the club began to host monthly dances. Meyers assured readers, many of whom were members of other all-male clubs:

> [T]his feature is naturally one of the most attractive to the members, and among the ladies themselves the club is a very popular place. . . . It has not

> so far interfered in the smallest degree with the exercise of the members' privileges, as they can use all the club's advantages on these occasions. . . . Ladies, by telling their friends of the beauty of the club-house and the enjoyment to be obtained on its ladies' days, have induced their male friends to join the club. (447)

The Jersey City Athletic Club's new policies demonstrated the negotiations of clubmen to maintain the previously masculine space of the club while at the same time allowing for the expanding range of activities and participants in club life. At the Capital Bicycle Club in Washington, DC, a similar process occurred, as scrapbook accounts of dances and picnic outings became as plentiful as the aforementioned sublime stunt rides (Capital Bicycle Club ser. 2, box 5). Whereas the club's 1883 Anniversary Literary Exercises had included a series of toasts that reflected the masculinity and exclusivity of the audience,[3] evidencing that the event was attended by members only, the 1887 celebration featured a mixed audience of club members' wives and dates and included a toast to "Our Club Sisters," "At whose sight, like the sun, All others with diminish'd luster shone." These ladies even delivered some toasts of their own, including a presentation that "succeeded in convincing its hearers that double tricycles do not run themselves when off concrete" (Capital Bicycle Club ser. 2, box 5). In asserting the tricycle's inappropriateness for off-roading, so popular among male Ordinary riders, women riders were voicing their perspectives on the purposes of riding, articulating the limitations of the machine designated for their use.

Beyond the clubhouse, many club runs shifted to new spaces, including paved urban roads that were more appropriate for the kinds of leisurely riding implied by the tricycle. Riders aboard both Ordinaries and tricycles ventured on shorter runs focused less on physical challenge than on enjoyment or wholesome appreciation of the outdoors. Gone were the Capital Bicycle Club newsletters' enthusiastic descriptions of technically difficult stretches of road or path. In contrast to the challenging terrain of club leader Owen's previous birthday runs, the scrapbook reports that his 1888 birthday run involved a picnic lunch (with lunch order form) and a scenic destination. Wheelmen were accompanied by "a number of lady friends," and the newsletter reported later that "[t]here was no very rapid riding, ten miles an hour being the maximum speed" (Capital Bicycle Club ser. 2, box 4). Another run to Shenandoah Mountain was advertised that year with the following promise:

"No wheeling during the heat of the day. Will take things easy so as to have an enjoyable and beneficial tour, making 25 and 30 miles per day. The Route will be confined wholly to carriage roads" (Capital Bicycle Club ser. 2, box 4). These reports confirm changes in the spaces and priorities relevant to club life. Whereas the bravado of racing and stunt riding had previously dominated discussions of club activities, the club now seems bent on reassuring riders of the accessibility of the trip, as well as on making the journey a pleasant one for men and women together.

In general, the tricycle's increasing popularity—and the patterns of use encouraged by its association with femininity, health, and accessibility—had shifted the network of American bicycle club life, helping women riders access new agency in influencing the development of bicycle technology and culture. The young girl in Ruth Hall's poem at the beginning of this chapter, quietly waiting for her beau to return home from his ride aboard the Ordinary, had been an outsider both to bicycle culture and to the patterns of use that it engendered. Her inactivity had worked to stabilize the particular form of masculinity associated with the Ordinary, just as it had confirmed the "natural" reticence and domesticity of women. Aboard the tricycle, however, the female rider gained access to physical club spaces and, over time, expanded the range of club activities. Even as the tricycle materialized gender difference in its design relative to the Ordinary, the increasing visibility and participation of its rider in club life exerted a force of its own, marking the existing designs as inadequate in a way they had not been previously.

Incompatibility between the Ordinary and the Tricycle

Within a few years after the members of the Capital Bicycle Club celebrated the arrival of beautiful Belva aboard her tricycle, clubmen and their lady friends alike began to realize the shortcomings of mixed company aboard the Ordinary and the tricycle. In addition to its bulkier size, the tricycle had less acute steering capabilities than the Ordinary and was much heavier—a greater problem for female riders than for male tricyclists, who were generally stronger and more accustomed to physical exertion. In order for a mixed group of male Ordinary and female tricycle riders to remain together even on the best of roads, wheelmen aboard Ordinaries had to hold back and tricyclists had to push hard to keep up. In Oudshoorn's terms, this arrangement challenged the limits of the gender script of each machine. In an *Outing* article entitled "Women as Cyclers," Minna Caroline Smith reports on bicycle club outings among mixed groups of women and men:

> [T]ricyclists do not enjoy long runs of any kind. The bicycle-rider finds it a little tedious to accommodate his speed to the three-wheel, and to a lady rider the exertion of keeping up for a long distance is somewhat fatiguing. (318)

Although Smith identifies feminine frailty as a limitation for tricyclists, she also implies that the speed discrepancy between the two machines is a source of riders' incompatibility. Another rider, Marion Steele, offers the following commentary in *The Bicycling World and L.A.W. Bulletin*:

> Think how ridiculously the boasted civilization of the nineteenth century arranges the lots of the sexes. . . . The lightly dressed, strong man may ride the light-running, single-track, fifty pound bicycle. The thickly-dressed and long-skirted, weaker woman must trundle the lumbering, three-track, one hundred pound tricycle. ("On the Ladies' Wheel" 563)

Even as the tricycle provided a feminine alternative to the masculine Ordinary, riders were coming to recognize that the two machines were materially inadequate to the companionship they were increasingly called on to facilitate. Whereas the Ordinary thrived as a machine to distinguish its riders as men and allow them to distance themselves from the feminization of the white-collar workplace, the machine's very height, difficulty, and danger made it an obstacle for the possibilities of courtship and sociability that emerged alongside the tricycle. And whereas the tricycle had some limited use as a therapeutic machine and for courtship, its features prevented it from easy integration into club rides even as its presence was changing club culture rapidly by the later 1880s.

Some of these problems were addressed by the two-seated tricycle, or sociable, which better fit the changing nature of American bicycle culture. One writer, in a *Cassell's Magazine* article reprinted in *Outing*, offered the following prediction of the sociable's ascendance:

> The day is not far distant when these sociable tricycles, carrying their various loads along, consisting, perhaps, of a man and his wife, a fellow and his girl, two ladies, or a man and his mother-in-law, will be as familiar sights along our New England roads as have been for ages horses and buggies and the old one-horse shays. ("Our Monthly Record" 475)

So confident was this author in the sociable's ability to allow riders to share a common experience that he described the new machine as "the mechanical Moses that is to lead the enslaved race into the land of cyclic equality" (475). This lofty prediction about the sociable failed to manifest, however, as hobbyists of both sexes quickly moved past the novelty of simply riding together, wanting instead increased mobility and independence. The machine's width made it difficult for couples to ride on narrow pathways, and some designs even allowed one rider control over most operations of the vehicle. For example, a rider reported in *The Bicycling World* his wife's reaction to the couple's new sociable tricycle:

> Mrs. Ixion complains that in the new machine the last item of feminine control has been denied her . . . steering, braking, and back-pedalling are all denied her. Drive as fast as I please, she can do nothing but increase the speed or remain passive. I attempted to console her by explaining that there was nothing whatever to prevent her from working just as hard as she wanted to, and that the removal of distracting duties would enable her to concentrate more thoroughly her energies on the pedals. ("Tricycle Notes")

Mrs. Ixion's complaints demonstrate her increasing ownership over cycling as an activity she shares with her husband, rather than one in which she partakes only occasionally as a companion. Similarly, her husband's patronizing answer to her concerns suggests the sociable's users' preferences: the machine addressed the incongruity between the tricycle and the Ordinary, but it did not offer the balance of autonomy and companionship that women riders like Minna Caroline Smith envisioned.

In addition to its relation to club life, the tricycle proved increasingly problematic for a few women who—perhaps influenced by the possibilities for riding that club life offered male riders—sought not only the health-bringing, leisurely companionship with male riders that advertisements like the 1885 Pope ad promoted but also opportunities to demonstrate their own powers of speed and endurance. Though in their writings, most women tricyclists urged prospective riders not to push themselves too hard aboard the machine, several personal narratives reveal that women riders were not immune to the urge for competition. In an 1895 account, for example, Woman's Christian Temperance Union president Frances Willard recalls one of her first experiences aboard a tricycle a decade earlier, when she and her two companions competed in an impromptu time trial:

> Taking out my watch I timed them as they, at my suggestion, set out to make a record in going round the square. Two and a half minutes was the result. I then started with all my forces well in hand, and flew around in two and a quarter minutes. Not contented with this . . . I declared that I would go around in two minutes. (64–65)

Here Willard depicts herself not as the sedate tricyclist riding calmly alongside her beau, but as a tough competitor who attacked the race with "all [her] forces well in hand." Similarly, Arlo Bates, writing in *Outing* in 1885, reports somewhat condescendingly his amazement at his wife's competitiveness with two tricyclist friends, who claimed to have ridden four and a half miles in a quick thirty-six minutes (695). Though his wife complained that she must be able to best that time, he assured her that such a feat was impossible, adding, "[W]e clubmen understand these things from experience" (696). Other women sought to demonstrate their powers of endurance. Minna Caroline Smith, for instance, organized a Boston area ladies' tricycle tour in 1886, which she described in an *Outing* article, "The Ladies Tour to Kettle Cove." When asked by a friend why she wanted to invite only women on the tour, she replied that she "intend[ed] to show what women can do on wheels without any masculine help" (431). Such reports indicate a disjunction between the tricycle as manufacturers had intended women might use it and the range of uses to which they actually put it: not only in companionship with their male counterparts but also in the more vigorous exertion and displays of stamina that had been reserved for male riders. Manufacturers had associated the tricycle with ease of riding and gentle therapeutic results, but as more women became familiar with the culture of cycling, they sought something of the riding experience that had been coded as masculine.

In this sense, these tricyclists are users straying from the script provided by the design of their machines, demonstrating the blurring of the gendered boundaries that had once remained distinct through the containment of the physical space of the bicycle club. Tellingly, Willard crashed during her time trial and was injured when her tricycle overturned going around a tight turn—evidence of the inadequacy of the tricycle as a machine for meeting the desires of women riders to engage in friendly competition.[4] And Smith's ladies-only tour eventually became a couples' tour, as several invitees lamented that their husbands wanted to participate—a point that indicates that not every woman shared Smith's desire to stray from the script her machine provided.

Nonetheless, these individual examples demonstrate what Bijker refers to as the "interpretive flexibility" (74) of the tricycle. That is, when a technology is harnessed for purposes or audiences other than those for which it has been designed—or for which it is scripted—it becomes more malleable, more likely to change both materially and symbolically. Through its enlistment by riders like Willard and Smith, then, the tricycle participated in small ways in the dissolution of the gender order it appeared to uphold. As Oudshoorn asserts, a machine can only partially regulate the behavior of the individual rider; in use, individuals may always find ways to resist or transform the material dictates of the machine. And it is in these resistances, which gain strength through their repetition and through the repetition of discourse about them, that technological innovation begins.

Taken as a whole, these concerns—both of impaired sociability within the context of the club and of the tricycle's misfit for women's expanding interests—helped increase both machines' interpretive flexibility. Put another way, these concerns replaced the easy, unproblematic relationship between the Ordinary and its male user that had prevailed earlier in the decade with a different relationship—what activity theorists call a "present-at-hand" relationship, in which the machine and user no longer appear to be natural extensions of each other, and the tool is constantly made "present" because of its inadequacy to the task at hand (Winograd and Flores 36). Within the relatively closed space of the men's bicycle club in the early 1880s, young male riders' interests were well suited to their machines, and thereby the high-wheeler's design and use, but gradually this fit eroded through a shifting array of activities initiated by women's increasing involvement in cycling club culture. Under these conditions, old and new possibilities competed, mingled together, and reconstituted under the pressure of a changing social order enacted through the inextricable blend of embodied user performance and discourse.

Women and the Emergence of the Safety Bicycle

In 1888, amid riders' growing dissatisfaction with the Ordinary and the tricycle, a Scottish veterinarian living in Belfast made a remarkable discovery. Tinkering with the tires of his ten-year-old son's tricycle, John Dunlop discovered that an inner tube filled with compressed air could provide an effective cushion from road vibrations, rendering the vibration-cushioning height of the Ordinary technically unnecessary. A machine lower to the ground—long experimented with but not widely adopted on American soil during the Ordinary's reign—became practicable for riders desirous of comfort and accessibility.[5] Additionally, the new tires had an unexpected benefit: they improved bicycle speed. Soon European riders were breaking new records in races ranging from the mile to the (one-hundred-mile) century—all aboard Safeties cushioned by pneumatic tires (Herlihy, *Bicycle* 252).

Despite this apparent alignment of the Safety with male Ordinary riders' interest in speed, as well as the improved comfort of the new machine for all prospective riders, American riders and manufacturers were slow to embrace a new, lower-wheeled machine. How would such a machine fare among riders who cherished the challenge of mastering the Ordinary? Would American women really embrace a machine that required them to straddle a saddle and commit to sustained effort in learning to ride? Along with the tricycle, some form of low-mount bicycle could interest older, more safety-conscious riders, commentators conceded, but the Ordinary would retain its original following, who would continue to form the bulk of the bicycling community. As one writer predicted in *The Bicycling World*, the Ordinary would no longer "hold indisputable sway, as the only machine," as "[t]he element of safety is rather distasteful to a good many riders that prefer to run some risk, as it gives zest to the sport" (qtd. in Herlihy, *Bicycle* 246). Similarly, a different writer in the same magazine observed that while "[t]he rear-driving safety has come to stay, and while it is bound to run the old timer for honors on the road, it can never hope to crowd it entirely out" (qtd. in Goddard 84).

These commentators could not conceive that the Safety bicycle—its very name signifying an alternative wheel offering less excitement than the original—could offer riders anything approaching the "true" experience of (masculine, competitive, skill-based) cycling aboard the Ordinary. Certainly, the makers of the American Eagle—a "reverse" Ordinary in which the tall wheel was positioned behind, rather than in front of, the smaller wheel, so as to reduce the number of "headers" a rider might take—were referring to the Safety in their 1890 trade catalog, in which they offered the following commentary:

> If the Eagle offers greater difficulties to the beginner, it is because it gives much more in return when once mastered. There are very few accomplishments of any value that can be gained without practice, and that which takes the least time to learn is usually the least valuable when learned. (7)

The author's insistence on accomplishment and practice distinguish the Eagle from both the tricycle and the Safety, tacitly aligning the Eagle with the Ordinary at the center of (masculine) bicycle club life.

These assumptions about the Ordinary's staying power, however, reveal commentators' and manufacturers' failure to acknowledge the shifts under way within American bicycle culture. As more and more women entered the purview of the bicycle club, even the staunchest clubmen expressed a growing commitment to "practical riding," as the members of the Capital Bicycle Club described Safety riding in a toast at their 1888 Literary Exercises. More so than the sociable or even the "reverse" Ordinary, the Safety's material features matched riders' shifting interests and expanding numbers. The new machine required more skill in learning than the tricycle but less skill than the Ordinary. It was safer than the Ordinary but less cumbersome than the tricycle, and it could be made more cheaply—an important feature for its expansion beyond the genteel club environment. Additionally, it enabled mixed-sex groups of riders to approximate the same speed and to travel together with greater ease and enjoyment, scripting a common experience among riders of both sexes. Perhaps most importantly, and controversially, it offered both men and women a radically new technological script—one that enabled the emergence of a new feminine *habitus* and shifted men away from their daring feats aboard the Ordinary, toward more companionable riding. Whereas the tricycle had scripted riders to retain their long skirts and sit completely upright, their legs close together, the bicycle required more athleticism as well as altered dress; by necessity, the rider's legs straddled the seat and her upper body was, to some degree at least, thrust forward in the seat. And whereas the Ordinary had scripted riders to endure frequent falls and maintain their concentration on the mechanics of riding, the Safety allowed them to ride in a more leisurely manner with less fear of injury.

Perhaps because of the ways in which the Safety upset both the activity of riding and the gender order its predecessors had supported, manufacturers and commentators had difficulty envisioning a future in which the Safety would become *the* bicycle of choice for both sexes. To the surprise of both groups, however, the 1888 and 1889 cycling seasons brought with them an unanticipated surge in the popularity of the Safety, its riders including many converted women tricyclists. In major cities, women aboard Safeties participated in club rides, such as those of the Capital Bicycle Club. Occasionally, they formed their own clubs. One DC-based women's Safety club attracted over one hundred members in the spring of 1888 and made frequent trips of up to forty miles (Browne 75). That same season, a Baltimore women's club participated along with men in a League of American Wheelmen parade, riding Safeties. And by that fall, cycle magazines were commenting on the phenomenon, adopting the perspective of approving, if somewhat bewildered, onlookers. One anonymous commentator in *The Bicycling World and L.A.W. Bulletin* announced:

> [T]he tricycle is doomed. Dead as the typical door nail—both single and tandem . . . is there not a rhythm of motion about the two-wheeler, a sweeping flight . . . that is never experienced on the other? And will a woman handicap herself with a double weight when she can have a forty pound wheel? ("News and Comments" 441)

Another enthusiastic rider touted the following benefits of the Safety for women in comparison to the tricycle: "no knee movement, no bending of the shoulders, no walking up hill, no lagging behind the swiftest husband or brother" ("News and Comments" 497). Weekly reports of new women Safety riders peppered the papers: a rider from New Orleans wrote in to *The Bicycling World and L.A.W. Bulletin*, "The ladies' Safety is commencing to loom up. Two months ago there wasn't a rider, now there are three" ("Here and There" 263). Another writer proudly hypothesized, "We think Dunkirk, N.Y. has more ladies, in proportion, who ride safeties, to the inhabitants than any other place. There are five lady safety riders, and the population of Dunkirk is 7500. Who can beat the proportion?" ("News and Comments" 36). Though relatively few in number, these early women bicyclists helped secure the ascendance of the Safety bicycle and rejected the highly gendered "technological scripting" that distinguished the Ordinary and the tricycle in favor of a new blurred script, in which riders of different sexes could share similar experiences aboard their machines.

Despite the growing numbers of Safety riders of both sexes, however, manufacturers initially remained reluctant to abandon the notion that the Ordinary was the industry standard and the tricycle was the appropriate bicycle for women. A Pope Manufacturing Company ad in a June 1889 issue of *The Bicycling World and L.A.W. Bulletin*, for instance, featured a large image of an Ordinary and offered this assurance: "[M]ore Safeties have been sold this season than during any other season; yet the regular bicycles hold the riding lead." As the ad claimed, "All of the wheelmen of America are not forsaking the standard machines" (Pope Manufacturing Company Riding Lead 262). The 1889 Overman Wheel Company trade catalog, meanwhile, embraced the Safety but marketed its Victor model only to male riders, promising specifically that "[m]en, old and young, have found it a tractable and profitable steed" (17); the same catalog continued to describe the tricycle as "the ladies machine."

However, the following year, several bicycle makers responded more productively to women's interest in the Safety, likely as the result of women's demonstrated interest in the new machine. They did so not simply by advertising their machines to women, but by offering alternative Safety "ladies" models. The Overman Wheel Company's 1890 trade catalog betrayed some hesitation in marketing its Victoria Ladies Safety, as it offered no illustration of the machine and promised only that the machine was "in rapid process of construction" and "designed to meet the requirements of ladies, light-weight men, and boys" (20). There is no indication of what these requirements might be or how these disparate groups might even share requirements. And despite giving the wheel an obviously feminine name, the ad's mention of men and boys reveals that the company remained reluctant to market the Victoria exclusively to women. The Pope Manufacturing Company introduced its Columbia Ladies' Safety more confidently, with an advertisement and extensive description in the January 10, 1890, issue of *The Bicycling World and L.A.W. Bulletin* featuring the caption "Now Ready!" As the ad promised:

> *Appreciating as we do the benefit conferred by those ladies who have added themselves to the ranks of the cyclers, and that received by them, we could not do less than turn our best efforts and resources to the preparation of a bicycle particularly suited to their use. ("Columbia Ladies' Safety" 225)*

This model featured several adjustments "particularly suited" to female riders: a "drop" frame and "dress guard" over the back wheel designed to accommodate a rider's skirts, wide-set stationary handlebars, and a soft, wide seat.

With some variation, the features of this "ladies" model persisted throughout the next decade, as bicycle makers large and small continued to offer machines that materialized small differences between the sexes, even as they allowed for greater companionship between male and female riders. Whereas the tricycle and the Ordinary had scripted vastly different gendered behaviors, the specially designated women's Safety models offered a more nuanced script, attending to women's appearance and propriety aboard the wheel while allowing them the same basic mechanisms as men. The advent of the ladies' drop frame (fig. I.3) eliminated the standard diamond frame's crossbar bridging the seat and the handles (fig. I.4), enabling women to ride more gracefully in skirts. Although this important innovation allowed women to forgo both the discomfort of bunched-up clothing and the harassment they might receive in bloomers, it also weakened the machine, requiring a reinforced lower bar

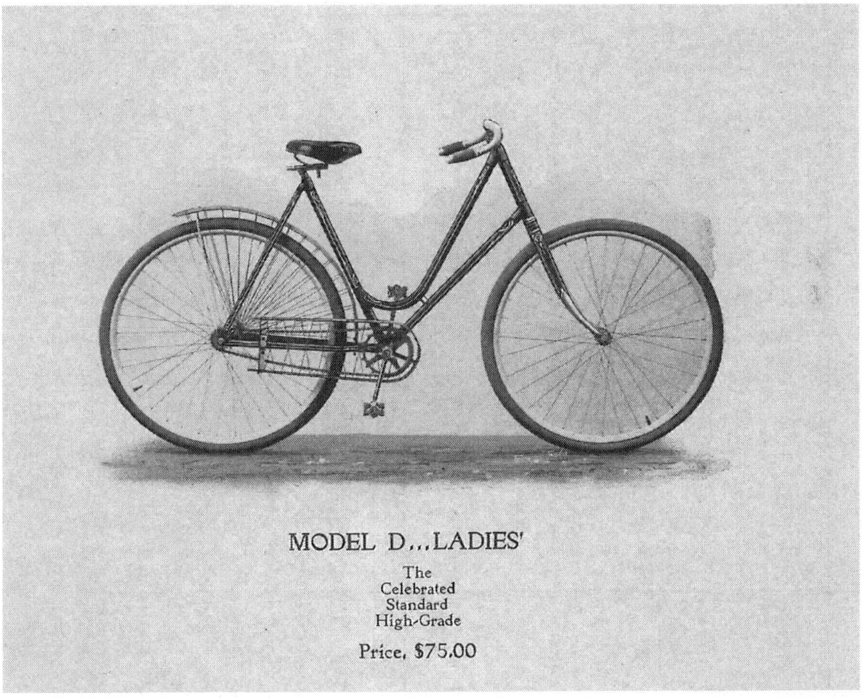

Figure I.3. Damascus Ladies' Model D with drop frame and wire skirt guard. Trade catalog image, 1897. Indiana State Library.

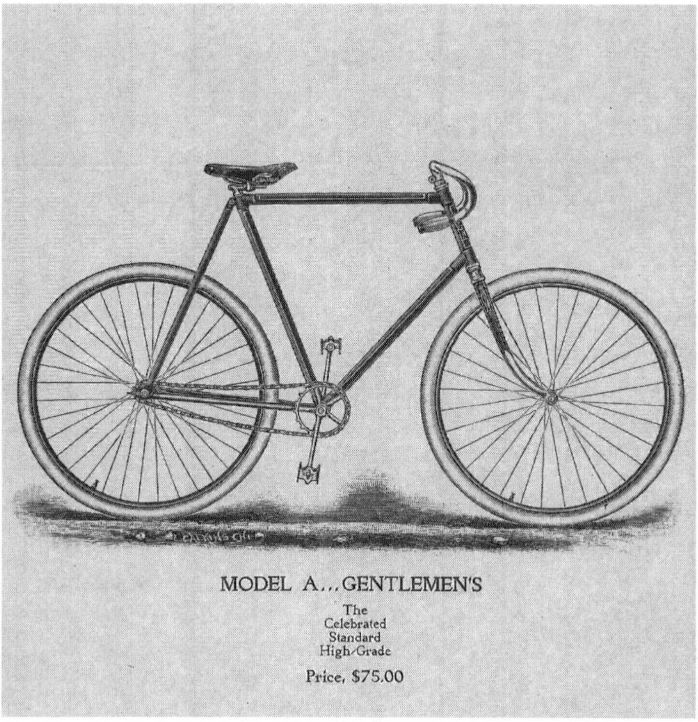

Figure I.4. Damascus Gentlemen's Model A with diamond frame and low handlebars. Trade catalog image, 1897. Indiana State Library.

that often made the machine heavier. Whereas by mid-decade most men's models weighed between fifteen and twenty-five pounds, depending on their components, the drop frame and the wire skirt guard often placed over the back wheel made for a machine often weighing between twenty-five and forty pounds. As the makers of the thirty-pound Ladies' Eclipse bicycle explained in their 1895 trade catalog, "It is difficult to get the weight off this model and yet retain all its features of strength and fittings especially necessary for ladies' use" (25).

Bicycle makers' selective offering of handlebar options to women riders also contributed to the gender script associated with the ladies' Safety. Whereas standard crossbar models, tacitly intended for men, featured a variety of handlebars ranging from low-slung "racing bars" to higher-set "touring bars," commentators complained about the unsightly appearance of women riders "scorching," or leaning low over their handlebars. In response to this concern, makers offered what the 1895 Eclipse Bicycle catalog describes as "bent up" handlebars on its ladies' model to encourage upright sitting. For lovers of speed, meanwhile, the men's Eclipse Special and Eclipse Racer models both featured "the most approved pattern of drop bar" (13), which literally forced riders into a racing position. Similarly, the Acme Bicycle Company's 1899 catalog offers a variety of options on its men's models, including "stationary Ramshorn, raised or drop-handle bars" (9), but only "stationary raised handlebars" on its women's Acme Belle model (11). An illustration in the 1897 Damascus trade catalog suggests the range of options available to men, in contrast to the single ladies' option (fig. I.5). Like the diamond and drop frames, these handlebars scripted subtly different gender performances onto the machine itself, encouraging women's erect posture and leisurely riding while allowing for a range of purposes and intentions for male riders.

In general, ladies bicycle models betray a subtle scripting of gendered performances aboard the Safety, as the features of these models enable slightly slower, more leisurely riding but discourage practices considered masculine:

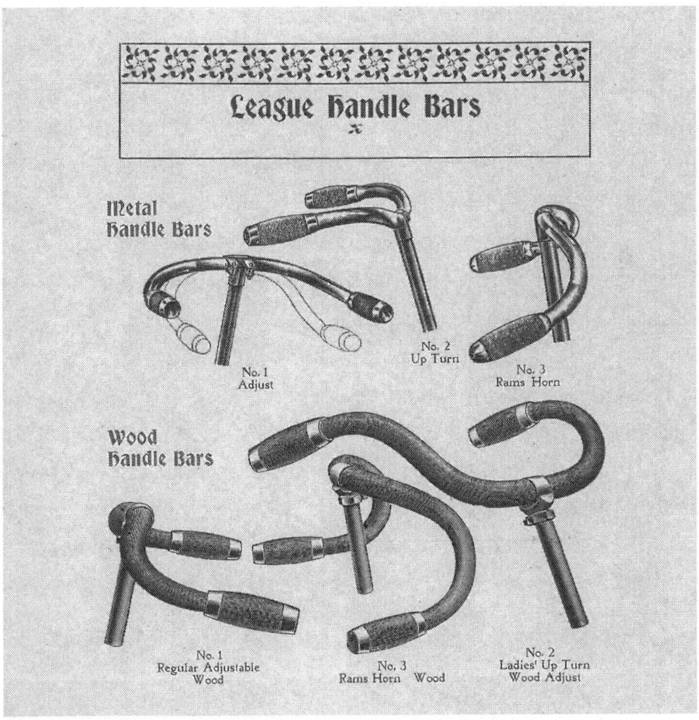

Figure I.5. Damascus wooden handlebars trade catalog image, 1897. Indiana State Library.

fast riding, racing, or leaning down over the handlebars. Trade catalog descriptions for these models betray bicycle makers' assumption that female riders would be preoccupied with the aesthetics of the machine and would ride for leisure only. For example, the 1896 Ariel Cycle Manufacturing Company trade catalog highlights "the essential feature of a ladies' bicycle: striking beauty of design" and describes the Titania's "exquisite dark maroon piano finish" and "unrivalled quality of nickel work" (11); in contrast, it emphasizes the masculine Ariel Roadster's capacity to navigate "precarious roads" and meet riders' "practical needs" (5). The scripting of gendered behaviors aboard the Safety, then, occurred through both material and rhetorical means, naturalizing women's apparent proclivities and the commonplace notions that they were weaker and more aesthetically oriented than their male counterparts.

Nonetheless, the emergence of the Safety marked a definitive shift in late nineteenth-century gender relations, addressing the obvious mismatch between the tricycle and the Ordinary and offering a machine better suited to facilitate a shared experience for men and women. Furthermore, the ladies' Safety increased the ranks of women bicyclists and signaled the industry's acknowledgment of women as a viable market for its wares. If the ladies' Safety distinguished the female rider from the male, it did so in much smaller ways than did the tricycle—and many women chose to disregard the feminine model altogether, donning bloomers in order to enjoy the relative stability and light weight of the men's machine. Annie Londonderry, for example, began her round-the-world journey aboard a Columbia Ladies' Safety but switched to a Sterling men's bicycle after reaching Chicago feeling discouraged and overwhelmed (Zheutlin 42). In general, the widespread enthusiasm among both men and women for the Safety transformed American bicycle culture from the masculine domain it had occupied during the 1880s. As more and more women took up the Safety, and as men began to view the Safety, rather than the Ordinary, as *the* bicycle, the network of actors and objects associated with bicycle culture expanded productively, and women riders wielded their influence on both the machine and the uses to which they might put it.

A Glimpse at the Bicycle Craze of the 1890s

As the Safety drove out competition from the Ordinary and the tricycle in the late 1880s, the American bicycle trade began to expand and diversify. Bicycle historian David Herlihy notes that the number of cyclists doubled nationally, numbering over 150,000 by 1890 (*Bicycle* 259). Whereas in 1887 about a dozen cycle manufacturers had competed for business, by 1890 that number had increased to about seventy-five bicycle makers (*Bicycle* 259), and the sale and rental of secondhand machines made riding available to a much wider range of Americans. Several companies, including the St. Louis Wheel Company and Rouse, Hazard, and Company, allowed buyers to pay using installment plans. The powerful bicycle clubs of the previous decades still dominated the cycling press and offered increasingly well-publicized and fastidiously organized races, but the province of bicycling was no longer exclusively theirs. The network of bicycling was dense and complicated, implicating a broad array of objects, people, and arrangements, and the activities it enabled undermined a nineteenth-century gender order that had distinguished men and women spatially, intellectually, and emotionally.

Whereas previously the Ordinary had dominated the bicycling scene, materializing a form of masculinity that heightened, rather than leveled, differences between the sexes, by the early 1890s the increasing popularity of a more recreational form of bicycling, available to a wider array of people, had ushered in new relational possibilities among riders of different sexes, ages, and classes. The tricycle's popularity floundered alongside that of the Ordinary, as it, too, materialized a classed and gendered experience that no longer reflected the spirit of American bicycle culture. Although the ladies' drop-frame Safety was not identical in form to the men's model, its differences were less pronounced and promoted new purposes and contexts for riding among members of both sexes.

Evidence of these new purposes and contexts is apparent not only in the changing designs of bicycles themselves but also in the expanding network of objects and accoutrements surrounding the machine. Ads for the portable Kodak camera, for instance, appeared in the 1889 issues of *The Bicycling World and L.A.W. Bulletin*, declaring that the product was "an article which every wheelman should possess and secure" for "a complete pictorial record of interesting scenes and incidents" (Kodak 15). The introduction of such an object into the network of American bicycling culture coincided with the rise of the Safety, suggesting an increase in leisurely touring amenable to both sexes and to the widespread use of cameras by riders. Similarly, cycling tour books circulated, solidifying the availability of touring beyond the intrepid, often uncharted, efforts of the Ordinary clubmen. One such book, the 1890 *Cyclists' Road Book of Connecticut*, features an illustration of a woman Safety rider gazing out at a distant forest and promises "information concerning the character of roads, choice of routes between places, distances, hotels, etc., as may be essential to the requirements of the cyclist as a tourist" (Huntington 5). Such a book reflects the shifting needs and interests of riders, who were less interested in "roughing it" than the clubmen had done previously. Finally, in conjunction with increased touring and sightseeing, roadside hotels and repair stations began to appear during the early 1890s, accommodating this same broader spectrum of urban riders desiring "a great escape" from the city (Tobin 842).

In general, the introduction of items such as the camera and the tour book, the increasing array of hotel options, and the Safety itself stabilized a broader and more diverse network surrounding American bicycle culture, enabling certain forms and understandings of the activity while diminishing the relative power of other forms, such as the masculine bicycle clubs of the previous decade. Though these clubs continued to flourish, they often diversified to allow women various membership roles. Connecticut's Colt Bicycle Club, for example, adopted the following amendment to its constitution on July 21, 1890:

> By payment of $2.00, L.A.W. Initiation fee and dues for one year, and L.A.W. dues of $1.00 for each year thereafter, ladies may have the privilege of wearing Club name . . . and appear on parade, but shall have no voice in the management of club matters, or claim on money in the treasury. (10)

This reduced role was problematic, revealing the extent to which clubmen had mixed feelings about the expanding presence of women among their ranks. The Capital Bicycle Club, similarly, divided its social engagements for 1891 into three explicit categories: club nights, club guest nights, and ladies' nights—a division that must have been difficult to maintain, as one newsletter writer felt compelled to remind readers that on club guest nights, "members are expected to bring their *male* friends" (Capital Bicycle Club ser. 2, box 5; emphasis in original). In general, club life continued into the 1890s, shifting to accommodate new riders and new contexts for riding, but the expansion of available contexts for riding exceeded those promoted within clubs. Meanwhile, the expanding network of activity enabled women bicyclists to experience their new pastime in ways previously not, or minimally, available. Mixed groups—or, increasingly, honeymooning couples—could travel together aboard bicycles over extended distances, and they could understand their riding specifically as leisurely or even romantic. Armed with new information and accommodations, aboard lighter-weight machines coasting down smoother roadways, female riders could even tour unaccompanied by clubmen.

Despite these enticing opportunities, women across the country still faced many obstacles to taking up the bicycle in significant number. Particularly outside of major cities, women riders attracted particular ridicule for perceived indecencies ranging from the unchaperoned nature of their bicycle outings to even slight alterations to their dress. Opponents of women's bicycling included Women's Rescue League leader Charlotte Smith, who describes the bicycle as "the devil's advance agent," charging that bicycling would bring about women's moral and religious demise (qtd. in Macy 22). Smith was not alone in her distaste for women bicyclists; one writer, Marion Steele, writes of encountering a group of women on the street: "If looks could have annihilated, wheel and rider would instantly have become an indiscriminate heap of bone, old rags, and scrap iron" ("On the Ladies' Wheel" 563). As one observer points out in 1889, "There is a heap of prejudice to be overcome in some sections before ladies can ride bicycles without adverse comment" ("News and Comments" 352).

Despite the frequency of insults directed toward women riders, the biggest obstacles to be overcome involved more subtle prejudice, often unspoken and sometimes even leveled by supposed supporters of women's bicycling. Sometimes in the guise of offering advice, fellow riders critiqued ladies' form aboard the machine, their appearance in bicycle dress, their sense of direction, and even their ability to make split-second decisions while riding. An 1889 commentary in the "Here and There" section of *The Bicycling World and L.A.W. Bulletin* offers the following advice:

> We do hope that anyone having a lady friend who contemplates cycling will give her a few lessons on the art of riding. We saw the other day a lady . . . whose knees . . . were at least two feet apart. Not only was the appearance bad, but the work must have been ineffective. More than half the ladies we have seen on the road do not have the first conception of the way to ride. (251)

Such criticisms, as well as the sense that even fellow riders were making generalizations about women on the basis of individual performances, served as a barrier to women's riding that many found difficult to overcome.

Additionally, because female riders remained relatively few, those who did ride subjected themselves to special scrutiny unlike that faced by male riders. One *Bicycling World and L.A.W. Bulletin* correspondent from Los Angeles, for instance, not only reports that a number of women in the city had taken up the wheel, but names and describes each rider's abilities aboard the wheel: "Miss Daisy Birdsall was the pioneer, and she rides gracefully a drop frame . . . Miss Tierney handles a ladies' safety with rare skill . . . Miss Josie Baraclough is the newest recruit" ("Here and There: Los Angeles" 442). In general, the highly public nature of riding deterred many women from attempting the new machine, even as riding schools opened up, prices dropped, and the new features of the ladies' model enabled riders to don less conspicuous dress.

Over the course of the 1890s, however, women marshaled their forces to address these problems, encouraging one another to ride and linking the activity not only to health and recreation but also to the enactment of a practical, capable new modern womanhood. Women commentators, inventors, fiction writers, and riders exercised the rhetorical agency afforded by the expanding network of American bicycling culture in order to produce social change. Within the changing material landscape I have just described, new possibilities for feminine habitus had become part of a grid of possibility in late nineteenth-century America. The Safety promised to facilitate greater mobility and independence of travel, scripted embodied practices that enabled women to discover their physical strength and discard exaggerated standards of propriety, and helped transform the late nineteenth-century gender order. The potential of this machine to promote change, however, was contingent on one essential element: women's use. Though manufacturers played a major role in encouraging women to use the machine, I suggest that women's widespread participation in the coming bicycle craze emerged largely through their own discursive and embodied efforts. Simply by encouraging more women to adopt the bodily script and habitus of the Safety bicycle, these writers contributed to a reorientation of the gender order of the day.

Chapter One

Women Riders and the Invention of the Modern Bicycle

> [T]he wheel was not taken up [by women] in a day. When a horseman wishes to mount his steed, he puts one hand on its mane, his foot in the stirrup, and vaults into the saddle. A woman must have her steed brought up to her for contemplation, see that it is satisfactory, and then ask for a lifting hand to give her a mount. It is the feminine method of approaching all hobbies. The lifting hand in this case was W. E. Smith, the inventor of the drop frame bicycle, and it was only given after his wife had looked the safety over and decided that she wanted to ride it. ("The World Awheel" 158)

Published in the April 1896 special bicycling issue of *Munsey's Magazine*, this brief account of the invention of the "drop frame" bicycle for women is telling in its tacit assumptions about gender and the nature of mechanical invention. Although the anonymous author credits a man, W. E. Smith, as "the lifting hand" and "inventor" of the machine, one can easily read that Smith's wife was the initiator of—and perhaps even the silent partner in—the design process that led to the "dropping" of the bicycle frame's crossbar to accommodate a woman's long skirts. That Smith's unnamed wife "ask[ed] for a lifting hand" in the first place is unrecognized as an inventive act; her involvement in this critical transition in the bicycle's development is, rather, essentialized and reduced to a background to her husband's seemingly heroic achievement.

Perhaps even more significantly, the story of the invention is reduced to a single moment—the stroke of brilliance of an individual man, nearly devoid of the larger context in which American women were struggling to accommodate their machines and their bodies to one another. In reality, similar bicycle adjustments—to bicycle frames, to women's clothing, to contexts for riding and social expectations—were occurring around the country and throughout Europe, and would-be inventors were busy filing patents describing their innovations. The "invention" of the drop frame bicycle was one product of these efforts and of other, less formalized adjustments that did not lead to patents but did assist individual women in riding more comfortably and confidently.

The drop frame contributed to the expansion not just of the network surrounding bicycle culture but, more specifically, to what historian Ruth Schwartz Cowan describes as a "technological system"—a complex linkage of interrelated and interdependent parts without which a technology cannot take hold in the lives of its users. As Cowan notes:

> Each implement [within a technological system] . . . is part of a sequence of implements—a system—in which each must be linked to others in order to function appropriately. . . . [A]n electric range will not be much good if electric current is missing, and a washing machine cannot function in the absence of running water and grated soap. (13)

In the case of the bicycle, the drop frame contributed to such a system, enabling more women to take up bicycling even as it materialized gender differences in its design. Because of its added weight and compromised stability, not every woman rider adopted the drop frame; nevertheless, the altered machine helped enlist new users who might otherwise have thought the bicycle too radical or cumbersome for their needs. For instance, the drop frame design certainly encouraged women who were hesitant to wear shortened skirts or bloomers or who were concerned about propriety in mounting and dismounting from the traditional diamond frame bicycle model. Also important was that the drop frame allowed working women to use the machine more easily for transportation, as they could wear acceptable work clothes while riding. In general, then, this single innovation made bicycling more attractive to a much greater number and diversity of women riders than would otherwise have been the case.

However, the drop frame was not the only crucial component of the technological system that emerged through women bicyclists' inventive efforts. Other, smaller accoutrements and adjustments to the machine also helped expand its usability and versatility for women. Just as smoother roads and roadside inns made distance riding feasible for both women and men, innovations in seating, bicycle umbrellas and shields, locks, and especially clothing made the bicycle safer, more comfortable, and more socially acceptable for women riders. And contrary to the assertions made by the anonymous author of the *Munsey's Magazine* article, many of these innovations were accomplished through the efforts of women riders themselves. These riders, as users of the technology with particular goals in mind that manufacturers often could not anticipate, were uniquely positioned to invent—to discover their needs while riding and then adapt the machine accordingly.

At a time when fewer than 1 percent of all American patents were filed by women (Gray and Peteu 27), over sixty patents were filed by women for a wide range of accoutrements and tools related to bicycling. Though this is still a relatively small number, it is evidence of the flurry of inventive activity that the new machine inspired among women. And even beyond those women who actually pursued the expensive process of patenting their achievements, many women bicyclists innovated the machine's technological system in less formalized ways, experimenting with dress and accoutrements and sharing their ideas for material innovation among themselves through women's bicycling newsletters and magazines. Far from being the passive recipients of male inventors' and manufacturers' "lifting hands," as the *Munsey's* author who opened this chapter suggests, American women played a crucial role in adapting the bicycle to the needs of female users, inventing a technological system that enabled riders to use their new machine in ways that the "lifting hands" could not have anticipated.

In this chapter, I consider the achievements of these numerous user-inventors as simultaneously material and rhetorical. That is, I situate women's inventions and innovations not only as corrections to the material limitations of the bicycle as a machine but also as responses to the circulating discourse about women's special needs and tastes as bicyclists. Women inventors responded to their own desire for greater social and physical comfort aboard the wheel and, often simultaneously, addressed through their inventions the concerns of commentators, doctors, and fellow bicyclists who worried about the impact of riding on women's health and morality. In an era in which, as art historian Martha Banta has argued, American women's bodies were themselves texts to be "read" by observers, women bicyclists came under particular scrutiny for their clothing, posture, and even facial expressions. A bloomer, a "mannish" pose, or a sunburned, squinting face all functioned as what Cara Finnegan has referred to as "image vernaculars": fairly specific visual arguments grounded in the shared, historically contingent social knowledge of creator and audience (33). The sunburned bicyclist, for example, not only had demonstrated a lack of concern for her skin or outward appearance but also had become inwardly hardened and weathered, her outward appearance mirroring the state of her spirit and possibly even portending a lack of empathy and nurture for her family. The fear of damaging one's skin or of otherwise becoming susceptible to a negative "reading," then, made some women understandably hesitant to attempt bicycling.

In response to this fear, women inventors created new implements that both addressed skeptics' interpretations of their experiences aboard the wheel and alleviated prospective riders' concerns about the negative attention they might receive while bicycling. Their innovations improved the fit between the machine and its female user, expanded the network of material objects that shaped the culture of bicycling, and helped quell the varied concerns of opponents or skeptics of women's bicycling. Women inventors resituated concerns about women bicyclists' health and propriety as "design problems"—not mere commonplaces about women riders' health or morality, but areas of misfit between the machine and its female riders that were ripe for their interventions. In general, design problems emerge when particular arguments about an object or its users begin to circulate widely, emanating simultaneously from many sources (for example, popular magazines, cartoons, newspaper reports, and medical journals) and from many stakeholders (such as satirists, users, commentators, and doctors); the result is a shared perception of a "problem" with the fit between a user and a technology. Satirical depictions of the mannishness of women bicyclists in bloomers, for instance, helped generate a flurry of inventive activity surrounding bicycle dress, thus indirectly promoting innovation.

In the discussion that follows, I consider the ways that circulating discourse about women's bicycling helped generate the design problems to which women inventors responded. Rather than point to any one invention or inventor as singular or uniquely worthy of note, I locate invention within the province of *all* women users' efforts both to rearticulate concerns about their riding and to adapt the bicycle to their own perceived needs. In doing so, I draw from Michel de Certeau's notion of the body's hidden, individualized "tactics"—ad hoc modifications to established or institutionalized "strategies" or ways of doing things that demonstrate both the limits of disciplinary power and the possibilities for individual agency. In their everyday encounters with the machine, as well as in their verbal articulations of the design problems that generated their innovations, individual women bicyclists exhibited tactical behavior that—through repetition and often codification through marketing or patenting—became "strategic" in de Certeau's terms and thus available to greater numbers of riders. Rather than privileging the dominant "top-down" notion of invention as a linear process undertaken by an extraordinary or technically trained individual to the benefit of the passive and acontextual user, this chapter situates invention within women's contexts of use, suggesting that users' conception of design problems, articulated through both embodied experience and circulating discourse, preceded and validated the sorts of "eureka!" inventor moments that are often most celebrated in the history of technology.

By locating technological innovation within the context of use, rather than expertise, this chapter also provides a model for accounting more productively for women's contributions to the history of technology. As Amy Koerber has pointed out, women's contributions have often been overlooked because of historians' tendency to equate all technology with highly public, expensive innovations, such as those involving military weaponry or computers ("Toward a Rhetoric" 60). When we consider how technology users innovate in small ways, often facilitating the development of larger technological systems rather than individual technologies, we encounter broader definitions of both technology and innovation. By examining all the "tools, devices, or systems designed to help users carry out specific tasks" ("Toward a Rhetoric" 60), as well as the many components of the technological system that surrounded and facilitated the emergence of women's bicycling in the late nineteenth century, this chapter combats the assumption, apparent in the *Munsey's Magazine* article, that women bicyclists were simply the lucky recipients of an already discreet, fully functioning technology.

Although women bicyclists experimented with and even patented a wide range of objects, including locks, lamps, and special carrying cases for bicyclists, I focus here on three particular calls to innovation to which women responded with ingenuity in their efforts to promote bicycling among themselves: the need to develop appropriate women's clothing for bicycling; the need to address widespread concerns about the comfort, safety, and morality of bicycle saddles for women; and the need to protect the rider's face from outside elements and moral censure. Women bicyclists responded to circulating commonplaces about the bicycle and its female riders, addressing these issues collectively through discussions in bicycling newsletters and advice columns in magazines and newspapers. Additionally, they drew from their discourse and embodied experiences in producing both singular, unpatented "tactical" innovations and more permanent, formalized "strategic" innovations that were patented and assigned for profit. In each case, the particular form their efforts took was shaped by the unique design problems that emerged through both use and discourse.

Women and America's "Age of Invention"

In an 1895 issue of the *Newark Daily Advocate*, the Press Claims Company of Washington, DC, announced a contest wherein a single reader would win a $100 prize for the best patent submitted to the company during that month. Neither the nature of the contest nor the company's objective—to serve as liaison between new inventors and the US Patent and Trade Office—was unique for the time period: late nineteenth-century Americans were enamored with inventors and inventions, for both their ingenuity and their profitability. The ad notes:

> *The idea of being able to invent something strikes most people as being very difficult; this delusion the company wishes to dispel. It is the simple things and small invention that makes* [sic] *the greatest amount of money. . . . Almost anybody, at some time or another, conceives an idea, which, if patented, would probably be worth to him a fortune. Unfortunately, such ideas are usually dismissed without thought.*

From 1870 until around 1910, America was immersed in an "age of invention," during which time inventor heroes such as Thomas Edison and George Eastman made headlines as inventor-businessmen embodying American ingenuity and progress. And with such claims as that of the Press Claims Company, that "almost anybody" could gain a fortune through his or her ideas, readers were encouraged to think of themselves as capable of profitable invention, regardless of their training or experience. Handbooks such as William Edgar Simonds's 1871 *Practical Hints on the Sale of Patents* and Fred G. Dieterich's 1899 *The Inventor's Universal Educator: An Educational Guide for Inventors, Patentees, Manufacturers, and Mechanics and All Others Connected Directly or Indirectly with Patents* were readily available for aspiring inventors pursuing patents. As Zorina Khan notes, application procedures were "straightforward" (165), including a one- or two-page declaration of specifications in which inventors described the components of their innovations and explained operating mechanisms, several paragraphs of claims to novelty, and two or three illustrations to which the specifications referred. For $20 to $50, inventors could hire a patent attorney to help draft the precise, highly codified language of the application. Such a fee was a significant but not entirely prohibitive sum for Americans eager to cash in on their ideas at the turn of the century. In an era in which, as Dieterich puts it in his patenting handbook, "there is no field so full of promise and hope of reward as that of invention" (20), there were many who felt the cost was worth the effort.

Even women were included in this widespread interest in invention, as the idea that "almost anybody" was capable of invention implies. In fact, in his handbook for prospective patentees, Dieterich dedicates a chapter specifically to women, celebrating the "remarkable, advantageous, and profitable results" of women's ingenuity and urging all those who have "a knack for mechanical structure" to patent their ideas in order to take advantage of "substantial financial returns" (60). Meanwhile, *New Ideas*, a hobbyist magazine for inventors first published in 1895, offered a column entitled "New Ideas for Ladies" that celebrated women inventors' successes and provided advice for would-be inventors (Macdonald 217).

Many newspapers and magazines, from the *Chautauquan* to *Scientific American*, generated a sense of exigence for women's inventions by speculating that as more and more women gained education and expanded their interests, they would continue to produce more and more valuable inventions. One author in the *Kansas City Daily Journal*, for instance, points out that "woman is rapidly coming to the front as an inventor," "filing thousands of applications for patents and improvements in articles generally adopted and intended for their sex [as well as for] implements with which men only as a rule are supposed to deal" ("Women as Inventors" 10). An 1891 article in *Frank Leslie's Popular Monthly* outlines the history of American women inventors, arguing that the rate of women's inventions during the late nineteenth century was such that "it is hardly possible to keep count" (Stevens 235) of them all. Some articles, such as Leon Mead's 1894 review of women's inventive capacities that appeared in the *Chautauquan*, even laud innovations that were not patented:

> The average housewife has many useful, if not ingenious, contrivances of her own conception. They may not be patented and on the market . . . but nevertheless she values them for their utility and as being concrete

> evidences of her own ingenuity. It not infrequently happens that the young ladies of our big country, with little or no practical knowledge or experience, devise something that, though trivial by comparison, yet is made truly serviceable. (464)

Mead goes on to argue that these innovations demonstrate that "women possess at least embryonic tendencies toward mechanical invention" (464), which will be developed as they "become familiar with the commercial and industrial operations and needs of the country" (467). Appearing in a magazine geared toward adult learners, Mead's article celebrates not only the lucrative possibilities for patented inventions but also the benefits of less formalized innovations that occur in the home. Though Mead tacitly suggests that such work is "trivial" in comparison to those inventions that respond to "the needs of the country," he engenders pride in readers for their resourcefulness and ingenuity, encouraging such behavior as evidence of the innovative character of "our big country."

Perhaps in response to the national enthusiasm for invention, the total number of patents issued to women doubled in the 1890s over the previous decade, a rate of increase more than three times that of patents issued to men during that time (Khan 165). There is even some evidence that women's patents during the 1890s were especially lucrative; Olive Gunby notes in a 1901 issue of *Scientific American* that "fully one hundred of the patents taken out by women within the past five years are yielding unusually large returns to the inventors" (21241). One inventor, Lavinia Foy of Massachusetts, was often touted as having earned an annual income of $25,000—a fortune at that time—for her seventeen patented corset inventions (Khan 186). According to Zorina Khan, women inventors were often single or widowed, and they frequently had financial motives for their work. Since patent fees and application processes could cost up to $100—or about one-quarter of the average non–farm worker's wages at the time—many women inventors sought out financial assistance, either by having their patents assigned to manufacturers, patent lawyers, or agents like the Press Claims Company or by sharing their patent rights with male coinventors (Khan 186). Still others who were more affluent or, like Foy, more established were able to pay their fees up front and keep the profits to themselves.

Stories about such successful women, circulating in magazines and newspapers, fueled women's interest in invention and encouraged them to look to their bicycles as possible sources of inspiration for innovation—even to see innovation as their national birthright. Inventions not only were potentially lucrative but also could provide acclaim, and they serve as evidence of late nineteenth-century American women's often-contested ability to contribute to the development of technology. This exigence helped riders take themselves somewhat seriously as innovators, tinkerers, and inventors. Rather than understand their relationship to technology as fixed or beyond their control, they saw it as their duty to undertake, for their own good and for the good of all women, adjustments to the machine and its technological system.

Nonetheless, many of the women who invented a cycling accoutrement or made a design adjustment did not obtain a patent for doing so. In addition to not wishing to incur the expense of the patent application fee, many women remained hesitant to enter the public eye by seeking remuneration or acclaim for their inventive efforts. These women's innovations simply appeared, receiving small note in newspapers and magazines reporting on the cycling world; an 1896 *St. Paul Daily Globe* article, for instance, mentions the sudden prevalence of the "bicycle belt"—a contraption similar to a fanny pack containing "a canteen . . . intended for small change, tickets, a watch, and other trifles." Though no inventor is named, the author hints at both the exigence or design problem that the bicycle belt addressed and the gender of the inventor, noting that "every woman knows how awkward it is to get at a pocket on a wheel" ("Belts for Wheelwomen" 18). Another article in the same newspaper references the emergence of the "bicycle bang," a fall of human hair fastened to the head with "numerous diminutive pins," carefully concealed and intended to remain in place on windy days, so that bicyclists can "escape the annoyance that is the consequence of possessing a full head of hair" ("Bicycle Bangs" 14). Such inventions circulated among riders through such newspaper articles and likely through word of mouth. Though they were not attributed or patented, they provide further evidence of how riding the bicycle invited women's inventive efforts, which contributed importantly to gradually improving the fit between the machine and its female users.

In general, women bicyclists' inventive activities can be thought of as performances of user agency or demonstrations of the extent to which technologies and technological systems continue to develop through use. As rhetorical agents, women bicyclists took advantage of the democratic spirit of innovation that surrounded them and the user knowledge derived from their embodied experiences aboard the machine in order to make small contributions to the

Safety bicycle's development. They reshaped criticisms or concerns about their riding into concrete, solvable design problems. The innovations they yielded, in turn, further shifted the material-rhetorical network surrounding women's bicycling, enabling a wider range of embodied performances—such as rides for practical purposes in bad weather—than manufacturers had anticipated in observing the activities of early riders participating in leisurely bicycle club runs.

The Invention of Women's Bicycle Dress

> If there is any object on earth which makes jubilee in the realm of unclean spirits, it is a "society woman" in masculine habiliments, straddling a bicycle, and prepared to make an exhibition of her immodesty on the thoroughfares of a great city. ("What Shall the New Woman Wear, Skirts or Bloomers?" 14)

This excerpt from a sermon by a prominent Atlanta reverend suggests something of the fervency of opposition to women bicyclists donning bloomers or other forms of pants during the 1890s. The association of such garments with both masculinity and immodesty, which had long been widely acknowledged and debated,[1] reignited during the 1890s as the popularity of women's bicycling increased. Another reverend, a Father Wilson of Terra Haute, Indiana, declared in an 1895 sermon his objection to them "on physical as well as moral, or spiritual grounds," as women "were riding to the devil in bloomers." And a young organist at a church in Ohio, Miss Ada Coleman, caused churchgoers to walk out of a service when she performed in a bifurcated garment after having ridden her bicycle from home; the following week, the young women of the church donned bloomers in support of their friend ("What Shall the New Woman Wear, Skirts or Bloomers?" 14).

But the backlash against bloomers was not limited to the church, or even to moralists who disdained all forms of women's athleticism. A group of young men from Connecticut went so far as to form an "anti-bloomer club," pledging the following:

> I hereby agree to refrain from associating with all young ladies who adopt the bloomer cycling costume, and pledge myself to the use of all honorable means to render such costumes unpopular in the community where I reside. ("What Shall the New Woman Wear, Skirts or Bloomers?" 14)

Whether these young men were themselves cyclists is unclear, but their attention to the bloomers' association with cycling suggests that they had cycling in mind as a particular context for their oath. Though in some urban quarters, such as New York and San Francisco, women's cycling costumes enjoyed great popularity during the early years of the craze, even inspiring "bloomer balls" in which women all arrived dressed accordingly, by 1896 the constant threat of resistance, judgment, and social discomfort had returned and the trend had receded. Even as the bloomers allowed women riders greater freedom of movement aboard their machines and potentially the ability to discard their heavier and sometimes less stable drop frame bicycles, they still had to contend with the likelihood that for many observers, the garments signified immodesty, brashness, masculinity, and even a loss of spirituality.

It is little surprise, then, that bicyclist-inventors throughout the 1890s saw bicycle dress as a significant design problem. A few inventors sought to accommodate less conspicuous forms of women's dress by modifying the machine itself, enabling riders to return to the long skirts that bicycles had previously required them to discard. The dress guard, for instance, was a wire shield placed over the back wheel to protect a rider's skirts from becoming caught in the spokes. Though several dress guard models existed during the 1890s, riders complained that the devices added weight to the already heavier and less stable drop frame model, that they were ineffective, and that they were difficult to install or adjust. Two women—Caroline E. Miller of Minneapolis and Grace T. Heineke of Birmingham, Alabama—patented dress guard designs in the late 1890s that sought to lessen the weight problem; both highlight weight as a problem in their patent applications. Heineke's design, for instance, consisted of "a single length of stout wire or other suitably strong and light material" (1) so "as not to impede the progress of the bicycle" (2). Heineke also cites the ease with which her design can be adjusted, depending on the length of the skirt and the design of the wheel (2). Miller's design, meanwhile, similarly consisted of "light-weight aluminum or similar metal in which lightness is secured" (1), and the inventor chose to highlight its functionality in heavy wind (1). Such innovations are evidence of women's efforts to make riding in skirts more feasible for women, enabling them to ride without worry of censure for conspicuous apparel and working to minimize the extent to which their modifications would weigh the machine down.

These designs materialized the assumption that women would adjust themselves minimally to their machines and rested on the adjustment of the machine to women—a choice that enhanced the convenience of bicycling as a means of practical transportation, particularly in locations in which altered dress was sure to attract ridicule. Nonetheless, such modifications could not allow women to discard the drop frame altogether for a diamond frame, which would put them on more equal footing with their male companions. The drop frame itself, along with the skirts it enabled, was at the heart of this problem. As the author of one 1894 article in the *Evening Dispatch* of Provo, Utah, puts it, "[T]he unscientific and clumsy frames devised for riders wearing skirts" amounted to "a discrimination against the fair sex, reaching the proportions of a grievance" ("Women on Wheels"). The solution, the author suggests, lay not in changing the bicycle, but in altering women's dress "to make all men and women free and equal bicyclers" ("Women on Wheels"). Improved designs for bicycle costumes were thus in high demand; as one headline in the May 24, 1896, *Los Angeles Herald* reads, "Chance for Genius: The Perfect Bicycle Costume Is Yet to Be Devised."

Fortunately, sewing clothing to address bicyclists' needs catered to women's already well-developed facility with, and access to, the materials required to participate in just this sort of call to innovation. By the late nineteenth century, most middle-class families owned sewing machines, and more and more women were using inexpensive patterns to produce clothing for themselves and their families. As historian Sarah Gordon has noted, women across the country purchased patterns from catalogs such as *Demorest's* or *Delineator*, owned by the Butterick Pattern Company, in order to achieve styles and standardized effects in their clothing that had previously been the exclusive province of tailors in urban areas. Many aspiring inventors took advantage of the popularity of dress patterns to produce and patent patterns for bicycle clothing.

Unsurprisingly, then, women bicyclists produced many more patents for bicycling clothing during this period than they did patents for adjusting the bicycle itself. This approach allowed them both to capitalize on their skills and to respond more directly to criticisms about the appearance of bicycle dress. Additionally, applying for design patents could be less expensive than applying for patents related to mechanical innovations; inventors of clothing patterns and other "ornamental designs" could pay just $10 for a three-and-a-half-year patent, whereas all other inventors paid $15 for an initial seven-year period (Dieterich 12). Inventors thus responded to the design problems associated with dress more often than they responded to design problems with the machine itself; they addressed the closely intertwined problems of *function* (by which I mean both safety and comfort) and *fashion* (by which I mean a sort of social comfort and acceptability).

The degree to which the public fixated on the question of appropriate women's cycling dress is apparent through the attention accorded to the topic in newspapers and magazines. These conversations helped women inventors both clarify the design problems to be addressed and generate—within limits—an atmosphere of collaboration and exchange about a wide range of clothing options, encouraging a *rhetoric of choice* that stressed the needs and desires of the individual bicyclist while at the same time regulating the use of garments, such as bloomers, that excited so much opposition. In fashion columns and in local bicycling newsletters, women riders were assured that there was no need to wear bloomers because of the innovation under way all around them. They were encouraged to find the style, fabric, and cut they found most comfortable and to share ideas they had with others. In this way, bicycling women established a collaborative approach toward addressing the need for bicycle dress, and they came up with a multiplicity of solutions available.

In both textual and embodied practices, bicycle enthusiasts emphasized choice: they suggested that what women might wear was ultimately their decision, and their own input was undoubtedly the best guide in addressing the design problems of function and fashion. Writing in *Harper's Bazaar* in 1893, for instance, Edith Townsend Everett notes that "a woman's individual taste is, as a general thing, the best guide in the matter [of dress]" (485), while another *Harper's* author observes two years later that "any one ought to be able to select from among the many a costume which suits her ideas as to comfort and appearance" ("The Outdoor Woman" 787). Clothing choice was even a matter of national pride; in contrast to English riders, Americans "have all varieties [of bicycle dress] in evidence, from the knickerbocker with scarce a suspicion of fullness to the ordinary long and full skirt" ("The Outdoor Woman" 786).

Significantly, the articulation of a rhetoric of choice, as well as an emphasis on the design problems of both fashion and function, was both echoed in patent applications that women submitted to the US Patent and Trade Office during the 1890s and materialized in the designs these inventors created.

Women patented novelties in material, in cut, and—increasingly as the decade wore on—in the mechanisms for transforming convertible garments for different contexts and different machines. Furthermore, they embedded in their designs options for riders to make their own adjustments. Whereas earlier patents were for simple bifurcated garments that, theoretically, appeared like dresses when the rider was away from the machine, later patents were for complex garments that, with adjustment, could be converted to bloomers, shortened skirts, or conventional long skirts. This increasing design complexity—from simple disguises to a range of choices—reflects in part the development of the rhetoric of choice in the popular press.

Margaret Hobbs Lawson's 1893 patent for what she describes simply as a "bicycle garment" is characteristic of the earlier wave of inventions. Lawson, a Radcliffe student from Boston, sought to "provide a combination garment for the use of female bicycle riders, which shall combine the desirable qualities of trousers and skirt." Her design involved what appears in her illustration (fig. 1.1) to be a skirt of several different layers or flounces, all tightly pleated to disguise that the hidden innermost layer was actually a loose pair of pants. Her one-page patent application declares:

> It will be seen that the trousers portion of the garment, presenting the appearance of a skirt when the occupant is riding, enables the wearer to readily mount a bicycle and ride the same without the inconvenience attending the use of an ordinary continuous skirt of usual length.

The tight pleating and layers constituted the novelty of the design, which required no physical adjustment when the rider was off the wheel. The pleats, however, distinguished Lawson's garment from a conventional skirt in appearance even if they disguised the bifurcation successfully; the design, then, remained aesthetically problematic for riders who, for example, might simply have wanted to bicycle to their workplaces.

Later patents demonstrate inventors' increased concern with wearers' ability to alter and adjust garments to suit their own needs, as reflected both by the nature of the designs they generated and by the way they characterized the novelty of these designs. In an 1895 patent application for what she calls a "bicycle and walking costume," Mattie Peck of New York City offered a garment consisting of a long, lightweight underskirt that could be raised up using drawstrings and hidden beneath a short overskirt for bicycling. Peck

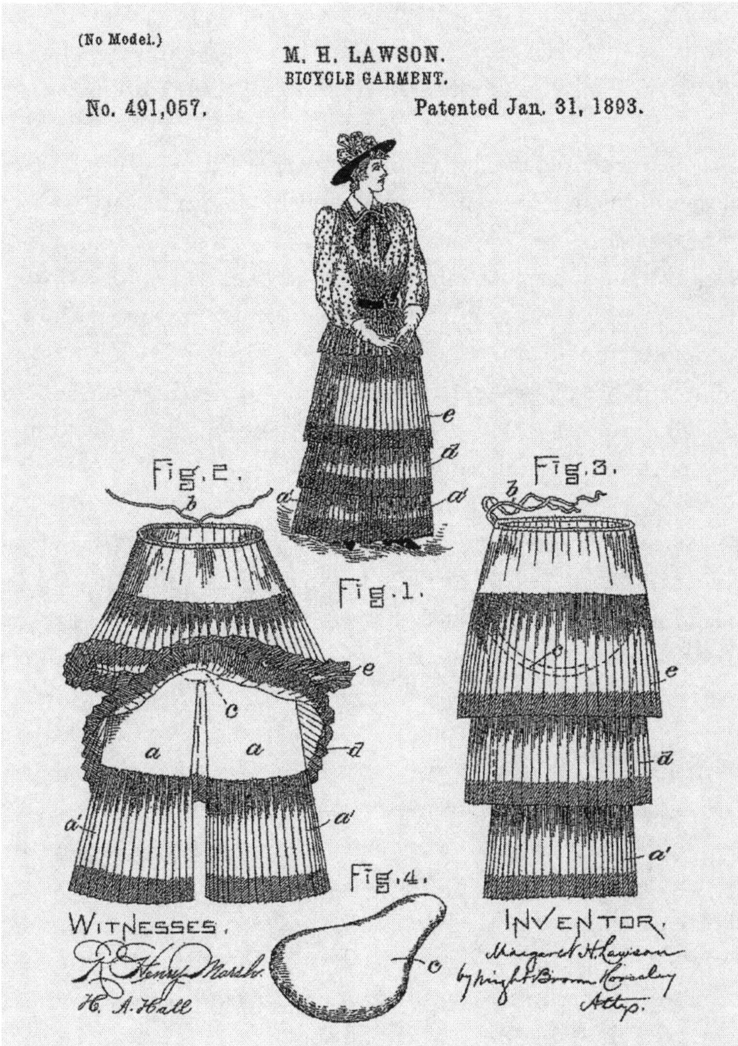

Figure 1.1. Margaret Hobbs Lawson's patented "bicycle garment," 1893. Image courtesy of the National Archives and Records Administration.

describes her invention in terms of both fashion and function, as "a costume which, when cycling, permits the utmost freedom of motion while not being unsightly or otherwise objectionable, and which may at once be transformed into a walking skirt indistinguishable from the usual style." Riders could raise and lower their skirts as they wished, and as she notes, they could re-create her invention according to their own wishes:

> I do not confine myself to the exact formation of parts and details herein set forth and illustrated, as the same may be changed or varied in many particulars to suit the especial grade or material of the costume.

Peck's interest both in declaring the novelty of her double-skirted drawstring invention and in enabling possible users of the design to vary it according to their wishes suited the dominant rhetoric of choice surrounding women's bicycling: women were both empowered and beholden to determine what style would work best for their own purposes, which might vary by climate, class, urban or rural location, or individual preferences.

Similarly, in her 1897 patent application for a cycling skirt, Eliza Voorhis of Brooklyn describes a "convertible" garment not unlike Peck's, but with a different mechanism for making alterations:

> [The garment] combines the essential features of a walking, riding, and bloomer costume . . . so constructed as to be readily adaptable for conversion into any of these said shapes which a user may arbitrarily select while the garment is being worn and without the necessity of removing the same from the body.

Voorhis's carefully annotated five illustrations reveal a skirt that can be raised or lowered using buttons and straps at the waist and even converted into bloomers by means of several drawstrings and straps (fig. 1.2), an improvement on Peck's design that suggests the increased acceptance of bloomers. Similarly to Peck, she points out that her pattern "can be cut after any desired prevailing style or pattern"—so that not only can the rider make safety adjustments to her clothing as she mounts and dismounts her bicycle, but she can also further adapt the garment to her own tastes and fashion.

Finally, Lena Sittig of Brooklyn created a variation on the need for convertibility that addressed an increasing problem for bicyclists who needed or wanted to ride in all terrain and weather conditions. Patented in 1894, Sittig's waterproof "skirt protecting garment" was the first and most successful of several inventions; it was intended "to be worn with or without other skirts according to the weather or season, serving . . . to inclose the other skirts and protect them from dirt." Sittig's waterproof "duplex skirt," as she calls it, consisted of a double-layered, "pocket-like" skirt within which a rider could position her other skirts as she traveled to work through rain, mud, or dirt.

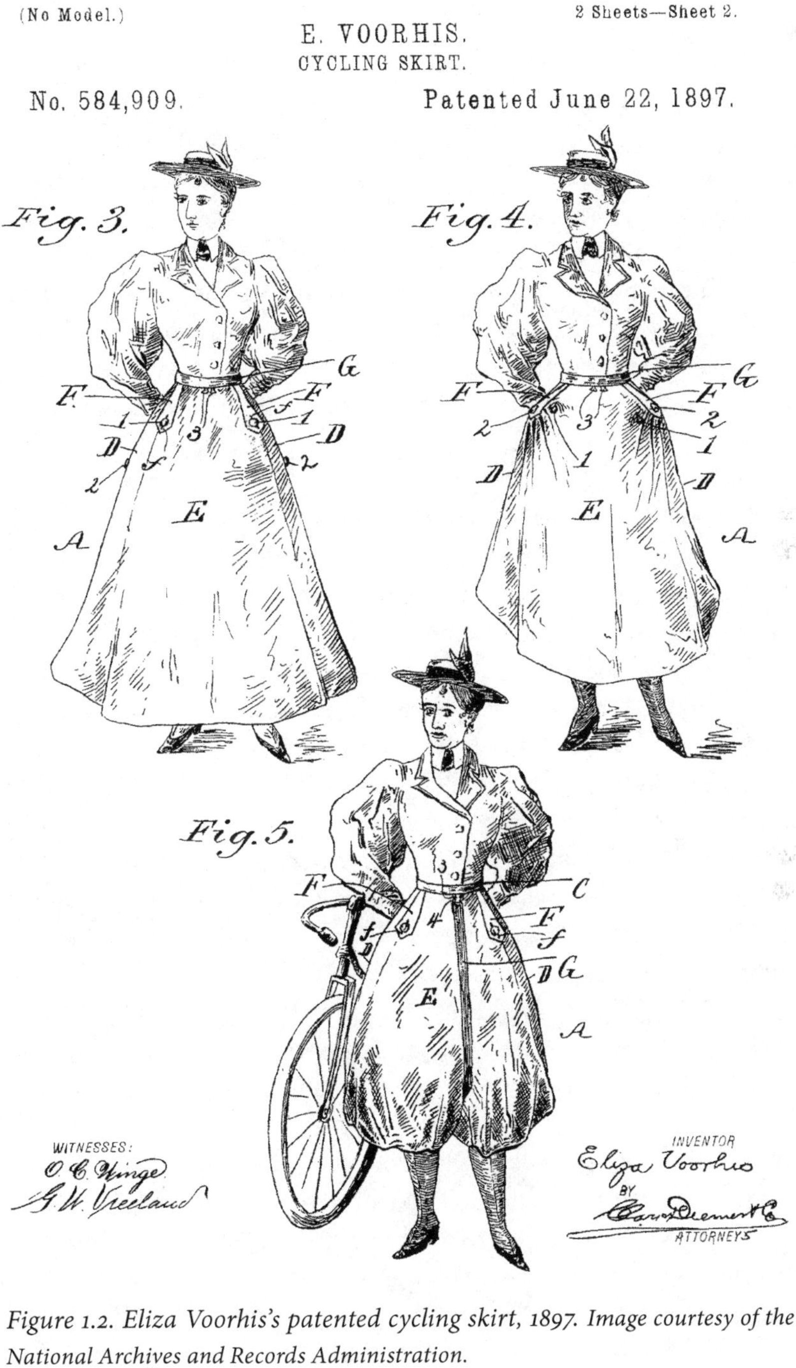

Figure 1.2. Eliza Voorhis's patented cycling skirt, 1897. Image courtesy of the National Archives and Records Administration.

Like Peck's and Voorhis's patent applications, Sittig's emphasizes the rider's many choices: she could travel with no additional skirt hidden within the pocket of the duplex, she could add leggings or a "trunk" that could be "of any length," or she could fasten the trunk to the inner skirt "by sewing or by button-holes." Sittig's waterproof skirt contributed to the diversity of contexts in which women could ride, preserving a rhetoric of choice in the specifics of its design in the process.

The rhetoric of choice apparent in women inventors' patents survived in the pattern catalogs through which most women gained access to the patented designs. The original owners of the patents are not mentioned in these catalogs—the clothing patterns stand by themselves, available for readers to select and adapt according to their own purposes. An 1895 *Delineator* description of "Misses' Cycling Trousers" (fig. 1.3) indicates that the trousers are "to be gathered or dart-fitted in front" and are intended "for wear with or without skirts" ("Misses' Cycling Trousers" 313). In general, phrases such as "as desired" or "as preferred" pepper the increasing number of pages dedicated specifically to bicycle garment patterns during the mid-1890s. And the images of the garments, priced at 10 to 30 cents apiece, reflect in their design a similar rhetoric of choice, featuring multiple versions of different pieces so that readers could imagine many possibilities for their athletic wear.

Although these possibilities were necessarily tied closely to the types of patterns included in the catalogs, they offered women the explicit sense that they had some choice in designing their own bicycle dress. In addition, they generated a tacit sense that women riders could, through their own design efforts, further expand these choices without public reprimand. That is, they could select from among patterns and further modify them in terms of cut and fabric in order to suit their own purposes unanticipated by the *Delineator*'s pattern designers. In the sense of de Certeau's notion of tactics, they could defy or extend the strategic or generic modes of action promoted within dominant institutions by selecting and reshaping patterns to suit their own purposes (xix).

Surviving bicycle garments made from patterns suggest that women often did this. In comparing two legging-skirt combination costumes made from the same Butterick pattern, for instance, historian Sarah Gordon identifies wide variation that exceeded even the options in the catalog. The catalog costume was short-sleeved and made of serge, whereas one of the artifacts Gordon describes is long-sleeved and woolen without an accompanying skirt,

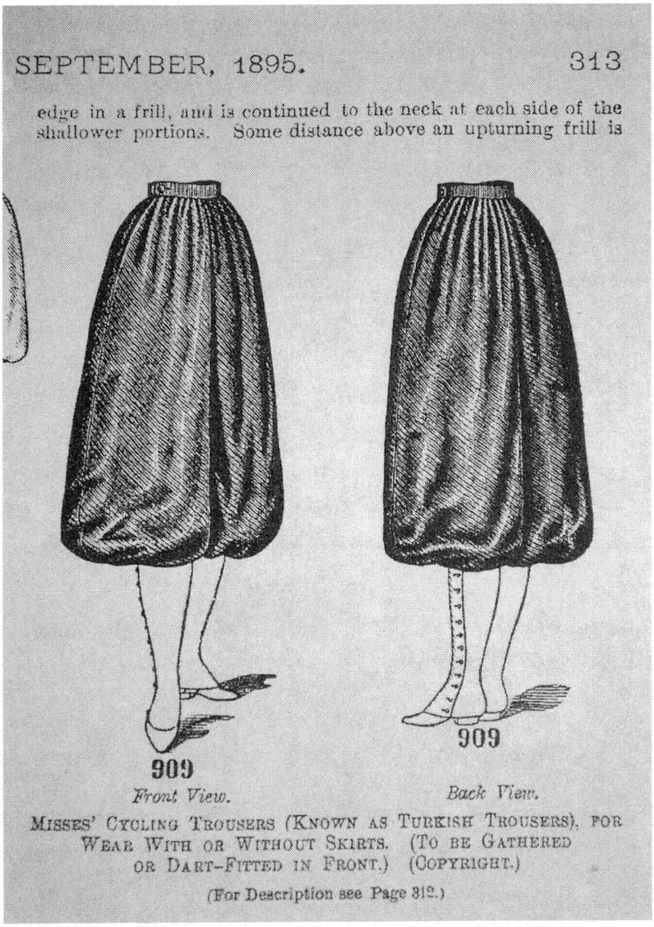

Figure 1.3. Misses' cycling trousers, worn with or without skirts. Delineator, *September 1895.*

and the other is short-sleeved and silk. The lighter fabric on the latter costume perhaps indicates the need for a rider to remain cool even when wearing the two-layered legging-skirt combination (Gordon 34–35). Similarly, some riders varied their attire not in sewing and construction but in actual wear; a costume I examined at the Connecticut Historical Society features a nearly unworn skirt with threadbare bloomers of the identical fabric, indicating that the rider discovered through her experiences riding that she did not require the skirt. These examples demonstrate the tactical behaviors that women riders exerted over their adoption of clothing patterns, promoted by the rhetoric of choice in play in magazines, patent applications, and pattern catalogs. Though not every woman rider patented or even publicized her personal innovations, the tinkering enabled by cycles of use, sewing, and commentary helped women isolate specific design problems to address and provided fertile ground for invention.

Riders drew from both their sewing knowledge and their own riding experiences in producing new designs and variations that, in turn, were attempted and adjusted by other riders. Importantly, the combined force of all of their inventive efforts—whether tinkering, writing, or patenting new designs—both validated and addressed hesitant riders' perceived problems with bicycle dress, constituting a material response to critics of women's cycling who cited their clothing as evidence of their loose morality or lack of femininity. By selecting from among a growing variety of options for their bicycle dress, and by contributing through their own experiments to these options, women cyclists came to see the design problems of fashion and function as surmountable through collective effort. As a result, the number of bicyclists increased and diversified throughout the 1890s, including not just the fashionable urbanites who had originally taken up the new activity at the start of the decade, but a much broader range of riders.

The Invention of the Women's Bicycle Saddle

In an 1895 *Sporting Life* article entitled "New Saddle Needed: The Present Article Not Suited to Female Riders," an anonymous author complains about bicycle manufacturers' failure to design a saddle to meet the unique "bodily requirements" of wheelwomen:

> The pommel is high; it interferes with the dress and chafes the body; and if this part is tilted downward one slides forward on to the narrow shank of leather, and the comfort of wheeling is destroyed. Stout women condemn the narrowness of most saddles, while many of less weight object to a seat of more than ordinary width. Out of fully a score of saddles that are satisfactory to men not one is pronounced good by the mass of women; not one, they say, is adaptable by any possibility to woman's structure. (16)

The author's tone betrays a sense of urgency and dissatisfaction often articulated in the cycling press of the day by both male and female commentators. That women required a saddle wholly different from men's was fast becoming commonplace by the mid-1890s; few people dismissed women's discomfort from the bicycle saddle as a minor concern, and little attention was devoted to similar complaints from men. However, unlike in the case of bicycle dress, commentators did not always share the same ideas about precisely which design problems with existing saddles needed to be addressed. As the *Sporting Life* author suggests, different riders sought out different solutions to their discomfort while riding, and often a solution to one problem led to difficulties in new areas. Turning the pommel down, for instance, might prevent some physical pain, but it made staying on the saddle and riding with speed over significant distances very difficult. Yet doctors often asserted that women should not ride far or fast, and "scorchers" who did so were criticized for hunching down over the handlebars—which was materially impossible to do with a downturned pommel. Though bicycling commentators employed a *rhetoric of urgency* that prompted a push for innovation in saddle design and saddle accessories, they did not offer a specific articulation of the design problems that ought to guide that innovation.

At the same time, medical commentators contributed to discourse that made the saddle, like the bloomer, a source of potential moral censure for women bicyclists. Writing in the *American Journal of Obstetrics and Diseases of Women and Children* in 1896, Dr. James Prendergast complains not only that "[d]ealers and riding teachers in general are very ignorant of the wants of women riders" but also that existing high-pommeled saddle designs resulted in sexual arousal (250). As he puts it, somewhat cryptically, contact with this peak could lead to "friction and heating of the parts where it is very undesirable and may lead to dangerous practices" (250). Similarly, in another medical journal article from 1895, Dr. Theresa Bannon isolates the conventional saddle's high peak as in need of remediation, warning that the very touch of the hard surface

> presses upon the soft tissues which form the pelvic floor, finding its first bony rest at the pubic arch and the coccyx, compressing the soft parts that cover them . . . the evil results of which cannot yet be estimated. (142)

Finally, in another 1895 article, Dr. Robert Dickinson singles out the rider, rather than the saddle, as the perpetrator of illicit sexual activity, arguing:

> The saddle can be tilted in every bicycle as desired, and the springs of the saddle can be so adjusted as to stiffen or relax the leather triangle. In this

> way a girl . . . could, by carrying the front peak or pommel high, or by relaxing the stretched leather in order to let it form a deep, hammock-like connectivity which would fit itself snugly over the entire vulva and reach up in front, bring about constant friction over the clitoris and labia. This pressure would be much increased by stooping forward, and the warmth generated from vigorous exercise might further increase the feeling. (34)

This elaborate description tacitly suggests the role of the bicycle in contributing to women riders' sexual depravity, as Dickinson's hypothetical rider is actively engaged in arranging her saddle for masturbation. Within this configuration, both the high pommel and any contact between the rider's body and her saddle might signify a female rider's depravity.

Plagued by both general concerns about the physical injuriousness of the bicycle saddle for women and more specific assertions that women bicyclists were prone to masturbation aboard their machines, women inventors and bicycle manufacturers alike undertook a variety of innovations to alleviate riders' physical discomfort and social anxiety. New women's saddles generally featured both a shorter peak, or pommel, and a wider, shallower seat, often with a hole or gap in the middle to ensure that women's genitals did not touch the saddle. For instance, one 1896 advertisement for a Sager saddle (fig. 1.4) notes that the product "holds the rider like a chair, the entire weight being supported by the bones of the pelvis, which alone touch the saddle" (Sager Manufacturing Company). Similarly, an ad for the Newell Manufacturing Company takes a more explicit approach, claiming that "[e]very intelligent woman knows that it is very injudicious . . . to sit astride a Pommel saddle when cycling. We are pleasing hundreds of women riders, among them well-known physicians." The Newell saddle "poise" was a mere ring on which the rider would balance, ensuring that the woman had little contact with the bicycle saddle.

Taken together, these saddles not only responded to medically authorized implications of women's sexual impropriety but also contributed alongside women's wide, high-flung handlebars to scripting a certain kind of riding for women that differed from that of men. With only a short peak or ring, the female rider could not lean forward and "scorch"; rather, she was compelled to maintain a tall, ladylike posture while riding at a leisurely pace.

Two women inventors patented saddles with similar features to those offered by bicycle manufacturers. Their patent applications, like women's commentaries and advice columns, did not reference sexual activity explicitly.

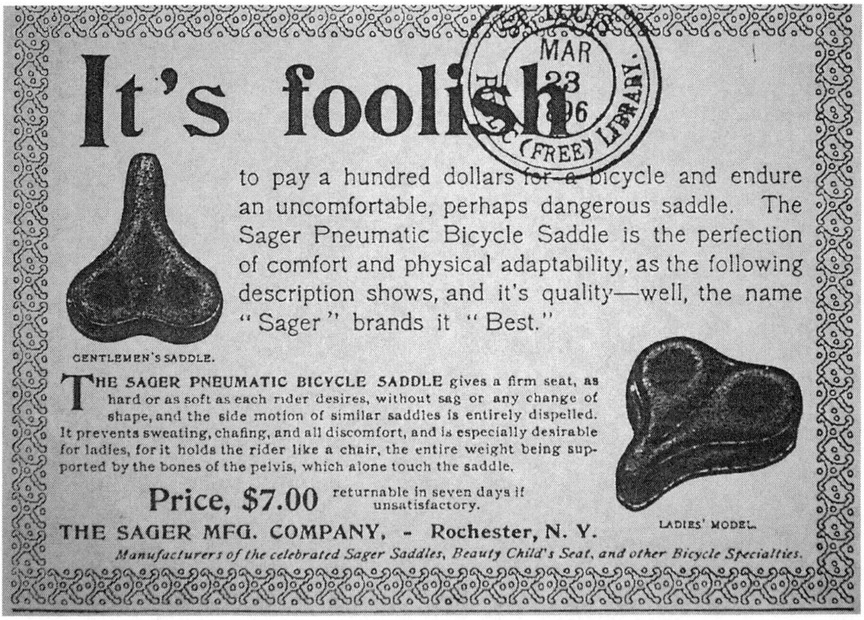

Figure 1.4. Sager saddle advertisement. Godey's Magazine, *April 1896.*

Rather, they addressed women's minor physical pain and social apprehensions about mounting and dismounting from a long-pommeled saddle. In their 1893 patent application, for instance, Sarah L. Naly and Mary Scott Jones of Philadelphia provide the following rationale for their bicycle saddle:

> Aside from being uncomfortable to a female rider, [the existing saddle style] has the important objection that the point or projection at the forward part catches upon the skirts of the rider when getting on or off the bicycle, often causing considerable mishap, to say nothing of mortification.

Naly and Jones reference physical pain only in passing as a justification for their patent and female masturbation not at all; their attention is instead focused on the "mortification" of getting one's clothing caught on the long-stemmed saddle. Though the two inventors describe a design that "shall greatly widen the forward part of the saddle upon which the rider sits, and preferably reduce the depth or the distance from front to back," and that features a small indentation in its center, they explain their design choices in terms that suggest a lingering concern with apparel, rather than with rider sexuality (fig. 1.5).

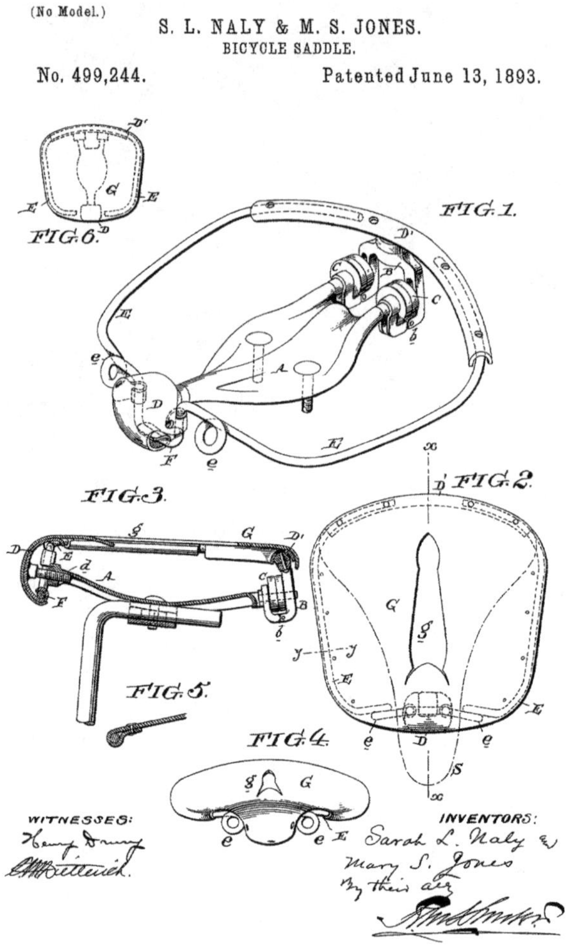

Figure 1.5. Naly and Jones patent illustration, 1893. Image courtesy of the National Archives and Records Administration.

Perhaps surprisingly, some women bicyclists cast doubt on the assumption that such designs were necessary for women at all. These riders called into question the urgent rhetoric deployed in the cycling press and in medical journals. In an 1896 *Harper's Bazaar* article, for instance, Dr. Frances Oakley rails against the "[m]any men [who] have lately written about the bicycle saddle for women" and urges readers to consider the "teachings of practical experience" over the "irresponsible clamor of discussion." A cyclist since the late 1880s, Oakley emphasizes the suddenness with which the safety concerns about women's saddles had arisen:

> I can not recall ever suffering even temporary discomfort from any saddle prior to 1895. Suddenly the slight difference between the male and female pelvis in certain anatomical measurements was magnified into a vague and portentous mystery. A new saddle for women was demanded which should discard familiar structure, and on new lines present an ideal, unfelt support. Manufacturers groped in the dark after this imaginary ideal. Experimental fallacies based on wrong anatomical premises were inflicted upon the community of perplexed wheelwomen. Freak saddles multiplied to the confusion and distress of beginners, and 1896 seems likely to outdo itself in this respect. (29, 11)

Drawing from her expertise as both doctor and cyclist, Oakley distances women riders from those who are dissatisfied with existing saddle designs, denying even slight discomfort from riding and indicating that the "wrong anatomical premises" of manufacturers' new designs might deter beginners from riding. Rather than respond to a design problem that she does not feel exists, Oakley supplies a counternarrative in which experienced women riders deny the problem altogether, and male doctors, commentators, and manufacturers are simply seeking "to serve their own ambitions" (29, 11). She offers suggestions for traditional saddles that "adher[e] to the material and classical lines of construction which long experience has proved to be the best" (29, 11). Such saddles would enable women to ride in a wider range of contexts than would the new anatomical saddles.

Though not every woman shared Oakley's approach, other women riders sought to reframe the design problem by considering the issue of saddle comfort and safety without introducing their own new saddle designs—an indication that they, too, felt that these design problems could be addressed without radical changes that would circumscribe the possibilities for women's riding. Mary Foote Henderson of Washington, DC, for instance, dismissed on economic grounds the notion that women required an entirely new saddle. Rather than change the saddle itself, Henderson patented a bicycle saddle attachment design in 1896. She hoped her design would save riders money by allowing them to make their existing saddles more comfortable and by preventing "the necessity of absolute change in the structure of the saddle"—an indication that she was concerned that the hollow seatlike design would be difficult to ride. Her "padded saddle-covering appliance" could be placed over any saddle, preserving riders from "inconveniences . . . which resulted in some cases in physical injury, in many cases in excessive fatigue, and nearly all in local pains of a more or less passing nature." Henderson deemphasizes the urgency of "local" and "passing" "inconveniences," revising the concerns of the doctors and manufacturers of women's bicycle saddles who proposed radical changes to existing designs by positing minor alterations instead.

Other women inventors took a similar approach to Henderson's, rejecting the mandate for an altered saddle and instead patenting clothing items that featured padding to protect the rider from the narrow pommel or to prevent the sort of "mortification" with which Naly and Jones were concerned. Margaret Lawson's 1893 patent included "a cushion . . . which is sewed or otherwise secured to the trousers at the crotch . . . supplementing the saddle and enhancing the comfort of the wearer." In an 1898 patent for a bicycle skirt, meanwhile, Bertha Ellis Martin of Asbury Park, New Jersey, featured an insert in the crotch designed to "enable the garment to properly adjust itself to the saddle" and to prevent "the skirt from pulling or drawing at any part while the wearer is mounted and the wheel is in motion." Finally, in 1896, Elizabeth McCartney of New York City patented a convertible bicycle skirt that featured an optional "pad or cushion" sewn into the crotch area "to afford perfect protection to the wearer" and to allow her "to ride an ordinary diamond frame bicycle" as opposed to a drop frame. The "ordinary diamond frame" bicycle likely would feature a conventional seat—a combination that would maximize women's ability to use the bicycle for distance and speed.

Taken together, these patents suggest that women inventors sought to alleviate their minor pains without resorting to an altogether redesigned women's saddle that would circumscribe their riding activities. Inventors articulated their innovations as solutions to design problems related to discomfort, propriety, and convenience rather than sexual impropriety or even serious injury, and in doing so, they revised the sense of urgency that doctors were expressing.

In short, then, the controversy surrounding the women's bicycle saddle was characterized by several different, overlapping design problems. Women riders' innovations served as responses both to the sense of urgency that some doctors and manufacturers articulated and to the radically altered saddle designs these groups produced. Their efforts offered prospective women riders assurance that bicycling would not contribute to their depravity and also constituted a counternarrative to the circulating discourse indicating the danger of bicycle saddles for women. Additionally, the alternatives they produced helped maintain the availability of a wider range of riding purposes and postures for women who, aboard a short-pommeled "safety poise," might have been compelled to sit erect and limit their experiences aboard the wheel to very brief leisurely rides.

Notably, women's own sentiments regarding the safety of the saddle remained unresolved. As late as 1904, two women physicians debated the issue in an article in the *British Medical Journal.* Writing in response to a young woman's request for expert advice about selecting a saddle, Dr. Mary Gordon complains that women's saddles are "made too wide and often too soft," causing riders to hunch forward uncomfortably on the peak; she recommends that "hard saddles without springs, and keeping the rider rigid with the machine, are the most comfortable to women who will really try them" (1079). Nonetheless, her pointed reference to the worth of hard saddles as the most comfortable for "women who will really try them" evidences her awareness that trying such a saddle required a willingness to ignore or defy conventional wisdom about women's purposes for doing so. In response, Dr. Sarah Gray writes that Gordon's recommendations are "mistaken" and "dangerous." Gray argues instead that the woman bicyclist ought to ride "with one's feet," so that the saddle becomes "a mere fulcrum," while the saddle peak is "entirely useless" (1139). Neither doctor references the masturbation hypothesis directly, yet the nature of their disagreement suggests their awareness—and possibly different opinions—regarding its validity.

The continued disagreement regarding the saddle, nearly ten years after Dickinson, Prendergast, Bannon, and others articulated their concerns about women's sexuality aboard the bicycle, indicates that—unlike in the case of bicycle dress—riders, the cycle press, and doctors could not agree on a clear design problem to address. Rather, these groups each envisioned the bicycle saddle differently—as a crucial problem or a minor annoyance for women; as the source of moral ruin or mere social awkwardness; or as a physical discomfort unique to women or continuous with the minor discomfort of men. Nonetheless, women inventors and commentators addressed what they saw as riders' most pressing issues—public embarrassment and physical discomfort—and they developed riding strategies for cyclists to use in response to doctors' links between bicycling and sexual immorality. Just as women's adaptations to dress encouraged more prospective riders to take to the new technology, so, too, did these efforts encourage more women to look beyond the moral surveillance that doctors were dispensing, in order to make their own decision about the dangers saddles presented to bicyclists.

Protecting the Bicyclist's Face

Many prospective women riders worried about the effect that bicycling would have on their faces. The long-standing classed ideal of pale skin for Caucasian women persisted into the 1890s, and cosmetics were considered both indecent and dangerous, as they often contained toxins (Setnik 40). Thus maintaining a youthful, blemish-free face meant, for ladies, avoiding the sort of prolonged exposure to the sun that a bicycle tour or even a particularly long day ride might require. Many women were accustomed to carrying parasols or umbrellas, which were also signs of gentility because they denoted that the holder did not require her hands for manual labor. Spending large amounts of time on a bicycle, without the protection of the nearly ubiquitous sunshade, was a serious concern for many prospective riders. Christine Terhune Herrick warns in the *Minneapolis Journal* of "the effect of wind and sun on the [bicyclist's] complexion," reminding the reader that "the outdoor life . . . is bound to leave its mark on a woman's face and bearing" (2). Such warnings of the possible irreversibility of sun damage only militated further against women's willingness to ride the wheel at certain times of day or for long periods of time.

This general concern was exacerbated by a more specific threat that was not confined to women but earned them additional censure from those who opposed women's bicycling: the mysterious ailment of "bicycle face," which one writer in an 1895 article in the *Yakima* (*Washington*) *Herald* describes as "a wild and haunted look of the eyes" together with "strained lines" on the face due to "a general focus of the features indicative of extreme attention directed to a spot about two yards ahead of the front wheel" ("Bicycles during 1896," image 4). Together with other bicycle-related maladies that emerged in the 1880s and 1890s—"bicycle hand," for instance—"bicycle face" received a great deal of attention in the popular press. Though some doctors and riding enthusiasts scoffed at the existence of such a malady, others took it seriously; one writer in the *Minneapolis Tribune* characterizes it as a "physiognomic implosion" that "once fixed upon the countenance can never be removed" (qtd. in Robert A. Smith 70).

In addition to the specific perils of "bicycle face," women riders' faces were subject to special scrutiny on other grounds. Faces could be read, for instance, for evidence of sexual depravity in the form of masturbation aided by the bicycle seat or simply for vague evidence of a loss of femininity. One avid cyclist reports her difficulty in controlling her facial expression while riding to avoid appearing to be enjoying herself too freely—possibly a sign of masturbation:

> The only difficulty I have is that I cannot prevent my unruly features from expressing the exhilaration which I feel. My sons constantly said to me, "Mamma, you must not look so pleased when you are riding, it isn't good form." But with every fiber of my body tingling with delight, how can I help it? (qtd. in Lucy Hall 1)

Though this rider's testimony appears in a promotional pamphlet for women's bicycling, it points to women's—and observers'—consciousness of their facial expressions while riding.

Perhaps more ominously, Dr. Arabella Kenealy suggests this consciousness in "Woman as an Athlete," her 1899 critique of bicycling and other athletics, in which she details the physical and moral deterioration of a young bicyclist named Clara. Dr. Kenealy argues that the cyclist had compromised not only her health but also her facial appearance: "the haze, the elusiveness, the subtle suggestion of the face are gone" (639), she notes. This subtlety has been replaced by a hardness, assertiveness—perhaps a uniformity of color—in contradiction with feminine propriety. "Now one could paint her portrait with ease. Formerly only the most ingenious and sympathetic art could have reproduced her subtle and mysterious charm" (640). This "face of muscular tension," as Kenealy describes it, is the result both of sunburn and physical exertion and of the moral depravity that these physical signs portended: coarseness and a loss of feminine modesty.

Finally, a *Godey's Magazine* article seeking to educate women riders about proper etiquette advocates "grace" aboard the wheel and warns riders against excessive strain, on the grounds that, in addition to ruining their delicate health, it would show on their faces:

> The woman with . . . her face scarlet with exertion is neither fascinating nor attractive; she takes on an anxious, worried, look in her eyes, has her muscles developed at the expense of her feminine grace, and her complexion coarsened by the rude contact of wind and weather. ("The Feminine Scorcher" 446)

Fears of the harm bicycling might do to a woman's face, then, were vague and attributed to a wide range of sources, including wind, sun, overexertion, a loss of feminine modesty, and stress from mastering the wheel. As a result, the need both to prevent one's face from betraying too much pleasure or exertion and to shield it from the elements must have been a significant component of the bicycling experience for women. Advice columns direct women explicitly to attend to their faces; the aforementioned *Godey's Magazine* article, for instance, instructs readers to wear "a light net or gauze . . . [to shield] the complexion from wind and sun" ("The Feminine Scorcher" 446). Indeed, doing so protected the rider's complexion not only from actual harm but also from social censure, as such a garment could be used to convey the rider's appropriate feminine attentiveness to her physical appearance. However, wearing a net over one's face while bicycling must have been challenging both to the rider's physical comfort and to her range of vision.

Such recommendations must have not been wholly adequate, though, as women bicyclists articulated concerns about "bicycle face" and sun exposure as design problems to be addressed through material invention. These enthusiasts invented additional, more substantial means of protecting their faces from the elements and, in the process, of demonstrating that their feminine modesty had remained intact, contrary to the warnings of Kenealy. Several women patented contraptions for shading a bicyclist's face from the sun and rain. In May 1896, for instance, Effie Battenberg of Decatur, Indiana, invented an adjustable attachment for bicycles and tricycles that involved several clasps within which one could secure an umbrella, "so as to afford protection to the rider against the rain or sun and still leave the hands of the rider free for guiding the bicycle or for other use" (2). Additionally, Battenberg says that her design "permits its angle to be quickly and conveniently changed in a direction to the front or rear or to either side" (2). Later that same year, Mary Hicks of Hartford, Connecticut, patented an alternate design including a rotating and collapsible arm that would allow the rider not only to adjust the parasol as needed—to "afford ample protection to the user against the rays of the sun"—but also to store the entire contraption alongside the bicycle handlebars when not in use. In describing her invention, Hicks emphasizes its replicability, noting that "anyone skilled in the art [of umbrella making, presumably] can make and use the same" (2), indicating that she hoped others would take advantage of her ingenuity. Additionally, she includes with her description an illustration that explicitly shows her umbrella alongside a woman's bicycle, suggesting that she had women specifically in mind when developing her idea (fig. 1.6).

Finally, Alice A. Bennitt of Elgin, Illinois, patented a bicycle canopy, also in 1896. This design apparently afforded greater protection than either umbrella design, because the recommended size of the canopy was almost double that of the umbrellas. Bennitt points out her invention's usefulness for "protect[ing] the rider from the angular rays of a morning or evening sun" through the use of removable, adjustable clamps. Although her sturdier design was probably

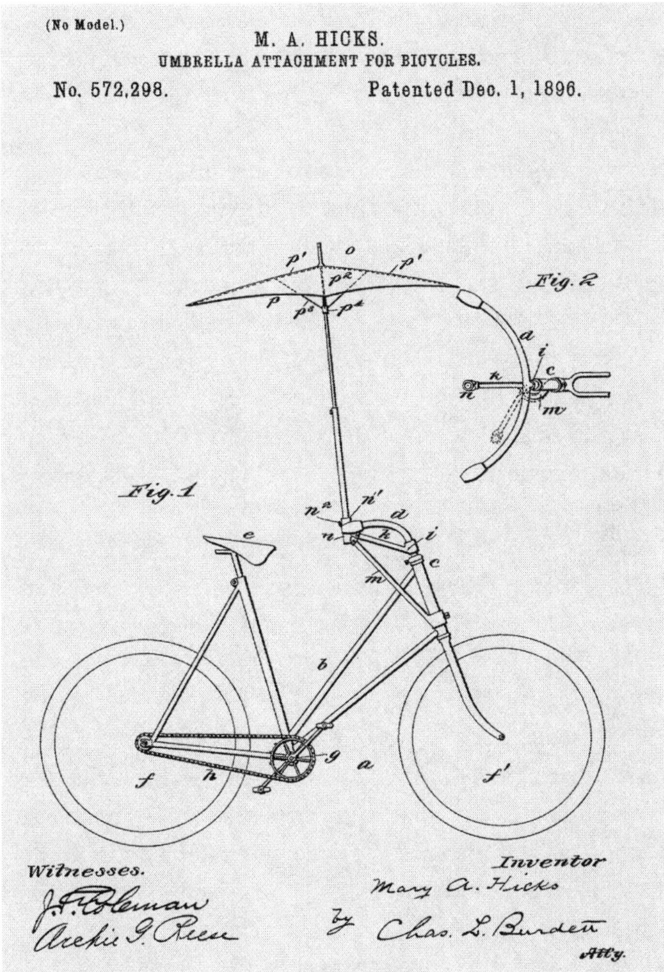

Figure 1.6. Mary Hicks's patent application for umbrella attachment, 1896. Image courtesy of the National Archives and Records Administration.

less easily adjusted than Hicks's and Battenberg's designs, she points out that her canopy is "lightweight and easily manipulated" and can be "readily adjusted to shade either side of a rider"; moreover, it is compact, easily folded when not in use, and could be "cheaply manufactured" (2). In general, these patented designs enabled women riders to prolong their journeys—and expanded the use of the bicycle to include riding in heat or inclement weather, which would be necessary for someone commuting to work, for instance—while diminishing their possible fears of sunburn or the general "coarseness" against which bicycle skeptics warned.

In addition to patenting solutions, riders shared recommendations in popular magazines and newspapers for alleviating the effects of the sun on their faces while remaining fashionable. During the 1897 and 1898 seasons, for instance, women bicyclists touted the popular tam-o'-shanter cap because, in addition to its fashionable appearance, it could be "easily and cheaply made" ("The Tam"). As one author puts it, "Anybody with a grain of ingenuity can make a Tam out of a 'wheel' of cloth and an old brim. It requires no trimming except a quill at one side, which can be stuck smartly to one side" ("The Tam"). In a *Richmond Times* article in which she details how to make a bicycle suit without a pattern, Adeline Rivers advocates the tam for similar reasons, noting that "[i]t protects the face, is cool, and has a certain 'style' about it that makes it a favorite." The author instructs readers to begin the project of making a tam as follows:

> Make two circular pieces, the same size. They need not be exactly round, as a slight variation in the brim produces a pleasant tilt. . . . Cut from the underpiece a circle as large as the crown of the head. (image 9)

Despite the specificity of her instructions, Rivers tells readers to follow their own "personal tastes" in determining the size of the hat's brim, echoing the assurances provided by the innovators of bicycle clothing. She notes that the hat can be made out of material leftover from making the bicycle suit, cutting costs and ensuring that the rider's apparel will match appropriately.

In this way, patenting and tinkering solutions to the vaguely defined design problem of facial protection aboard the bicycle expanded both the range of women bicyclists and the range of possible uses to which riders might put the bicycle. Whereas, for instance, the woman wearing a gauze net lacked visibility in sunlight and could not ride in rain, the woman with a collapsible, adjustable umbrella could ride in both conditions. With a tam-o'-shanter—a popular hat for both nonathletic and athletic wear—she could signal both her desire to adhere to contemporary fashion dictates and her concern for her complexion in the outdoors. Such innovations addressed the design problems associated with "bicycle face" and coarseness of women bicyclists' faces, as well as the implied coarseness of riders' morality.

Invention as User Agency

An 1893 *New York Times* article honoring Lena Sittig, inventor of the waterproof duplex skirt, celebrates the garment as "a great boon for women," enabling the female rider to remain comfortable and dry while riding, without sacrificing style or propriety. The author notes that Sittig's invention renders it "impossible for the skirts to become drabbled" and observes that "a few seconds in the dressing room will transform the demure, darkly-clad wheelwoman into the gayest of summer maidens." Despite this enthusiasm for the novelty of the invention, however, the author takes care to emphasize Sittig's amateurism, describing her as "an attractive society woman, musician, philanthropist and writer of pretty little children's stories" who "lack[ed] preparation" to become an inventor and would not have even thought to patent her invention had it not been for "a man, a prominent Brooklyn cyclist" ("A New Bicycle Skirt" 18), who encouraged her to do so. This characterization of an inventor who not only patented several athletic garments during the 1890s but also actively marketed her designs among bicycle enthusiasts,[2] before selling them to Best and Company for a profit (Macdonald 203), suggests something of Americans' conflicting attitudes toward women inventors during the 1890s. While American women's ingenuity was often encouraged and celebrated in the popular press, it was simultaneously feminized and distanced from men's ingenuity—framed as the product of serendipity rather than hard-won expertise or deliberate strategy, and as extracurricular rather than professional. Lena Sittig's inventions are celebrated, in part, because they apparently did not conflict with her role as a wife, mother, and society woman. In some senses, this treatment of her accomplishment is not unlike the *Munsey's Magazine* treatment of the wife of the drop frame bicycle inventor; Sittig, like Mrs. Smith, is characterized as a recipient of good luck more than as a shrewd businesswoman or inventor.

Yet women inventors saw themselves differently, and whether they were motivated by the desire simply to promote women's bicycling or by aspirations of fame or financial security, they were uniquely positioned to discover, articulate, and fill holes in the existing technological system surrounding women's bicycling. As users of the new technology, women bicycle riders drew from their own embodied experiences and from existing discourses about women's bicycling in order to articulate the design problems to which they responded. In a recursive process of use, discourse, and material inventions, they produced myriad small innovations that accumulated, working together as a technological system surrounding the bicycle and supporting women's participation in the new activity. If we conceive of technological change in this way—as a cumulative "collected" process in which inventors respond to the exigencies emerging from particular contexts of use, rather than as an acontextual individual achievement demonstrating only the originator's genius—we do much to level the landscape of invention. Innovations that by themselves may appear trivial—such as the bicycle umbrella or the bicycle bang—become significant for the cultural work they perform collectively in persuading users to invest in the technological systems that surround them.

Although it is impossible to know exactly how many more women were persuaded to ride bicycles during the 1890s because of any one individual invention, the plenitude of bicycle-related inventions and innovations that emerged during this era demonstrates that women bicyclists were active in adapting themselves and their machines to one another. And though it is unclear how many of the patents obtained by women bicyclists were actually assigned to manufacturers, many of the designs they generated closely resemble the advertisements in the magazines, newspapers, and pattern catalogs of the day. This resemblance demonstrates that regardless of whether a particular patent yielded a manufactured product or a fortune for its owner, women inventors' efforts were part of a larger movement toward innovation that was shaped by—and that transformed—both the rhetorical and the material environments in which bicycling took place during the 1890s.

In general, women inventors helped produce the sort of environment in which many more women were encouraged to take up the new activity and, in the process, to blur through their bodily actions the lines between the domestic and the public spheres, traveling more widely and independently than they would otherwise have been able to do and reconceiving of their bodies' capabilities and limitations in the process. In this way, rhetorical agency emerged through women inventors' embodied interactions with the machine they sought to innovate. This work yielded, in turn, a broader and more diverse audience of riders whose repeated bodily actions aboard the bicycle accumulated, making more visible the altered gender order that the network surrounding bicycling enabled. Though, as Marilyn Cooper has suggested of rhetorical agents more broadly, as individuals these inventors were likely not aware of the impact of their actions beyond these immediate design problems, collectively their efforts contributed to the changed material environment—the technological system—in which women bicyclists enacted a broad array of other changes in their lives.

Inventions such as the divided skirt, modified seat, and bicycle umbrella transformed the material environment not only for inventors but also for riders, who could combine specific elements within the growing network in order to accomplish specific tasks, such as traveling to work on a rainy day. For example, the working bicyclist could wear Lena Sittig's duplex skirt and carry a bicycle umbrella, making possible an independent, inexpensive commute. Similarly, riders could combine these elements to perform important cultural work, adding a tam to a convertible bicycle skirt, for instance, to deradicalize their appearances aboard a bicycle. And through the repeated embodied performances of such riders, this network gained traction, further encouraging similar performances among other riders. Hence tactical responses to design problems, such as tinkering with one's skirt length, sometimes became strategic responses that were codified through patents and distributed by manufacturers, increasing the visibility, as well as the practicality, of women's bicycling and facilitating the development of new experiences and even new identities for women. In the next chapter, I consider another dimension of this cultural work: the production and domestication of short stories, travel narratives, and commentary articles, which together produced fairly stable, socially acceptable narratives about women bicyclists in popular magazines.

Chapter Two

Popular Magazines and the Rise of the "Bicycle Girl"

There is a flower within my heart,
Daisy, Daisy,
Planted one day by a glancing dart,
Planted by Daisy Bell.
Whether she loves me or loves me not
Sometimes it's hard to tell,
And yet I am longing to share the lot
Of beautiful Daisy Bell.

Daisy, Daisy, give me your answer, do,
I'm half crazy all for the love of you.
It won't be a stylish marriage—
I can't afford a carriage,
But you'd look sweet upon the seat
Of a bicycle built for two.

Daisy, Daisy, give me your answer, do . . .

I will stand by you in wheel or woe
Daisy, Daisy,
You'll be the bell which I'll ring, you know,
Sweet little Daisy Bell.
You'll take the lead on each trip we take.
Then if I don't do well
I will permit you to use the brake,
beautiful Daisy Bell

According to popular legend, the hit song "Daisy Bell," by Harry Dacre, was first performed in 1892 before a fashionable crowd in the Bowery neighborhood of Manhattan. Dacre, the pen name of a British songwriter who had come to the United States to visit, was apparently intrigued by the phrase "bicycle built for two" when he arrived on American soil and composed what was to become a big hit on both sides of the Atlantic. Sheet music to Dacre's song circulated widely, and imitators composed alternative verses in which Daisy accepts or rejects the speaker's offer. The song captured and perhaps helped establish the playful mood of the 1890s, providing a counternarrative to that advanced by those who asserted that women bicyclists were sexually depraved or masculinized. In general, Dacre's song suggests the extent to which many Americans were disregarding the warnings of old-fashioned moralists and falling in love with bicycles—whether built for one or for two—as instruments for a fun, uniquely modern brand of heterosexual courtship between lively, spirited young men and women.

"Daisy Bell" was scarcely an anomaly in its advancement of the bicycle as a vehicle for courtship and modern masculinity and femininity. Songs like George Rosey's 1897 "Scorcher March and Two-Step" and Ella Herman's 1895 "The Bicycle Race" similarly characterized the new activity in playfully irreverent, flirtatious ways. And the young people who enjoyed these songs rode their bicycles to "bloomer balls," occasionally celebrated bicycle weddings in which attendees arrived aboard their machines, and often honeymooned aboard tandem bicycles. Whereas in the mid-1880s, male bicyclists had spent their time racing and performing stunts, a decade later racing was just one facet of the bicycling experience, which had become an appropriate pastime for women and a catalyst for the sort of modern courtship that "Daisy Bell" captures. Within this brand of courtship, men and women abandoned the separate spheres of the nineteenth century in favor of a mutual journey, in which couples experienced both adventure and adversity together, and lively, fun-loving, and opinionated young women shirked outdated notions of feminine propriety.

Yet negative depictions of bicycle courtship, and of the woman bicyclist, persisted alongside these upbeat characterizations. As literary historian Patricia Marks has documented, women bicyclists were often critiqued or caricatured in the popular press as ridiculous, selfish, unattractive, or masculine. As one commentator complains in 1895, the appearance of a bicycling woman "violates all your accepted standards of the eternal fitness of things," looking "neither graceful nor refined." "If women must indulge in bicycle riding, and if an awkward appearance is the inevitable penalty, then all that each individual may for herself consider is whether the game is worth the penalty" ("Woman on a Wheel," image 1), this author concludes, suggesting the extent to which even straddling a bicycle in public must have been a nerve-racking enterprise for many women. Other critics attacked bicycling women for their perceived selfishness and immodesty. For instance, "The Natty Bicycle Girl," an 1898 poem appearing in the *New York Times*, includes the following sketch:

> Before she got her bicycle she sometimes used to make
> The beds and wash the dishes, and help her mother bake.
> She would even sweep the parlor and dust the bric-a-brac
> And once she did the washing, though it almost broke her back.
> But now she's got her bicycle she doesn't do a thing
> About the house, but day and night she's always on the wing . . .
> She looks extremely natty in her brief bicycle skirt.
> She often talks to strangers, and she has been known to flirt.
> Her health was never better; brown and rosy is her skin
> But her mother, if you'll notice, is looking worn and thin. (6)

Though this bicyclist is "natty"—fashionable, attractive—in appearance, she is inappropriately flirtatious and forward, talking to strangers and flaunting her good health and appearance while her mother's needs go unconsidered. Even if a woman managed to escape criticism for putting her body on display in bloomers or short skirts, she was still subject to this sort of moral critique.

Bicycle courtship was not universally well received either. Caricatures of large, bloomer-clad women alongside tiny, effete men abounded, indicating lingering skepticism about the modern brand of masculinity implicit in songs like "Daisy Bell." One such caricature, a stereograph entitled "The New Woman—Wash Day" (fig. 2.1), depicts a broad-shouldered bicyclist, cigarette in mouth and bloomered legs spread open, towering over a timid, feminized husband washing clothing (Underwood and Underwood). Cartoons offered similar images, emphasizing the ridiculousness of both the bicyclist and her beau and, in the process, suggesting the simultaneous dissolution of both the home and the gender order.

Such conflicting representations of women bicyclists and bicycle courtship, from the gay optimism of "Daisy Bell" to the mockery of "The New

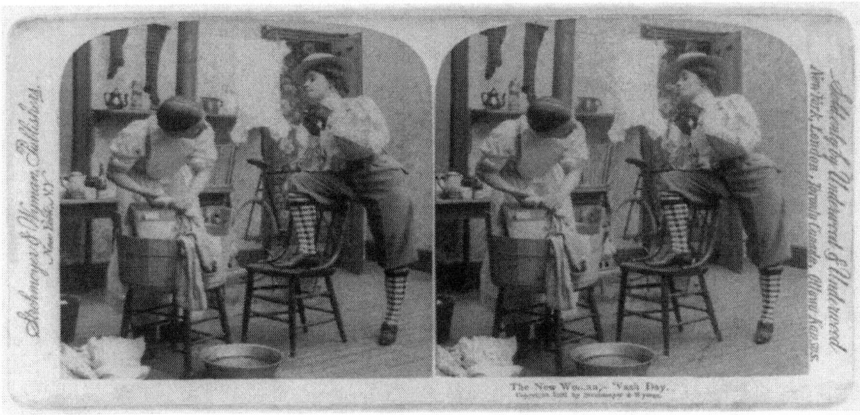

Figure 2.1. "The New Woman—Wash Day." Image courtesy of the Library of Congress.

Woman—Wash Day," demonstrate Americans' lingering ambivalence about the bicycle's role in the changing gender order of the day. The tensions between these opposing representations also provide some clue to the difficulties that bicycling presented would-be riders during the 1890s—particularly women, who were confronted with both the promise of ushering in a new era of feminine independence and the threat of moral censure and mockery for attempting to do so. In this chapter, I consider one important means by which women worked to resolve these tensions and allay Americans' fears: by publishing bicycle-related fiction, commentary articles, and travel writing in the new print venue of the nationally distributed popular magazine.

As literary historian Ellen Gruber Garvey has noted, the popular magazine possessed a distinctly modern, irreverent attitude toward tradition and propriety that made it an effective location from which to promote a controversial activity like women's bicycling. Whereas Garvey limits her analysis to the work of manufacturer advertising and fiction within generalist popular magazines to promote "a non-threatening model of women's riding" (*Adman*, back cover), I consider a wider range of genres authored by both amateur and professional women bicyclists, appearing in both generalist and hobbyist publications. I maintain that women writers used the popular magazine to perform cultural work that contributed to, but also exceeded, the "non-threatening" model of the woman bicyclist that Garvey explores. Within a wide range of popular magazines, women writers—including fiction writers, essayists, and travel writers—worked not only to increase the social acceptability of the woman bicyclist but also to give depth and complexity to her character: to give her a particular ethos that blended her modern femininity with qualities often considered masculine, including humor, courage, and integrity.

According to Nedra Reynolds, ethos does not consist solely of "measurable traits displayed by an individual," but rather "a complex set of characteristics constructed by a group, sanctioned by that group, and more readily recognizable to others who belong to that group" (327). These characteristics are historical in their resonances, meaning that they come together in particular ways at particular cultural moments—or locations, as Reynolds suggests. They negotiate, as Karen Burke Lefevre asserts, the "point of intersection between speaker or writer and listener or reader" (46). In the case of the woman bicyclist's appearance in the popular magazine, these traits overlap accepted feminine qualities with a broader array of possible qualities, providing a bridge from the familiar to the new that, as Kenneth Burke might argue, illustrates "that irony of historical development whereby the very strength in the affirming of a given term may the better enable men to make a world that departs from it" (*A Grammar of Motives* xix). In other words, women writers drew from the popular magazine in order to construct a culturally viable ethos for the woman bicyclist that carried within it the potential for social change even as it reassured audiences that the figure would not threaten the existing social order.

In doing so, these writers drew from both the material and the generic contexts in which they worked. Within their writing, they made what Julie Nelson Christoph has described as "material associations," or local strategies writers use for establishing ethos by positioning themselves in particular ways in relation to objects, locations, tastes, and educational levels. Christoph writes that "individually, [material associations] contribute little to the writer's ethos, but the accreted weight of them constructs an image or images of a particular kind of person" (672). Women writers constructed for the woman bicyclist—or, as she was often called, the "bicycle girl"—of the period a viable ethos by performing such associations, situating their characters and personas in relation not only to the bicycle itself but also to the landscapes and people they encountered in their adventures aboard it. And as Risa Applegarth has argued recently, the specific constructions of ethos these writers enacted emerged in part through the varying genres in which they wrote ("Genre"). Bicycle fiction, personal commentaries, and travel narratives all provided women writers with unique rhetorical resources through which they shaped the particular contours of the bicycle girl's complex and shifting ethos.

Rhetorician Casey Kelly has noted that agency involves "the capacity to recognize moments in which socioeconomic and cultural structures are vulnerable to reinterpretation . . . so groups of individuals may act to resignify the social order" (205). In this chapter, I consider the transformation in print culture under way in late nineteenth-century America as such a moment, within which women took advantage of shifting cultural structures to promote change indirectly, harnessing the wide readership and high demand for contributors that the popular magazine's rise helped produce. These writers sought to influence the American popular imagination through their widely circulating popular fiction, commentary, and travel writing, and they drew from the rhetorical resources of each of these genres in reassuring readers that bicycling would neither "unsex" riders nor contribute to their moral degradation. Ultimately, their efforts helped construct a more robust and transformative identity for the woman bicyclist.

Within popular magazines, women writers fashioned a more nuanced ethos for the imagined figure of the bicycle girl, complicating and expanding on the popular and fun-loving, but often vapid or incompletely drawn character type depicted in advertisements and exemplified by "Daisy Bell." In the discussion that follows, I first provide more context for the rise of the popular magazine in order to demonstrate how this new print venue offered writers both wide-ranging opportunities and productive constraints for their characterization of bicycling. Next, I consider each of three genres from which women writers drew in their characterizations of bicycling, demonstrating how each afforded particular constructions of ethos for the woman bicyclist. Finally, I revisit the impact of women writers' interventions on Americans' uptake of the bicycle, considering how these writers simultaneously worked to defuse the threat of the new machine and suggested its potential to promote new identities for women and men alike.

Bicycles, Advertising, and the Late Nineteenth-Century Popular Magazine

Though both magazines and newspapers had been staples in middle- and upper-class households throughout the nineteenth century, the 1880s and 1890s marked a tremendous expansion in the circulation and scope of magazines in particular. While the average circulation of daily newspapers increased impressively from twenty-six hundred to fifteen thousand (Starr 252) during this time, the expansion of the magazine industry was even more startling. Encouraged by innovations in printing technology, monthly magazine publishers embraced advertising for the first time in the early 1890s, enabling them to slash subscription prices in half and take advantage of expanding literacy rates. Between 1890 and 1895 alone, national magazine circulation tripled, with particularly successful magazines reaching an unprecedented readership of five hundred thousand. For the first time, people of different regions and classes were united by common reading material (Schneirov 5). And for the first time, they could enjoy specialty magazines geared toward their hobbies, political affiliations, and demographic groups (Starr 252). So dramatic was the combined effect of these two complementary shifts—one enabling a shared national culture, and the other enabling the emergence of a great diversity of new publics within that culture—that Richard Ohmann attributes to it the creation of a new social order within which people's social identities were refigured entirely, enabling the emergence of new affiliations, divisions, and imagined communities.

The development of this new social order was facilitated not only by the popular magazine's wide distribution but also by its distinctive tone and range of content. As media historian Paul Starr notes, both newspapers and magazines underwent significant changes in the last decades of the nineteenth century, moving from a primarily informational or educational model to an entertainment model (254). Whereas throughout the nineteenth century, monthly "quality" or "house" magazines had served as markers of high culture tasked with upholding traditional morality, the new "popular" magazines sought instead to dazzle readers and distance themselves from the stuffiness of their predecessors. *Munsey's Magazine* editor Frank Munsey, for instance, sought to immerse his readers in "the whirlpool of life" and saw his role as a facilitator of experience. "We believe that the time has come to throw conservatism and conventionality to the winds," he pronounces in his magazine, urging prospective writers to deal with "live subjects" (qtd. in Schneirov 85), such as sports, vacation destinations, and contemporary figures. This commitment to *entertaining* readers, rather than informing or disciplining them, led popular magazines to both a more open stance toward spectacle and innovation and, as Munsey's comment suggests, a subtle shirking of traditional morals. In many cases, readers were encouraged to see themselves as distinct in their manners and morals from previous generations of "fuddy-duddies"—as witnesses to the dawning of a new era unburdened with the stuffiness of the nineteenth century.

This irreverent orientation, in turn, lent itself to the promotion of new, modern activities like bicycling, which involved both mechanical innovation and, for women in particular, a shirking of old-fashioned morals. Large-scale bicycle manufacturers took advantage of the popular magazine's unprecedented embrace of advertising, investing in big, colorful ads that conveyed—often in few words—their product's alignment with the fun, irreverent modernity that popular magazines were coming to represent. These ads featured not only bicycles but also images of young, fashionable women, illustrated in popular styles that imitated contemporary art. For instance, the Overman Wheel Company invested heavily in Aubrey Beardsley–style Art Nouveau ads, while other companies featured images of women bearing the iconic "Gibson Girl" look of Charles Dana Gibson's illustrations: tall, willowy, and vivacious, with upswept hair.

A representative Overman advertising poster, designed by well-known artist Will Bradley, features a youthful, glamorous-looking woman sitting tall on her bicycle, riding leisurely as a male admirer, leaning forward as if also riding a bicycle, looks on approvingly (fig. 2.2). The reader's gaze is situated alongside the male bicyclist's, with the ad's focus on the woman bicyclist. Such an arrangement tacitly counters concerns that the bicycle would unsex the female rider or emasculate her beau. Because the woman rider does not look directly at the viewer, she appears appropriately demure and not alarmingly flirtatious; because she is not wearing bloomers but a long skirt, she does not appear radical or threatening. A different Overman advertisement that appeared in the April 1896 bicycling issue of *Godey's Magazine* features a young woman standing beside a bicycle and gazing off into the distance, surrounded by nature and framed by an intricate garland of flowers that similarly directs the reader's gaze (fig. 2.3). In each ad, the young woman cyclist, instead of the product itself, is the object for consideration, as the reader is encouraged to consider not merely a machine but a particular identity—the bicycle girl identity—that the machine affords.

In general, bicycle ads took advantage of the visibility of the popular magazine to counter skeptics' concerns that women bicyclists were masculinized, ungainly, and immoral, offering images of demure but distinctly modern female riders whose new hobby enhanced, rather than detracted from, their

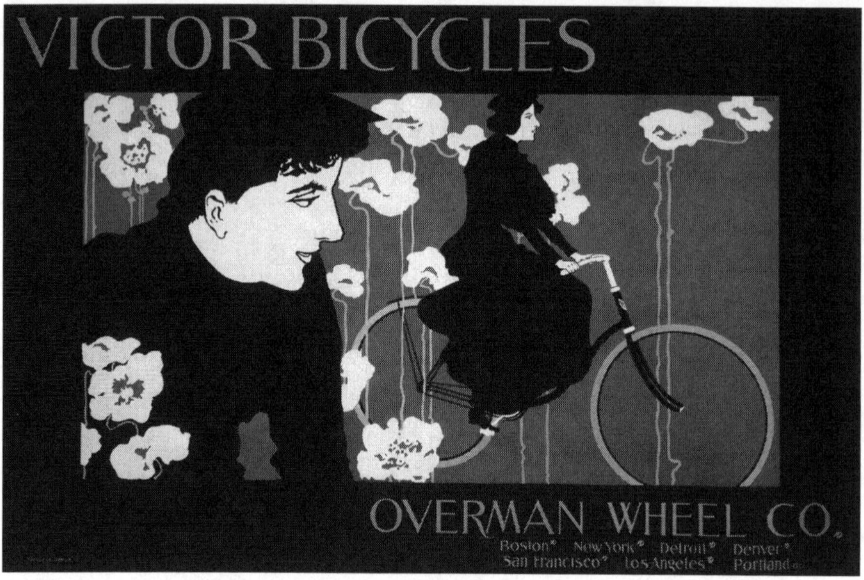

Figure 2.2. Will Bradley's Overman Wheel Company advertising poster.
Image courtesy of the Library of Congress.

femininity and their appeal as spouses and companions. Bicycle ads were also plentiful; Frank Presbrey reports in his 1929 book, *The History and Development of Advertising*, that it was not uncommon for bicycle copy to occupy a fifth of all ads in a given magazine during the 1890s (412).

As Garvey has noted, ads for bicycles often reinforced or appeared alongside short fiction about bicycling that sought to deradicalize the new activity. In popular generalist magazines, bicycling was a regularly featured topic. *Munsey's*, *Godey's*, and *Scribner's* magazines all published special "bicycle issues" during the height of the bicycle craze, with articles about topics ranging from the history of the machine to descriptions of its use by different groups, including royalty and the military, to discussions of appropriate dress for riders. Other magazines—*Frank Leslie's Popular Monthly* and *Harper's Bazaar*, for instance—offered regular columns about athletics and "the outdoor life" for women, in which cycling figured prominently.

Unsurprisingly, perhaps, the new activity made up the core of the content in the hobbyist and manufacturer-subsidized *Outing* magazine (Schneirov 123), formerly the Pope-owned League of American Wheelmen newsletter, *The Wheelman*. Whereas in 1886 this magazine had enjoyed a circulation of just eight thousand, by 1896 it had expanded to over eighty thousand subscribers

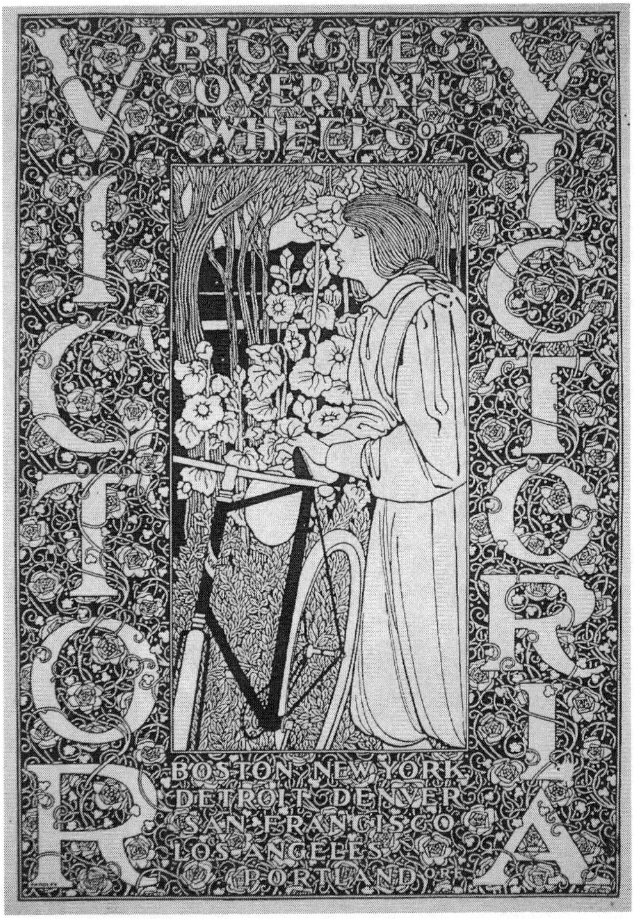

Figure 2.3. Victor-Victoria Overman Wheel Company advertisement. Godey's Magazine, *April 1896.*

(Mott 633). Notably, the magazine's contributors were often amateur riders and readers of the magazine who earned a small amount of money for their own stories, travel narratives, and opinion pieces. The magazine's early editor, S. S. McClure,[1] recounts traveling to bicycle events around the country and encouraging contributions from "enthusiastic wheelmen"—a practice so successful, he reports, that he received "articles on everything that had to do with bicycling" (152–53). Soliciting work from readers not only provided McClure and later editors of *Outing* with a way to fill the magazine's pages inexpensively but also blurred the lines between producers and consumers, enabling consumers—or users—to articulate their understanding of bicycle culture in a way that could influence fellow readers' understanding of the machine. And though McClure does not make special note of women readers' efforts to publish their work, the pages of *Outing* testify to their activity, as nearly every issue of the magazine features a woman-authored travel narrative, short story, or commentary piece.

In general, the proliferation of popular magazines opened up opportunities for a much wider population of writers to participate in the dissemination of ideas. As historian Jean Marie Lutes observes, "In almost all circumstances, it is easier to publish one's writing in ephemeral media, which require less of a material investment than book publishing" ("Beyond the Bounds" 339). Women in particular "played a central role in the lively tangle of publications" ("Beyond the Bounds" 337–38) that emerged during this time period, taking advantage of the new opportunities to publish their writing. According to Janice Radway and Carl Kaestle, the emergence of the print culture of the late nineteenth century created an important opportunity for both writers and readers to "accomplish particular ends . . . to address others, to learn, to constitute a sense of self, or to express their beliefs" (19). And because popular magazines were relatively accessible venues for women to publish their writing, they provided a particularly fertile ground for women both to exert their influence over public opinion and to encourage the formation of new identities for women.

As I assert throughout this chapter, women writers played a critical role in deradicalizing the bicycle, and they did so by drawing from the rhetorical resources of many different genres. Garvey focuses on the ways in which bicycle advertising and bicycle-related fiction mutually reinforced and substantiated the same messages about bicycling, conveying that it was fun and modern and that it would have a beneficial, rather than detrimental, effect on a woman's commitment both to her beau and to the domestic sphere. In fact, however, fiction was far from the only genre through which these and other messages were conveyed, as popular magazines also contained other writings—travel narratives, commentary articles, informational history pieces, and even poems. Examining the writing that women did in some of these other genres, and considering women-authored bicycle fiction alongside the larger body of bicycle fiction produced during the 1890s, reveals the extent to which the popular magazine functioned for these writers as a location not only for affirming but also for exceeding the fun-loving, modern bicycle girl identity advanced by bicycle manufacturers and songwriters like Dacre.

The Bicycle Girl in Fiction

The rise of popular magazines in the early 1890s elevated the cultural status of short stories, making these pieces "the literature of choice for an emerging mass audience" (Maik 3). Short stories performed a certain kind of cultural work, implicitly helping readers adapt to the new consumerist worldview exemplified by the popular magazine. Editors, as Mary Ellen Zuckerman has observed, sought out stories that "avoid[ed] the unpleasant" (83) and contained "no shocks, no surprises" (84). Hence, short stories often centered on successful courtship, and heroines embodied the spirit and vitality that the popular magazine sought to engender in its readers. Also, as Garvey has noted, short stories served implicitly as advertisements, situating characters in relation to particular products and technologies manufacturers wished to promote ("Reframing" 67). Women writers of popular fiction complicated this narrative in productive ways, not radicalizing the characters but using their courtship entanglements as a means of establishing, in their heroines, an ethos that blurred the lines between appropriate feminine and masculine traits.

However, not every work of short fiction endowed its female characters with these attributes; much fiction about bicycling—written by both men and some women—simply emphasized heroines' youth, beauty, appropriate femininity, and suitability for a match with a dashing male bicyclist. These heroines generally lacked depth or character development, making them little more than illustrations of the range of qualities that manufacturers' advertisements suggested the bicycle girl might possess. *Outing* magazine contributor Herman Rave's "The Tell-Tale Mirror: A Bicycle Courtship," for instance, tells the story of a "a beautiful girl, brown-haired, grey-eyed, neither tall nor short, always unimpeachably but simply dressed" (488), who weds her beau after spending many months timidly watching him ride past her home on his bicycle. Rave's short story is confined to generalities about the characters, who possess little more complexity than the images in bicycle advertisements: the beau is simply "a modern knight, riding the steel-built wheel instead of a steel-clad warhorse" (488), and must overcome the girl's "dignified" father's unfounded objections to bicycling. Finally, the young man teaches the girl to ride alongside him as the father looks on approvingly, until "at last . . . the young woman and the young man ride down the avenue abreast on wheels. . . . They say that the wheelman's club has been invited to a wedding in October" (489). The story moves the bicycle into what is otherwise a conventional courtship narrative, reinforcing only that the woman bicyclist is a conventionally desirable and demure figure.

John Seymour Wood's "A Dangerous Sidepath: A Story of the Wheel" similarly advances the courtship narrative implicit in advertisements. The story is told in the third person from the perspective of an outside observer, an unnamed friend of the hero, struggling law clerk Sam Selover, who by story's end has married fellow bicyclist Nathalie Sedge. Though we learn of Sam's love of nature, his willingness to sacrifice to take care of his ailing mother and sister, his artistic talent, his shyness, and his popularity among everyone he meets, we gain little more of Nathalie's character than we do of the unnamed heroine in "The Tell-Tale Mirror." Rather, Nathalie simply exemplifies the bicycle girl's physical and social attributes: we learn that she possesses wealth, beauty, agility, flirtatiousness, and nursing skill, which she applies to Sam's wounds after a bicycle accident. As one of Sam's friend's notes, "She's as full of fun as fun can be, by Jove! She's a terrible flirt, too!" (211). Predictably, however, Nathalie's flirtatiousness is neutralized when she cares for him after his bicycle injury; as he recovers, she "administer[s to him] assiduously" and proves herself "simple, quiet, [and] sincere" (214) during their conversations about his financial troubles. In the end, Sam and Nathalie are married and have replaced their bicycles entirely with another wheeled vehicle: a baby stroller. In general, "A Dangerous Sidepath," like "The Tell-Tale Mirror," substantiates and extends the courtship narratives of manufacturers' advertisements, establishing the woman bicyclist as an appealing figure but maintaining her role as an object of desire and admiration to whom the reader has only limited access.

To be sure, women fiction writers situated their bicycle heroines within courtship narratives similar to Rave's and Wood's. Their heroines conformed outwardly to the image of the bicycle girl that was emerging through advertisements and larger popular narratives of bicycling courtship: this heroine was youthful and attractive, and she possessed modern vitality and pluck, which distinguished her from her more staid and physically weaker foremothers. However, within many woman-authored short stories, the bicycle heroine became a more complex figure—one who grappled with the question of whether to marry at all. Whereas in Rave's and Wood's stories, the bicycle functions simply to assist a deserving male hero in finding an appropriate mate, in much woman-authored popular fiction, particularly that appearing in *Outing*, it functions more primarily to signify the heroine's independence, capacity for introspection, and physical bravery, as well as to distinguish her beau as an appropriate match.

Caroline Shelley's 1896 *Outing* story, "A Friend in Need," provides an example of how women authors often inserted the bicycle into their tales in ways that highlighted the depth and complexity of their female heroines, even while maintaining the coherence of the young and marriageable bicycle girl. Like the women in advertisements and the heroines in Wood's and Rave's stories, protagonist Katherine Whittier is attractive in a Gibson Girl fashion: "tall" and "slender," with "a radiant smile" and "a few stray curls" that continually escape the "thick, brown waves" of her hair (169). She is athletic and fun-loving, going yachting and dancing with groups of friends throughout the story. However, Shelley continually complicates her heroine's status as a simple, fun-loving bicycle girl, emphasizing her desire for solitude, her capacity for introspection, and her sensitivity to nature.

For instance, when the story opens, Katherine has recently rejected Tom Norreys's offer of marriage because she knows that in her youth and inexperience, "everything ha[s] the glitter and freshness of novelty." She requests more time to consider his offer, noting that she "wants to be very true to [her]self" (166). When they find themselves thrown together during a stay at a common friend's home, she insists that he keep his distance from her and instead works out her feelings for him while bicycling alone:

> She sprang on her bicycle one afternoon and drew in a long deep breath of satisfaction in her freedom, as she flew down the hard, white road that led into as fair a country as the heart of a wheelwoman could wish for. She toiled up the steep hills with the noonday sun pouring on her heated face, and coasted down the other side with breezes straight from the ocean blowing the tendrils of hair across her face and the scent of the sea to her nostrils. (171)

Shelley's characterization of this solo ride indicates that Katherine appreciates solitude and physical exertion, a conventionally masculine activity, as well as that she values her capacity to choose her own future and is conflicted about her feelings for Tom.

Interestingly, Shelley casts Tom as less conflicted in his own feelings for Katherine. Repeatedly, she notes his preference for Katherine's tall, willowy figure over the "plump," "pretty blonde fluffiness" (169) of Mrs. Thorne, another (nonbicyclist) character whom he courts halfheartedly because Katherine is unavailable. "Every turn of [Katherine's] head, every intonation of her low, sweet voice was dear to him," Shelley says, demonstrating the depth of his affection for Katherine in contrast to Mrs. Thorne, whom he confesses is "nothing to him" (172). By situating Tom in the story in this way, Shelley suggests that the modern courtship narrative is made possible not simply by the fun-loving athleticism of the bicycle girl, but also by the sincere affection of the modern beau, who seeks something more than surface companionship in his ideal mate.

When Katherine's bicycle tire is punctured while she is on a particularly long solo ride, however, she reveals some feminine vulnerability (she is the "Friend in Need" of the title) and is rescued by her former suitor. Though Katherine apparently does not know how to repair the tire, Tom quickly assesses the situation and reassures her that the problem is "the old story"—familiar and fixable because he has the necessary tools. Katherine is appropriately feminine, with a "trembling voice" (171), tears, and the confession that before her tire was punctured, she had lost her way entirely. As they repair the tire together, it is Katherine who confesses her love to Tom, rekindling a relationship that, we are at least led to believe, will lead to marriage. Both in casting Katherine as a reluctant bride and in enlisting her, rather than Tom, to renew the romance, Shelley affirms Katherine's agency as a partner in the bicycle courtship and alludes that her marriageability derives as much from her depth of character—her capacity for introspection—as it does from her attractiveness or her sense of adventure.

Similarly, Florence Guertin's 1895 story, "The Wheel of Time," depicts a bicycle-centered courtship and eventual engagement between a practical but somewhat vulnerable heroine and a chivalrous but modern hero. The heroine, Katharine Clark, looks the part of the modern, athletic bicycle girl. As her beau, Dwight Matterson, notes in describing his admiration of her physical attributes:

> [T]o some people she might appear more attractive in the full regalia of evening dress; but cycling was the time when he admired her most. Her cheeks glowed and her eyes shone with full enjoyment of the sport, and she looked like a girl of eighteen. (350)

Like Tom Norreys, Dwight appreciates his beloved's athleticism and expresses no doubt about his affections.

Similarly to Katherine Whittier in "A Friend in Need," Katharine Clark has already refused Dwight's offer of marriage, demonstrating her levelheadedness and maturity; Guertin notes that though Katharine "had no particular aversion to matrimony," she had not felt sure that Dwight Matterson was "the right man" (347) and thus had turned him away. Also like the characters in "A Friend in Need," the two protagonists maintain a common understanding despite their presumably failed courtship. Guertin presents segments of their letters to one another as evidence of the candid humor they share; at one point, when he is traveling in the West, he admits to Katharine that he is going bald, while she makes fun of her poor bicycling abilities. Though Dwight receives attention from Blanche Warden, a flirtatious and attractive young nonbicyclist, the attention she offers is "of a different kind" from Katharine's; Blanche goes into "raptures" and effuses his every gift "with superlatives until he refuses to listen" (349), suggesting her superficiality and her insincerity. Meanwhile, Dwight longs for the depth and candor of his friendship with Katharine:

> He was conscious, when with Katharine Clark, of a comfortable feeling of being understood, and of the best that was in him brought out . . . there was nothing in which he was interested that he could not talk of to her, from the price of the stock market to the art of Aubrey Beardsley. (349)

Dwight is not satisfied with the superficial formality of a relationship with a woman like Blanche; neither does he appear to long for the masculine friendships that bicycling men had pursued in the previous decade through men's bicycle club membership. Rather, Dwight seeks companionship with a woman like Katharine, whose ability to speak about both the stock market and Aubrey Beardsley signals not only her class status and educational level but also her modern views.

Notably, Dwight earns this opportunity in a similar scenario to the one that unfolds in "A Friend in Need." Like Katherine Whittier of that story, Katharine Clark reveals herself as appropriately vulnerable despite her wit and personal restraint; she loves to ride her bicycle but requires Dwight's chivalrous assistance in navigating some of its mechanical challenges. When the two are separated from a party of riders, Katharine's dress becomes stuck in her pedal, causing her to twist her wrist and narrowly miss falling off her wheel. As the two talk confidentially, Dwight cuts the ruffle out of the wheel and then treats her injured wrist, lessening her pain so that she can ride home safely. Just as in Shelley's story the female protagonist initiates the rekindled courtship, it is this event that prompts Katharine to let Dwight know her feelings for him, leading him to propose marriage a second time. The two thank (and pun) "the wheel of time" for bringing them back together.

The bicycle, in these stories, provides a way to distinguish both male and female modern protagonists from their nineteenth-century counterparts. In both stories, the courtship hinges on heroines who, while appropriately youthful, attractive, and fun-loving, possess independence tempered by vulnerability and are also marked by personal characteristics: a love of solitude in nature in Katherine Whittier's case and a sense of humor in Katharine Clark's case. The bicycle is a mechanism for displaying these qualities, rather than simply for bringing the couples together, and the beaus are modern not simply in their appreciation of bicycling or in their desire for young women who bicycle but also in the depth of their emotional connection to their beloveds, as signified both in their statements and in their willingness to wait for acceptance.

Additionally, women writers sometimes depicted female protagonists as adventurous heroines, athletic and fearless in their lifesaving feats aboard the wheel. Flora Lincoln Comstock's "Rosalind A-wheel," which appeared in the April 1896 special bicycling issue of *Godey's Magazine*, is a strong example of such a story. Consistent with the popular magazine's rejection of old-fashioned attitudes, Comstock's main character, Ethel, deceives her "stern" father and traditional mother by pawning a diamond pin she received as a gift. With the money she gains, she buys her own bicycle, which she stores and learns to ride in secret because her parents disapprove of bicycling women. After Ethel plans a secret bicycle trip and dons a boy's costume as a disguise, she recognizes a fellow bicyclist, Vernon Darrington, as the brother of a schoolmate. She travels with his friends through the countryside, even daring to dine and set up camp with them. Ethel enjoys her disguise until the group is awakened in the middle of the night by yells from a burning house. While the others work to stop the fire, Ethel must ride her bicycle to the nearest doctor to save a badly burned man:

> I rushed for my bicycle and was soon flying along the road, seeing all the time the terribly burned man and hearing his groans. The ground flew from under my wheel, and before I realized that I could be so near I saw the white fence. (390)

In an act that provides suspense for the story, Ethel helps save the man's life and participates fully in helping his family put out the fire. In her disguise, she is privy to the life of a young man and is clearly exhilarated by the experience—suggesting to some extent that the clothing and the bicycle make the person.

However, once the adventure is over, Ethel is exhausted from the stress and exertion of her ride and in need of appropriate masculine assistance. Similarly to Katherine Whittier and Katharine Clark, she punctures a tire and confesses that she "knew nothing about mending it." Though she tells herself to "[b]race up . . . ; be a man," she is able to return to camp only after Vernon finds her and escorts her there. Not only does he reveal that he has known her secret from the start, but he opens his heart to her and tells her that he admires her for her heroic and athletic deeds. Despite his frank profession of love, however, Vernon insists on escorting Ethel from camp back to her parents' home, where she is punished (and thus brought back into the familial fold) but allowed to begin a courtship with her beau, Vernon Darrington.

Physically, Ethel is the picture of the Gibson Girl, reporting that her boy's costume fits easily because of her "length of limb and general slenderness" and commenting about her conveniently short curls. She celebrates her "delightful freedom from skirts" (389), as well as the speed with which she is able to change her clothing without "so many hooks and eyes to fasten as usual" (390). However, later, when she senses that Vernon has discovered her true identity, she laments that he must view her as "a romp, an unsexed girl perhaps, an extreme version of the 'new woman'" (392), demonstrating that her defiance has not rendered her unmarriageable. Hence, the reader is reassured that despite her courage, athleticism, and sense of adventure, Ethel is a modest and marriageable young woman.

In "A Fin de Cycle Incident," appearing in an 1896 issue of *Outing* magazine, Edna C. Jackson offers another example of an adventurous female heroine. The female protagonist, Renie, is slender and attractive while exercising, as Jackson emphasizes in her description of Renie swinging Indian clubs:

> Her eyes sparkled; a soft flush came into her cheeks; the lace sleeves fell back from the rounded arms, and the supple form swayed to and fro as she swung the clubs with lightning speed. . . . Altogether it was a pretty picture and told of long and patient practice. (193)

Like other bicycle heroines, Renie looks the part of the bicycle girl, with her sparkling eyes and "soft flush" on her cheeks. She is also appropriately spirited, giving her bike "a small kick with her slippered foot" after she falls off, declaring, "I don't see what skirts were made for, anyhow! They are always in the way!" (193), and returning to her bicycle the next day donning "full Turkish pants of blue, blouse, and saucy cap crushed over boyish curls!" (194).

Yet Renie is conflicted about her conservative fiancé, Horace, who staunchly rejects female athletes and women who participate too boldly in public life, a fact that Jackson suggests makes him inadequate as a partner for Renie. During visits to Renie's house, for instance, he announces that he abhors women's "mannish posing" as athletes, as well as "the bold ways and language of the so-called fin de siecle girl" (192). Throughout much of the story, Renie struggles with her fear of even telling Horace about the secret bicycle lessons she is receiving from her brother Jim. "I must get those antiquated ideas of his remodeled to the present century!" (192), Renie insists.

She finds an opportunity to do this when she discovers a plot hatched by hoboes who plan to attack him at his work. To save his life, Renie must beat his train to its destination and warn him about the danger; doing so involves the intrepid act of riding her bicycle through a train tunnel and outrunning the train. Jackson's language in describing this moment is dramatic and suspenseful, demonstrating Renie's bravery and athleticism:

> Not once does the brave wheel slacken; not once does its rider waver! Into the black cavern she speeds and is swallowed up in darkness. She bends lower over the machine, of which she seems to have become a part. Perhaps the angels are clearing the way . . . perhaps she calls on them softly . . . she is hardly conscious; all life seems to be merged in feet and close-set lips. She begins to see a dim opening before her; how faint it is! Nearer, nearer! A scream that reverberates deafeningly against the rocky walls makes her heart leap and stand still. It is now or never a race for life. (198)

Thus Renie risks her life in order to warn her suitor, who is quickly converted and becomes a bicyclist himself. As the story ends, the two are married at last and are seen riding around town together.

Like Ethel, Renie undertakes a heroic feat, responding to an emergency that forces her to demonstrate her bravery, quick thinking, and athleticism. Interestingly, both authors construct the plot so that neither character is forced by necessity to take on a decidedly unfeminine role. Motivated by a dangerous fire or the threat of impending murder, Ethel and Renie are forced to reveal their capacity for heroism through decidedly masculine acts, even as they possess the bright-eyed vivaciousness and fun but demure companionship of Nathalie Sedge.

In general, these stories retained the basic features of the short fiction genre as it manifested in the popular magazines of the 1890s: their protagonists are young, fashionable, modern, and marriageable, embodying the energies and capacities for action that distinguished the popular magazine from its predecessor, the nineteenth-century house magazine. Just as in "The Tell-Tale Mirror" and "A Dangerous Sidepath" bicycling leads to a marriage and a conventional ending, "A Friend in Need," "The Wheel of Time," "Rosalind A-wheel," and "A Fin de Cycle Incident" each culminates in a happy union between likeminded modern individuals, serving to appease skeptics' concerns that bicycling would radicalize or masculinize women. At the same time, these stories exceed this narrative in small ways, suggesting different possibilities both for the woman bicyclist's ethos and for the nature and depth of her courtship. Whether through her capacity for introspection or her courageous actions, the bicycle girl emerges from women-authored short fiction not merely as an object of desire, but as a subject with complex motives that aid, rather than impede, her success in courtship.

The Bicycle Girl as Commentator

In addition to fiction, women authored commentary articles in popular magazines about the state of bicycling for their sex. These pieces often served a variety of purposes that overlapped with, but remained distinct from, short fiction about bicycling: though they maintained mostly domestic contexts for riding, they afforded authors the opportunity to explicitly defend and promote women's bicycling, offer preliminary advice to prospective women cyclists, inform readers about the history of women's riding, and construct for themselves an ethos that transcended the role accorded to the bicycle girl within fictional courtship narratives. More specifically, they enabled writers to create the sorts of "material associations" that Julie Nelson Christoph argues are central to writers' construction of ethos, linking themselves to particular natural images, cultural tastes, and objects in order to demonstrate the bicycling woman's particular capacities and interests.

Additionally, women-authored commentary articles provided, for fellow riders looking for terms in which to describe their own experiences and persuade others of the worth of women's bicycling, what Kenneth Burke describes in *A Grammar of Motives* as "representative anecdotes." While individual perceptions are unique "selections" and "deflections" of reality, Burke allows, such anecdotes gain strength in repetition, mediating perceptions and codifying them in terms of certain metaphors or narratives that share similar "selections" and "deflections." In this way, the representative anecdote presents itself as descriptive but contains within it a prescriptive element (60). Reading a range of commentary articles, as many women bicycle enthusiasts must have done, helped riders not only develop arguments in favor of their new sport but also gain a certain common understanding regarding the types of emotional and physical benefits they might report, as well as the tone and language of the observations they might share about their experiences. For instance, commentary articles often argued that bicycling would restore women's humor, making them more productive and agreeable wives or workers; they also advanced a celebratory history of women's bicycling, in which riders had "defeated" their detractors and the future, as a result, was infinitely brighter for all women.

Appearing in *Outing* magazine in October 1891, Grace E. Denison's "How We Ride Our Wheels" is an early example of the commentary. Denison was a frequent contributor to *Outing*, authoring a series of articles reporting on her cycling trip to Ireland in 1893 as well as several accounts of her adventures riding near home. Throughout her commentary, Denison outlines a history of women's bicycling often repeated in later commentaries: she emphasizes the hardship and criticism that earlier women cyclists faced at the hands of their detractors, indicates that this hardship has been overcome very suddenly, and then declares the woman bicyclist's struggle for acceptability "over." Denison's tone is celebratory and reassuring, situating women's bicycling as a formerly radical pursuit that has already been domesticated:

> [L]ady cyclists were at first looked upon with strong disfavor, and the hue and cry of reckless tampering with our lives and limbs . . . would have discouraged us had we not grown to love our wheels. We lived down, or rather rode down, our enemies, until, instead of remarks calculated to disturb the equilibrium of a woman on her own two trusty feet . . . we meet with encouraging smiles and admiring comments. (52)

In 1891, Denison's claims were overstated, as women riders remained relatively few in number and women's Safety bicycle models were only beginning to emerge. The "encouraging smiles and admiring comments" of supporters of women's bicycling were scarcely the only reaction new riders must have received. Nonetheless, by simultaneously describing a social transformation and positioning it in the past tense, Denison lessens the sense that the new activity will excite opposition and thus encourages a larger, less radical range of women to participate.

Echoing the emphasis on the woman bicyclist's capacity for introspection that Shelley gives her protagonist in "A Friend in Need," Denison's "How We Ride Our Wheels" also uses poetic imagery to intimate that the author's enjoyment of bicycling derives from her sensitivity and attunement to her natural surroundings, rather than an immodest desire for attention or a masculine urge to "scorch," or ride fast. Her attention to the senses conveys her facility with language, implying that she is well read but also a woman who has spent time outdoors, just enjoying the beauty around her. For instance, she advises

> starting early when the roads are fragrant with the scent of new-mown hay, the shy wild violet, the vagrant brier or the dainty honeysuckle, or when behind their delicate leaves the ruddy raspberry or the gleaming blackcap peep temptingly, or as the year fades the wheels may come back at night aglow with ruddy trophies of maple and sumac and Virginia creeper. (54)

Denison's references to specific plants, her use of adjectives, and her attention to the changing seasons are all material associations that help her position herself as not merely a fun and flirtatious bicycle girl, but someone with a deep sensory appreciation for nature—one who understands the landscape intimately. Additionally, she offers a representative model for how readers ought to understand and describe their own riding: as a poetic, almost spiritual experience divorced from masculine physical exertion or competition, but suggestive of the rider's capacity to appreciate nature in all its fine detail.

Appearing five years later, in *Scribner's* 1895 special bicycling issue, actress and playwright Marguerite Merington's "Woman and the Bicycle" is another example of a general bicycle commentary. Merington was well known in her day, having authored the popular play *Captain Letterblair* five years previously. Because of her fame, her contribution to *Scribner*'s—a magazine with a broader and more diverse distribution than *Outing*—signifies the development of the sport between 1891 and 1896. Nonetheless, Merington draws from many of the same rhetorical strategies as Denison, describing the experience and rewards of riding in similar terms and carving out a similar ethos for herself as a woman bicyclist.

As did Denison, Merington uses poetic language to convey the type of enjoyment women receive from bicycling. Her vivid descriptions establish the greater vitality and sensibility that bicycling provides the rider and distance her from the selfish, hypercompetitive "scorcher" that critics feared her to be:

> Far-reaching dreams of summer may bear the traveller of the wheel through clean stretches in the Berkshires, on sunny lanes of Normandy, among Welsh mountains . . . but all the workaday year there are highways radiating from the heart of the city to the borderland of the country, where one may breathe new inspiration for the world—the world that we persist in having too much with us in the getting and spending efforts that lay waste the powers. (704)

Even more explicitly than Denison, Merington establishes herself as both a literary-minded rider, referring to William Wordsworth's "The World Is Too Much with Us," and a well-traveled tourist, referencing both domestic and European scenes of picturesque travel. Her ethos is cultured, literary, and feminine in its appreciation for natural surroundings, and she tacitly supplies one particular reason for bicycling that women might draw from in their explanations of its benefits: its use in restoring the city dweller's health and vitality in the country. Whereas other claims—such as the freedom to travel without a male chaperone—were absent from women's commentaries, this commonplace that the bicyclist would be a city dweller in need of relaxation in the country was often voiced in support of both men's and women's bicycling.

Despite the worldiness of her own travel references, however, Merington suggests that bicycling's restorative powers will not detract from riders' commitment to their domestic duties and that the location for most women's riding is not far from home. As she notes:

> Now and again a complaint arises of the narrowness of woman's sphere. For such disorder of the soul the sufferer can do no better than to flatten her sphere to a circle, mount it, and take to the road. An hour of the wheel means sixty minutes of fresh air and wholesome exercise . . . it may be

> well to put down to the credit side of the day's reckoning with flesh and spirit. (703)

Interestingly, the "complaint" to which she refers is only occasional—something that happens "now and again" and that can be quieted by riding (703). At the same time, Merington acknowledges women's need for such an escape by asserting their right to seek it out. In general, her commentary does not imply a radical motive for the woman bicyclist, but it does highlight her cultural capital and her desire for relief from the monotony of her domestic duties.

Finally, writing in the same *Godey's* 1896 special issue in which "Rosalind A-wheel" appears, Mary Bisland offers a commentary on women's bicycling in her article "Woman's Cycle." Bisland, like Denison, appears to have been a hobbyist who wrote other articles about bicycling, including one detailing manufacturing processes at the Pope Manufacturing Company factory in Hartford ("The Making of a Woman's Bicycle"). The fact that she, like Merington, wrote for a general magazine rather than the hobbyist publication *Outing* indicates again the popularity of bicycling by 1896; *Godey's*, however, was at this time a less expensive magazine than *Scribner's* and thus appealed to a wider clientele. As a result, Bisland frames her arguments about the benefits of bicycling in slightly different terms than either Merington or Denison.

Similarly to Denison, Bisland emphasizes the rapidity of change that the bicycle has facilitated in women's lives and suggests—perhaps more accurately than Denison's earlier writing—that the change is already complete. Interestingly, her language implies not a steady progression of time, but a leap forward preceded by a long period of stagnation for women:

> Hampered through all generations, verily since Eve first essayed dressmaking in the Garden of Eden, by clothes that sadly restricted anything like liberty of action, the locomotion of women has been always passive and dependent. . . . Now, if a pitying Providence should suddenly fit light, strong wings to the back of a toiling tortoise, that patient cumber of the ground could hardly feel a more astonishing sense of exhilaration and gratitude than a woman experiences when first she becomes a mistress of her wheel. (386)

The rider's experience is simply a "then and now" shift—the past was stagnant and oppressive, and the shift to the present day is sudden and empowering. As

Bisland puts it, "In three years' time, the bicycle has created, not a revolution, but a revelation in the thoughts and actions of our worthy female citizens" (386). In Bisland's figuring, anyone who continues to object to women's bicycling has simply become outdated—a view that was consistent with most arguments against tradition put forward in popular magazines.

However, Bisland does not attempt in "Woman's Cycle" to convey the same cultured sensitivity to nature that Denison and Merington do in their pieces, directed at a more affluent and educated group of readers. Whereas Merington implies that bicycling may restore women's enthusiasm for her domestic "sphere," Bisland translates that argument for women who work at jobs during the day:

> One may ride five miles or fifteen, but at the end of one's jaunt the discontent with which drudgery clouds the impressionable mind is superseded by a wholesome calm of philosophy and a cheerful resolution. The world of tasks is more pleasant to endure, and fuller of compensations. Given a holiday, the average working girl prefers to spend it on her machine, in the sunshine and the open air, and thus the city toiler is brought into close communion with the country. (387)

Echoing the notion that the bicyclist would be a city dweller in need of escape, Bisland directs her attention to the "average working girl" rather than to the wife or mother stranded in the home. Like Merington, she notes that the bicycle will offer "cheerful resolution" rather than proposing it as a means to radical transformation—a way of reassuring skeptics and prospective riders alike that the woman bicyclist ought not to be perceived as a radical figure.

In their commentary articles, women writers composed a rough history of women's role in the bicycle craze, stressing the rapidity of change in popular attitudes toward their riding. In discrediting those who remained critical of women bicyclists, they drew from the rhetorical resources of the popular magazine, with its embrace of innovation and shirking of "outdated" traditions. Additionally, they often addressed arguments in opposition to their participation in bicycling by suggesting that the activity would help women embrace more cheerfully, rather than reject, their existing social roles. Finally, the commentary article afforded writers the opportunity to establish a sensitive, cultured ethos for the bicycle girl that further assured popular audiences that this figure was neither frivolous and self-involved nor unsexed. In general, commentary articles helped stabilize the range of arguments available for women bicyclists in favor of their activity, providing in their descriptions and observations a tacit prescriptive element that, often repeated, offered some reassuring commonplaces about who the woman bicyclist might be and why she might ride. Importantly, these commonplaces were congruous with, but distinct from, the courtship narrative established in bicycle fiction.

The Bicycle Girl as Traveler

If fiction provided women writers a forum for extending the popular courtship narrative, and if commentaries allowed writers to transcend that narrative, bicycle-related travel writing enabled writers to display the bicycle girl in action: as an adventurer, with or without a husband or beau, drawing from both her past experience and her innate coolheadedness in her encounters with the sorts of difference and adversity that travel affords. In rhetorical terms, the woman travel writer could construct an ethos for herself—and, by extension, for the bicycle girl—in relation to the places and people she encounters along her journey, by demonstrating her response to physical, financial, and mechanical adversity or mishap and by conveying her sense of humor through first-person narration.

Much travel writing penned by women bicyclists maintained or extended the bicycle courtship narrative by featuring the adventures of a modern bicycling couple on honeymoon—something that male-authored travel narratives generally did not do. Such writing enabled authors to simultaneously emphasize their own "modern" personal traits, such as mental and physical toughness, frugality, practicality, and culture, and enact the shared experience of the modern couple along the way. For instance, writers conveyed their like-mindedness to their husbands in contrast to people they encountered along the way, their shared sense of humor in these encounters, or their collaborative problem solving in the face of adversity. Whereas courtship fiction tended strictly to demonstrate how common feeling might bring a well-matched couple together, travel writing provided writers the opportunity to frame their own marriages as exemplars for the sort of companionship they believed distinguished modern relationships from previous arrangements.

Alice Lee Moque's travel narrative "A Bohemian Couple Wheeling thro' Western England" offers one example of such a honeymoon account. The author opens her narrative by announcing that she and her husband decided to undertake their "bohemian" cycling journey because they sought to "see as much as possible and leave style and high living to those who could better afford it" and because they did not wish to wait "until we are both gray-headed and may not enjoy the trip half as much as we do now" (186). Implied in Moque's statement is the sense that she and her husband are unified not only by youth but also by a common vitality—a thirst for experience—and by a disdain for hollow tradition that accorded well with the *Outing* audience for which she was writing. Repeatedly, she uses "we" to identify herself and her husband and to distinguish them from both the "Mrs. Grundy" traditionalists and the English people they encounter along their way.

In fact, Moque's ethos as a bicycle girl is difficult to distinguish from her husband's; she writes as though they are entirely of one mind. She reports on their shared planning, their common enjoyment of attractive scenery and roads, and their willingness to tour as frugally and as simply as possible. "It is really remarkable how well one can get along without many things that seem to be absolute necessities," she notes, adding that they each brought with them only "a change of underclothing and the few toilet articles necessary" (186). Even their exertion levels are interchangeable: "We arrived at Chester, feeling none the worse for our first spin. . . . We made good time, but we never scorch" (190). At no point does she highlight her femininity, other than to joke that her husband had to restrain her "enthusiasm" for seeing old cathedrals. In general, Moque uses the travel writing genre to identify herself as a tough and practical bicyclist and adventurer whose qualities unite her perfectly with her husband.

In another *Outing* piece, "Honeymoon on Wheels," Helen Follett describes her journey with her new husband from New Orleans to Washington, DC, aboard a tandem bicycle. Similarly to Moque, she constructs for herself an ethos that rests largely on *contrast*, although rather than contrast herself and her husband to the staid traditionalists she imagines might disapprove of their bicycling, she emphasizes their shared urbanity and sophistication to contrast them with the people she and her husband encounter as they travel through the American South. Rather harshly, she characterizes these southerners as sleepy, ignorant, "crude and provincial beyond description" (7), even "afflicted with strabismus" (5). In New Orleans, she notes, "pedestrians jumped out of the way and showed the same symptoms of fright that they would have had Tom and I been twin mad dogs" (6). This sense of contrast between herself and Tom and the people they encounter on their journey often sounds classist, regionalist, and racist to a contemporary audience, but it highlights the similarities between husband and wife and situates them as a fun-loving and sophisticated modern couple, urbane but also not afraid to rough it. So united, so adventuresome are they, in fact, that they steal a ride on a freight train to Mobile—an experience that Follett reports was "great fun" (6). Whereas Moque focuses on the frugality and practicality that she and her husband share, Follett constructs an ethos for her relationship that rests on spontaneity, adventure, and urbanity.

Other travel accounts centered on the ethos of the individual bicyclist and dispensed with the courtship narrative altogether, featuring riders undertaking bicycle journeys among groups of friends or even entirely alone. These accounts overlapped with Moque's and Follett's in the sense of contrast they established between their narrators and others, whether moral skeptics of women's bicycle touring, people they encountered along the way, or both groups. They often emphasized the cleverness and practicality of the authors as they escaped difficult scrapes, and some writers devoted much attention to the conditions of the roads they encountered—a practice shared by male bicyclists who wrote about their travels and likely intended to serve as both an aid to future travelers and a means of conveying expertise and credibility. In the absence of the courtship narrative from their accounts, some conveyed through material and moral statements the appropriate femininity of the riders, while others scarcely revealed their gender at all.

In "We Girls Awheel through Germany," an 1892 *Outing* account by someone identified only as "Martha," the writer describes her bicycle trip to Germany with four young female friends, spotlighting the many mishaps the group had, even though ultimately their trip was a success. The author refers to her friends as "girls" and often associates them with stereotypically feminine behaviors, even as they are backpacking through the countryside on bicycles that they themselves assembled after arriving abroad. The young women scramble helplessly around their hotel room to locate dropped ball bearings for one of the bicycles, for instance, and—in a lengthy dialogue—they complain about the dirt and rain they encounter along the way. Martha repeatedly mentions the shock of the German people that five women are undertaking such a journey, thus heightening the difference between her group and those they encounter and suggesting specifically her enjoyment of the novelty of their trip and their situation as female bicyclists. She notes, for instance, that when they disembarked from their ship, the officer at the dock asked "where the owner was and why he had five wheels" (298), observing that during their travels they caused "some astonishment and aroused people's curiosity" (299) in a particular town, answering "innumerable questions" (300) posed by townspeople amazed by their appearance. This contrast between themselves and the people they encounter, too, is heightened by Martha's many appreciative comments regarding the German people and countryside. Echoing the sentiments expressed in commentaries by women bicyclists, Martha situates herself as a person who appreciates natural beauty, one endowed with curiosity about the world and unafraid to ask questions in order to learn more. Her ethos reflects both the travel narrative genre in which she writes and the larger cultural context of the popular magazine, with its appreciation for direct experience and vitality, in which she is writing.

Grace E. Denison, author of the commentary article "How We Ride Our Wheels," also wrote about her bicycle trip to Ireland in five installments published in *Outing*. Though she was joined by a male cousin for much of the trip, Denison emphasizes her own planning, expertise, and judgment in describing her adventures, opening with a narrative about how she decided to undertake her journey in the first place. After reading favorable reports of riding in Ireland, "with the quickened interest of the true lover of the wheel," she began to work out the details and overcome the difficulties: "daring, planning, working to get through the barrier, which was two-fold wide, and long, and deep, and strong. A managing editor's will, and the yeasty, briny Atlantic Ocean!" Her casual reference to "a managing editor" reveals that she is not simply an amateur writer, but a paid and valued worker. Additionally, she scarcely references her gender either as a cause of others' surprise or as a shaping force in her trip, other than to mention that her initial focus on her apparel, rather than her itinerary, is "a confession of sex" (30). However, when noting the opposition of her friends, who offered "various gratuities in the line of advice and discouragement," including the claim that "*you'll* never ride that distance" (28), Denison does not intimate that her sex might account for their doubts about her abilities. Rather, she establishes herself as an independent operator whose gender is scarcely a factor either in her riding or in others' opinions of her.

Similarly, Denison stresses her expertise as a rider, suggesting both her physical toughness in overcoming difficult terrain and her ingenuity in working through mechanical difficulties. When her chain guard comes loose and becomes whirled into a "shapeless lump of twisted wires" (31), for instance, her cousin Tim wants to go back to get it mended, but she does not:

> I was too much afraid that if we turned back we should never get started again, to listen to such a suggestions; so I climbed on my wheel after freeing the pedal of its bedeviled necklet, and by dint of sitting on the skirt, contrived to keep it from catching in the chain. Of course it wasn't pretty, nor very comfortable to the cyclist . . . but it was better than the misery of turning back . . . and in the beauty of the mountains and the smoothness of the road, I soon forgot to consider appearances. (31)

Denison thus situates herself as someone more capable of enduring discomfort than her male cousin—someone who finds solutions to problems when others give up. Additionally, she establishes the authenticity of her touring and cycling experience by differentiating herself from the novice who might blindly trust the advice of guidebooks and strangers. She points out that their advice conflicts:

> [I]f one enthusiast affects the South, and assures you that the Northern or Western roads are abominable and uninteresting, there always follow him two more ready to pick up the gauntlet in defense of the disparaged localities, and to belittle the beauties of the Wicklow hills. (31)

In general, Denison establishes an ethos that rests on distinguishing herself as a tough and practical-minded professional. She writes herself as bicycle girl completely out of the romantic narrative advanced within advertisements and popular fiction.

Finally, Margaret Le Long recounts her journey from Chicago to San Francisco in a two-part series in *Outing*, published in 1898. Like Denison, Le Long emphasizes her toughness, indicating that among her packed items at the outset of her trip were only "a suitable skirt, a few toilet articles, a clean 'hanky' . . . and a pistol" (492) and asserting that she endured opposition "from every friend and relative who was on hand to register a protest" (492), as well as others who did so through the mail. Incredibly, Le Long travels through deserts, squats at a cattle ranch, cooks for strange men over an open fire, and is forced to shoot her pistol in order to avoid a stampede. Yet, unlike Denison, she genders her experience, crying disconsolately when she falls and has to ride several miles "through a mist of tears" ("From" 496), feeling dismayed at the lack of decoration at the Cazorus Cattle Ranch, and closing her narrative with advice to "my cycling sisters" ("Alone" 596) to always wear skirts and ride a drop frame bicycle. She notes that she "never once found a place where [she] was willing to doff [her] skirts and appear in bloomers" (596). Le Long's combination of adventurousness and respect for traditional decorum distinguishes her from many other bicycle tourists who wrote with amusement and satisfaction of the shock people registered when they wore bloomers while riding.

Le Long also establishes the authenticity of her experience, as well as her expertise as a rider, in her characterization of the roads she encountered and the maps that she feels failed her. For instance, she says that in Iowa, after enduring "fifteen miles of alternate sand and mud, hills and bogs, and a cold wind blowing," she "decided to stop in the next town and spend the rest of the day expressing [her] opinion about the League map of Iowa, which is a snare and a delusion" ("From" 492). Likewise, in Wyoming, she complains that her map is misleading, giving the impression that the territory was "thickly settled," when in fact it consisted only of "side-tracks and section-houses" ("Alone" 595). These comments highlight Le Long's role as an independent traveler, self-reliant and capable of both following and critiquing a map.

Writing firsthand accounts of bicycle touring not only allowed women a way to publish their own experiences but also offered them some latitude in moving away from both the courtship narrative that proliferated in the popular press and the commonplace claims in favor of bicycling that writers of commentary articles helped circulate. Whereas popular fiction reinforced the notion that the flirtatious and modern bicycle girl type would eventually marry a worthy beau, and commentary articles suggested that she would be happier and more introspective for having taken up the bicycle, the travel narrative facilitated a much wider range of identities for the woman bicyclist: she could establish for herself a cultured, resourceful, practical, or feminine ethos; situate herself alongside a husband or demonstrate her ability to succeed on her own; and use a humorous or serious tone in conveying her experiences. As a result, first-person travel narratives often strayed far from the type of bicycle girl established in manufacturers' advertisements and short fiction, individuating authors and demonstrating a much wider range of purposes to which women might put the bicycle.

Significantly, this stronger version of the bicycle girl emerged not in generalist magazines and newspapers, but almost exclusively in *Outing*, in which editors solicited contributions from both male and female cyclists recounting their travel experiences aboard the wheel. Though the circulation of such publications remained wide, the audience consisted of cycling and outdoor enthusiasts, "insiders" of sorts likely to be receptive to a more radical redefinition of femininity than that advanced in *Harper's* or *Godey's* magazines. Nonetheless, these narratives did circulate, helping readers imagine themselves not just as bicycle girls or wives but also as adventurers.

The Rise of the Bicycle Girl

During the 1890s, women's bicycling gradually ceased to turn heads in America, becoming a familiar modern phenomenon in most urban and many rural locations across the country. The sheer number of riders increased dramatically, and Americans came to accept the fun and thoroughly modern bicycle girl advanced in a wide range of popular narratives, including not only song, fiction, and advertising but also commentary articles and travel narratives. Rather than understand the woman bicyclist as a ridiculous, unsightly, immoral, or potentially radical figure, more and more Americans embraced her as a benign and even welcome sight—one capable of courage, introspection, resourcefulness, and a host of other qualities.

Though this transformation in the popular imagination came about for numerous reasons, in this chapter I have demonstrated the critical role that women themselves, writing within the new cultural venue of the popular magazine, played in bringing it about. They were not always aware of the collective impact of their rhetorical efforts, but women bicycle enthusiasts took advantage of both the wide circulation of the popular magazine and the specific rhetorical resources afforded by the genres within it to bring both shape and complexity to the ethos of the so-called bicycle girl. In doing so, they provided readers with particular ideas about who this figure might be—how, with whom, and under what circumstances she might use the new technology of the bicycle—as well as on what grounds her relationship with a male beau might be built and in what particular ways she might (or might not) promote women's bicycling to others. Indirectly but importantly, women's writing in popular magazines contributed to the uptake of the bicycle by American women, not only persuading them to ride and helping silence their detractors but also modeling for them *how they ought to understand* their riding.

As I have suggested, the agency that these writers wielded was both enabled and constrained by the material and social contexts in which their work was published. The emergence of new printing technologies at this time facilitated changed attitudes toward advertising and lowered subscription costs, while the broader scene of expanding literacy across the country helped generate a much broader, more diverse market for periodicals than had existed previously. These forces shaped the popular magazine, which emerged as a print venue for generating new consumer values—including the shirking of genteel tradition in favor of a cheerful consumerism, as well as a sense of hope and optimism for the future—that accorded well with the nascent bicycle industry's interest in attracting women riders. Women's writing about bicycling—in fiction, commentary pieces, and travel writing—was shaped by these values, just as it was enabled by the increased demand for published material that the popular magazine helped generate. As a result, the popular magazine did not provide a venue for advancing radical views or promoting explicit social change.

Yet women fiction writers, commentators, and travel writers did not simply replicate the nonthreatening version of the bicycle girl that manufacturers' advertisements promoted. Though the protagonists within their stories eventually married, and their commentators affirmed their commitment to domestic and work responsibilities, these figures also expanded and humanized the bicycle girl's interests, capabilities, and desires. And though the self-characterizations in travel narratives they published exhibited the youthfulness and energy that exemplified the bicycle girl, they also emphasized a wide range of other qualities that did not fall within that figure's usual range of possibilities. Drawing from the rhetorical resources of both specific genres and the larger cultural and material context in which they wrote, these authors produced works that alternately overlapped with and diverged from one another, coming loosely together to construct an ethos for the bicycle girl that influenced the particular way in which the bicycle became woven into the fabric of American culture.

Chapter Three

Women's Written Instructions for Change

> Women learning to ride wheels have been much in print; too often, however, blunt fact is made subservient to a picturesque story. ("Still the Wheelwoman: A Talk for the Daily Increasing Army of Beginners" 21)

So begins one 1895 *New York Times* article in which an anonymous bicyclist offers advice to prospective riders. The problem the author seeks to address, as her opening sentence implies, is the disjunction between the romanticized depictions of women's bicycling in popular culture and the substantial, even overwhelming, challenge that many women faced in actually learning to ride. Whereas the bicyclists in advertisements and fiction tended to be girlish, confident, and content to ride for leisure alongside a male companion, the real flesh-and-blood women who wanted to learn to ride represented a more diverse crowd—some were older, some were poorer, some were in need of practical transportation, and many simply found the task of adapting their embodied habitus to a machine like the bicycle much more difficult than the dominant image of the bicycle girl suggested it might be. The disjunction between this image and the needs and concerns of real women created an exigence for riders to share advice, instructions, and experience among themselves.

The *New York Times* author, for instance, offers her own story as a reassurance to other new bicyclists. Writing from a third-person perspective, she admits up front that "the author has a cautious nature, and, moreover, is not in the first flush of youth" ("Still the Wheelwoman" 21), and—though manufacturers and bicycle riding schools often promised that learning to ride the bicycle would be a matter of a few short lessons—she describes a "'going to her own execution' feeling before each lesson." After coming home from her first attempt covered "in black and blue marks," this terror even causes the author to dream that night that "she careened through the streets like a ship without a rudder—embracing lampposts with fervor—being dragged from under ice carts and run down by trolley carts." This dread emerges from her timidity, from her age and lack of fitness, and even—as she confesses—from the fact that "the average instructor does not know how to instruct" ("Still the Wheelwoman" 21).[1] The author goes on to tell her own story of perseverance and to explain such tasks as how to stop the machine, how to evaluate the instructor's work, and how to select appropriate clothing for riding.

In authoring this advice for prospective bicyclists, she offers a counternarrative to that of the breezy, youthful bicycle girl of the popular magazine; in her narrative, simply mastering the bicycle is made visible as a significant, hard-won achievement available to all women who are patient and hardworking. Though this counternarrative had its variations in tone and content, it circulated widely during the bicycle craze, as women pioneers offered various instructions to smooth the path for subsequent riders for whom manufacturer advice proved inadequate. Manufacturers might strive for women to buy their wares, but they did not always work hard to ensure that buyers mastered or actually practiced riding. It was largely up to women bicycle enthusiasts to correct this oversight by operating as what Miles Kimball (drawing from Michel de Certeau) refers to as "tactical" technical communicators: not working for manufacturers, but acting "in the gaps" between organizations and institutions to "recreat[e] technology to suit their own purposes" (65).

Riders' written efforts, which ranged from advice columns to technical descriptions to full-length monographs, helped, alongside the work of inventors and fiction writers, mediate the integration of the new technology of the Safety bicycle into the fabric of late nineteenth-century American culture. The texts riders produced elaborated on and revised popular and manufacturer conceptions of who might ride, for what purposes, and in whose company they might do so, shaping women's physical habitus aboard the bicycle and expanding the boundaries of necessary knowledge for women's riding from mere locomotion to mechanical expertise. Through their technical advice, these writers also influenced women's apparel and deportment while riding. As Bernadette Longo and others have argued, technical communication is not simply a transparent conduit linking users and machines; it is a historically situated practice that "can be seen as working to legitimate and value some kinds of knowledge while marginalizing and devaluing other possible knowledges" (16). By recording and disseminating their anecdotes, pointers, and procedures related to bicycling, bicycle enthusiasts were asserting the significance of particular kinds of knowledge—from mounting to tire changing to self-instruction—for a particular group of users to whom that knowledge would otherwise have been unavailable.

Additionally, in offering advice to one another, women bicyclists came to understand themselves as a somewhat coherent group through the texts they authored. Like the 1960s emergence of the Québécois, about which rhetorician Maurice Charland has written, they *constituted* a group identity through the narratives they generated and repeated. As Charland suggests in his landmark 1987 article, group self-identification develops as individual subjects come to hear and identify, collectively, with particular narratives about themselves (141). Whereas the Québécois came to understand themselves as a coherent group by articulating shared sentiments of state separatism, women bicyclists conceived of themselves as a public of "wheelwomen" through the instructional texts they circulated among themselves. More than the short stories, commentaries, or travel narratives within popular magazines, these instructional texts offered a forum in which riders spoke directly to other riders, articulating a self-legitimizing narrative that bridged the gap between the glamorous, youthful ideal of the bicycle girl and the object of mockery often caricatured in the media. These texts named an identity—or technology user role—that associated bicycling with physical effort, mechanical expertise, personal autonomy, practical convenience, and greater community among women bicyclists. By constituting such a group, authors and readers alike expanded the ranges of both the contexts for women's riding and the people invited to participate. They helped politicize the bicycle, wresting it from the realm of leisure and investing it with significance as a means of women's emancipation.

In this chapter, I outline the conditions under which most women were learning to ride the bicycle in the early 1890s, describing the prevailing attitudes about less capable women novice bicyclists that, together with the bicycle girl representations promoted within popular magazines, circumscribed the range of women who were invited to become users of the new technology. To demonstrate how instructional materials often reinforced this limited invitation and, in the process, prescribed a limited role for women bicyclists, I consider the male- and manufacturer-authored bicycle manuals in circulation during the 1890s. Finally, I examine three different full-length bicycle manuals authored by women bicycle enthusiasts and a handful of advice columns on riding, care, and apparel for bicycling. As technical communication, these texts demonstrate a variety of strategies for adapting the bicycle to their audience. Some, such as the above anonymous *New York Times* author and Woman's Christian Temperance Union president Frances Willard, offered conversational prose and narrative, rather than explicit directives, in order to empower users to take what Marika Seigel has described as a "system-disrupting" stance, positioning them as experts rather than novices and inviting readers to critique manufacturers' assumptions about the bicycle's use (77–78). Others, such as cycling experts Maria E. Ward and Lillias Campbell Davidson, framed their advice and instruction as conventional and authoritative, tasking novice readers with "mastering" the detailed content they provided in their lengthy handbooks. Taken together, these widely circulating enthusiast instructional and advice materials provide evidence of women's efforts to counteract the shortcomings of the plentiful male-authored and manufacturer-produced materials published during the 1890s.

Negative Representations of Women Learning to Ride

> For while Winslow's bicycling was all that could be wished, and he flung himself in the path of the on-coming wheel with marvelous celerity and precision, he had not the power to withstand the never yet revealed number of pounds carried by Miss Lorania, impelled by the rapid descent and gathering momentum at every whirl. They met; he caught her; but instantly he was rolling down the steep incline and she was doubled up on the grass. (Thanet 189)

This apparently comic moment from Octave Thanet's story "The Stout Miss Hopkins's Bicycle," which originally appeared in *Harper's New Monthly Magazine* in 1897, suggests something of a flip side to the romantic narrative of the youthful, agile bicycle girl: the public censure directed at women riders who did *not* fit this narrative of youth and proper modern athleticism (Thanet 189). Often affectionate but still unmistakably mocking, this censure was usually directed at those riders, such as the fictional Miss Lorania Hopkins, whose "never yet revealed number of pounds" or advanced age made them conspicuous aboard the bicycle. In Thanet's story, the thirty-three-year-old Hopkins is a hopeless bicyclist, spurred to join the fad only by social pressure and a desire to lose weight. Like the anonymous *New York Times* author, she is secretly terrified of riding and spends most of her lessons simply struggling not to knock over her instructor. Fortunately, however, the valiant but shy (and very small) Mr. Winslow saves her from the above disaster, and the two reveal their mutual romantic interest at the end of the story, thus ending Miss Hopkins's bicycle career. Thanet's tale—and her lovable but slightly ridiculous protagonist—subtly reinforces dominant ideas about who should and who should not ride and hints that many women bicyclists are simply pretending to enjoy themselves for the sake of fashion or romantic opportunities.

Many women began to ride in indoor bicycle schools like the one the *Times* author described in her article, learning alongside a male instructor for a fee. Indeed, much advice specifically directed new women riders to such schools, warning against the dangers of learning from a friend or family member (Clyde 65). Because tuition for a half-hour lesson at these schools ranged from 25 to 50 cents (the equivalent of $7 to $15 today), they were most accessible to middle- and upper-class women, to whom these schools often advertised especially. For example, the District Cycle Company Bicycle School in Washington, DC, notes in an 1895 *Evening Post* advertisement its "ladies sitting room" (7) as a special enticement to attract female riders. Similarly, the N. P. Curtice Company Bicycle School in Lincoln, Nebraska, states directly, "We want to teach a thousand ladies this season. It's the ladies we want especially" (9).

Despite the schools' efforts to promote their services to women, many characterizations of women bicyclists at bicycle schools were satirical, intimating the extent to which learning to ride in such a setting must have been a stressful experience. For instance, the author of an 1895 *New York Tribune* sketch entitled "Scenes at a Bicycle School" jokes that a "fair tyro" always receives more careful attention from the instructor than one who is "not fair," noting also that all women at a bicycle school "may be divided into two classes—those who think they can ride and those who know they can't." Additionally, he describes a pupil who "strains at the pedals like a lusty truck horse whose driver has overloaded him," and who "has about as much idea of the principles of equilibrium and of the preservation thereof as a cat in a fit" (21).

Similarly, a depiction in an 1895 *New York Truth* article of a "wobbler" engaged in a lesson offers additional detail, emphasizing both the unattractiveness of the rider's exertion and the heroism of the instructor for tolerating her ineptitude:

> Three times around the rink had she rolled her one hundred and eighty pounds. She had gotten red in the face, very red. Her hair was coming down and her hat was badly listed to port. . . . The instructor pushed the bicycle, Mary's legs involuntarily responded to the revolution of the pedals while he held her up, and in this way the first lesson was a success. She had done all she could to send the bicycle over to one side or the other, and she clutched the handle-bars in a desperate grip; but the man managed to keep her upright. He did it bravely through the half-hour, pushing against her with all his force when the wheel started to fall toward him, and clinging to it, as desperately as a drowning man, when it fell to the other side. (qtd. in Marks 195)

Here, both the instructor and Mary, the woman rider, are objects of comic ridicule; there is no sense that Mary has any real interest in learning to ride at all—only that she has landed in this rink because of some fleeting interest in the bicycling fad. Likewise, there is no sense that the instructor has any commitment to teaching her to ride; he is depicted as solely engaged in a struggle to keep her from toppling over. This narrative, like the romantic narrative of the successful young, athletic woman rider, appears repeatedly in the popular press during the 1890s and serves to tacitly circumscribe the range of actual women for whom riding was appropriate, potentially deterring many would-be riders from attempting an activity that could render them ridiculous. This narrative also highlights some of the fear and awkwardness that actual women experienced while learning to ride in a rink, seated close to a male instructor who was likely a stranger.

Implicit Representations of Women in Bicycling Instructional Materials

In their landmark essay from the 1980s, Ben Barton and Marthalee Barton describe the inherent narrativity of technical communication, as well as of other nonliterary texts. They argue that users, like characters, are positioned within instructional materials to "fulfill narrative, rather than logical, exigencies" (36) in their interactions with technological systems. Technical communication advances these exigencies by assuming particular trajectories of action and eliminating or diminishing other possible actions. Additionally, technical communication constructs these narratives based on certain assumptions both about a user's level of knowledge, interest, and experience and about the contexts in which he or she might be expected to use a technology. Instructional manuals and advice columns assist in the creation of such user narratives by providing or withholding details, definitions, images, and possible choices for action. As a result, these texts play an important role in regulating who has access to technical information and, as a result, who can gain mastery of a technology. Often, as was the case with most of the bicycling guides, handbooks, manuals, and advice columns published during the 1890s, instructional materials construct a narrative that reflects and advances dominant ideas about particular user groups.

Such materials abounded during the Safety bicycle craze, as they had during the early 1880s when the Ordinary emerged in the United States. Most manuals and user guides were authored by male enthusiasts whose bicycling experience dated back to this era and who saw themselves as seasoned experts tasked with expanding the sport for new audiences. Some were authorized by bicycle manufacturers such as Colonel Albert Pope, who wanted to generate as much excitement about bicycling as possible. As they had in years past when speaking of the Ordinary, these materials tended to celebrate the bicycle's restorative powers for the modern sedentary man, implicitly assuming that their readers would be lawyers, businessmen, and other members of the middle and upper-middle classes. In their references to women's bicycling, they rejoiced that the invention of the Safety had prompted their female companions to abandon restrictive fashionable dress but did not address women directly, as they often did men. Rather, these authors tended to view women bicyclists as, at best, a secondary audience, worthy of mention because they might serve as companions to the men who made up the bulk of readers. The concerns they perceived women as having—which mostly involved bicycling clothing and exertion levels—were confined to separate chapters or referred to only in passing. And adhering to the popular representations of women riders—positive and negative—these manuals and handbooks disregarded the interests of older, less athletic, and working women, thereby advancing the same narrative promoted within popular magazines: that the woman rider would be youthful, athletic, and affluent.

Published in 1895, Henry Clyde's *Pleasure-Cycling* offers an example of the way many instructional manuals for bicycling during the 1890s addressed women's bicycling. Clyde sets his manual in opposition to books that are directed to racers or serious hobbyists, spending a significant amount of time in his long introductory chapter, "Poetry in Motion," simply introducing the sport and espousing its benefits. Writing "solely for the instruction and benefit of cyclers in the pursuit of health and pleasure" (6), he does not exclude women from his audience in any explicit way and, in fact, offers sporadic advice specifically for them. However, throughout his book are suggestions that his primary audience is male; in his opening chapter, he advocates bicycling as a healing power for the "jaded business or professional man overwrought and weary with his year's work" and promises:

> Like other healthy and manly sports, this brings to the surface the boyishness latent in every man who is worth his salt. The wheelman is your modern Don Quixote, who finds his way beset with small marvelous adventures. His fellow wheelmen, met upon the road, are for him good comrades, or objects of mild, benevolent curiosity. (25)

This introduction implicitly situates Clyde's text as a guide for a certain type of man, perhaps older than the intrepid rider of the high wheeler but still eager for "small marvelous adventures" aboard the Safety bicycle. His discussion of women bicyclists involves the issue of dress—an important concern for women, but not one that will necessarily help them overcome all physical obstacles to learning to ride.

For instance, Clyde indicates that his reader should have little trouble learning to maneuver the machine—an endeavor that the anonymous *New York Times* author found challenging and even frightening. In describing the earliest efforts of a novice rider, he withholds detail, trusting the reader to master the basics without instruction and assuming that they will do so without much difficulty, likely at an indoor riding school. He says:

> In the riding school, you will first be placed in the saddle, and, upheld by the instructor, be made to ride around the track until you are able to balance with an occasional tumble, and to propel your machine, and you will afterwards be taught . . . to mount and dismount. (66)

This description prepares the bicyclist for a riding school experience that seems to be contained within a single session, dismissing the "occasional tumble" that the *Times* author complains gave her nightmares as a minor obstacle in reaching the goal. His cavalier attitude toward falling perhaps echoes the bravado of early Ordinary riders and implies that the "manly" bicyclist will not be deterred by a minor fall. Although he does acknowledge that some people will not learn to bicycle at a riding school, he mentions in passing that women will be in particular need of a professional instructor because of the challenge their machines present. "It is wholly or nearly impossible to learn riding on the lady's common . . . [drop frame] bicycle without the assistance either of a professional instructor or of some practiced amateur rider" (65), he notes, thereby affirming the authority of the riding instructor and suggesting that the woman rider will be someone able to afford paid lessons.

Perhaps most significantly, Clyde completely omits information about basic riding motion on the grounds that the rider cannot learn from this sort of elementary instruction. He asserts:

> A few hours' patience will teach you more than all the professors of the art can write. So, in what follows, the writer assumes that the beginner has learned already to balance himself in the saddle, to propel his bicycle, and in some fashion to mount and dismount. (68–69)

For the woman rider struggling with her riding lessons, this assumption reinforces the notion that if she does not pick up on the basics "naturally," she is simply not fit for instruction; the body should perform these tasks intuitively, through simple practice. Likewise, Clyde promises that the novice bicyclist who practices frequently for "a season" should be able to "take a fifty-mile run without appreciable fatigue" (101)—a significant and perhaps intimidating number for a rider who has had little exercise in her adult life. Though Clyde's book is clearly written to assist novice riders, it supports a narrative that assumes certain things about them—not only that they are likely male but also that they are eager for adventure, should find learning easy, and are likely members of a leisure class interested in riding strictly for pleasure. It is not difficult to imagine that a rider like Octave Thanet's Miss Hopkins might find in this book evidence that she is ill suited for bicycling.

Another handbook, *Dr. Neeson's Book on Wheeling*, offers a more sustained consideration of women riders than Clyde's book. Published in 1899, Victor Neeson's book features two separate chapters that pertain specifically to women, "The Bicycle for Women" and "The Morality of the Wheel," which he asserts "mostly concerns" women riders (79). These chapters do little to describe the process of learning to bicycle, however, as this information is covered elsewhere in Neeson's book in similar detail to Clyde's. Neeson remarks in "The Bicycle for Women":

> All that has been said in the previous chapters refers equally to women as to men. It should be understood, however, that a woman, being more finely organized than a man, cannot endure as much hard work, nor for so long a time. . . . She also suffers more nerve strain than a man; therefore her riding should be slower. (63)

This assertion that women were "more finely organized" and had reduced capabilities for speed and endurance constitutes the whole of Neeson's advice to women about riding; he makes no effort to address them directly and quickly moves on to a different purpose: to respond to perceived critics of women's bicycling, defending the activity on the grounds that it will improve their health. Whereas previously, Neeson argues, women's only "safety valve" for her "nervous troubles" was housework, bicycling has revealed itself as "particularly attractive to women on account of its novelty" (58).

Additionally, he asserts in a somewhat condescending tone that bicycling has at last "taught" women what they were previously too stubborn to see:

> It has taught her that the condition of health depends a great deal upon regular systematic exercise. Not that this is a new theory just discovered; it has been recognized for ages, and its precepts followed by the male sex generally and a few sensible women who have organized gymnasia and athletic clubs. (56)

The discussion—which departs from his second-person writing elsewhere in the book and refers continually to women in the third person—reflects Neeson's support of women's bicycling and even responds to the assertions of bicycling critics. However, it does little to help the woman rider navigate the challenges of learning to ride, and it reinforces the idea that most women are not actually serious about bicycling in the same way as men: they are only attracted to novelty, with the exception of "a few sensible women."

Also of note, Neeson's descriptions of actual women riding reinforce the notion that the machine is for the young bicycle girls of the popular magazines, rather than for women of all ages, classes, sizes, and energy levels. In talking about the healthful benefits of riding, he shifts from the term "women" used in the chapter title to an explicit description of the "bicycle girl" and notes that with riding come "the springy step, the erect carriage, the clear eye, the fresh complexion, the well-balanced poise of the head and body" (58). Neeson focuses on physical appearance and health without attending to other, more controversial, benefits of riding—perhaps because he intends to respond to women's bicycling critics. He ignores women's calls for dress reform, for instance, instead choosing to diminish the importance accorded to physical modesty by intimating that women themselves are the only people interested in its regulation. "It is amusing to observe the transitional stages of a woman's conception of modesty, as she takes up wheeling and progresses in it," he says, going on to document a woman's experiments with her skirt, which is shortened continually as she becomes more proficient as a bicyclist. "She will tell you, if interrogated, that her ideas of modesty have changed. She no longer considers it modest to endanger her life and health for the sake of keeping a few inches of her leg under cover" (88), Neeson says playfully—implying his own innocence in maintaining restrictive standards of dress for women. His manual perpetuates narratives of women bicyclists that suggest their novice status and their role as companions to the male riders who make up his primary audience; it also encourages this audience to look on them as somewhat reluctant, ridiculous novices who are not fully aware of the benefits of their new activity.

A third manual—distinct from Neeson's and Clyde's in that it was authored by a woman, reporter Ida Trafford Bell, at the request of the Pope Manufacturing Company—demonstrates how narratives that marginalize particular users, or that position them in limited roles, can emerge even when authors seek these users as a primary audience. In addition to this 1890 booklet, *Bicycling for Women*, Bell wrote several magazine pieces in favor of women's bicycling, indicating her personal investment in promoting the activity. Nonetheless, Bell's booklet betrays many of the same assumptions as Clyde's and Neeson's texts. Even in its length—a mere thirty pages in contrast to the full-length books directed at male audiences—*Bicycling for Women* affirms the notion that women users will need and desire a less thorough treatment of the subject than their male counterparts. And like the chapter about women's riding in Neeson's book, Bell's booklet devotes much of its attention to responding to critics of women's bicycling rather than providing information for riders. Just as Clyde's *Pleasure-Cycling* withholds detail about certain activities in the interest of brevity and conciseness, so, too, does

Bicycling for Women, which lacks information about bicycle maintenance, long-distance or tourist travel, and practical transportation.

Perhaps most strikingly, Bell asserts repeatedly that bicycling will make her readers happier wives and mothers—that it will enhance, rather than erode, their femininity. Throughout its pages, her manual reinforces the idea that the feminine bicyclist is a devoted domestic caretaker. Bicycling is a way for women to "best win strength and courage to meet their many household worries," (3) she says. Drawing, as Neeson does, from the contemporary notion that women possess fragile nerves, Bell proclaims that through this gentle exercise, "tempers will improve with buoyant health" so that "into the home comes radiant sunshine of all outdoors" (3). The new technology will not take women away from their domestic tasks, but it will ease their discontent with these tasks. Neither will the bicycle take women physically away from their husbands or families. While Bell concedes that the bicycle allows women a ready means for "a social call or brief errand" (18), she makes no mention of bicycling to work or of prolonged excursions as relief from domestic duties. In addition, she points out that beyond individual transportation for small errands, there is "another and more powerful reason why women should ride" (19):

> There are so many holidays, and half holidays when a man feels as though he must get away, but hesitates to do so because the wife or daughter or sister or sweetheart must be left at home. But if she ride [*sic*] a bicycle, she can go with him, thereby depriving him of neither his outing nor the pleasure of her society. (19)

In this configuration, women ought to learn to ride to serve as companions for the men in their lives—to save men from sacrificing their exercise and their whims and to create opportunities for women to develop or strengthen their marital and familial relationships. This narrative coincides with advertisements the Pope Manufacturing Company published in popular magazines, offering a consistent narrative of technological use within which the reader could insert herself.

Significantly, Bell emphasizes the ease of bicycling—a stark contrast to the *New York Times* author's account of her own experiences learning to ride. She reassures readers that "the first steps in bicycling will be found surprisingly easy and free from danger or harm" (6); in fact, "two or three lessons are usually sufficient for even the most timid to acquire acquaintance with and control of the machine" (7), so that riding is not a "serious undertaking by men or women of any age" (6). Additionally, she affirms both the assumption that her readers will learn through professional lessons affordable only to the middle and upper classes and the authority and infallibility of the instructor in assisting the rider: "The one word 'push' is what the instructor is constantly using. Taking his advice, the learner will soon find herself riding in a manner that will both please and surprise her" (9). Here the expert instructor is male, and the learner need only to take his advice, as riding is easy. In sharp contrast to the aforementioned scenes of stress and danger, the ease and enjoyment of the riding lesson, as well as the crucial role of the male expert instructor, are reinforced in an image of an indoor riding hall in which novice women riders wheeled in circles, held steady on their wheels by male instructors. Because bicycling was actually a far more difficult endeavor for some women unaccustomed to physical activity than Bell acknowledges, the booklet's strategy of emphasizing the ease of riding likely alienated some would-be women riders just as readily as Clyde's and Neeson's texts.

However—in striking contrast to Neeson's and Clyde's manuals—the booklet includes just one page dedicated to "The Adjustment of the Machine," and this page offers only generalities: "Properly adjusted, the bicycle should bring into play and strengthen every set of muscles in the body" (16). Information on how the bicycle is "properly adjusted" is equally limited; the manual notes merely that "[t]he saddle should be so placed that the rider's heel can just touch the pedals in their lowest position," not explaining how women might adjust the saddle other than that the saddle "can be adjusted by means of the screws provided for that purpose" (16). The lack of detailed information, in relation to the level of detail used in describing the process of mounting the machine, indicates the Pope Manufacturing Company's expectation that women riders would not be making these adjustments themselves.

In their assumptions about readers' gender, class, contexts for riding, ease in learning, and need for particular types of detail, these manuals demonstrate both bicycling enthusiasts' and bicycle manufacturers' tacit support for a particular type of women's bicycling: one in which women needed limited technical skill in order to participate, for leisure, alongside male companions, and one that upheld the popular narrative of the youthful, effortless modern bicycle girl. In positioning the bicycle as an instrument to enhance, rather than complicate, conventional standards of femininity—or, as in Clyde's case, downplaying women's need for particular information related to their new hobby altogether—these instructional materials authorized a limited context in which women interacted with the bicycle. Additionally, they likely contributed to some riders' difficulties in learning to ride, even as they encouraged others to participate. However, a new group of enthusiast-authored texts was emerging to complicate existing user narratives, promoting bicycling to women not as a healthy, pleasurable lark, but as a difficult challenge promising both personal and political transformation.

Women Enthusiast–Authored Advice for Beginners

In response to the proliferation of instructional texts that tacitly discouraged some would-be bicyclists from braving the physical and social challenges of learning to ride, as the 1890s continued, more and more women bicyclists began publishing their own forms of instruction and encouragement for prospective riders. These bicyclists used technical communication as an intervention in dominant narratives about both women and bicycle culture, seeking through their texts not only to encourage individual riders to overcome self-doubt but also to foster women's collective efforts to demonstrate, to both themselves and others, their physical and mechanical abilities aboard the new machine. Importantly, their texts were constitutive, not merely reflecting their preexisting awareness of themselves as a discernible group, but helping them see themselves as a group in the first place. By writing directly to one another, and by offering layers of advice overlooked in other instructional texts, these women developed a user narrative that revised and expanded the narrative offered by those texts. This user narrative offered the outlines of identity for the woman bicyclist for whom riding might or might not come easily, who might ride for many purposes, and who identified with neither the bicycle girl nor the Miss Hopkins–esque parody perpetuated in the popular press.

Many women enthusiasts' instructional materials performed the sort of "system-disruptive" stance about which Marika Seigel has written in a more contemporary context. That is, their instructional and advice writing did not simply insert users into existing dominant narratives, as did Clyde's, Neeson's, and Bell's manuals, but provided means for users to question or transform these narratives. Often this writing employed system-disruptive strategies that Seigel describes, such as "reopen[ing] questions of why and on whose terms certain procedures are recommended," positioning users as experts, and offering "a conversational, rather than prescriptive, mode for delivering instructions" (95). For instance, Frances Willard's 1895 *A Wheel within a Wheel: How I Learned to Ride the Bicycle* operates in this mode. Willard's book is a humorous, often self-deprecating narrative of her own process of learning to ride at fifty-three years of age, substituting the author's reflections on bicycling and life lessons for the detailed, step-by-step explanations of particular processes found in the manuals. Similarly, the anonymous *New York Times* author's "Still the Wheelwoman" article offers a painfully honest process narrative with sporadic tips and pointers, rather than systematic directives.

Other advice and instructional texts drew primarily from more conventional strategies, positioning their authors as experts addressing novices, as Neeson, Clyde, and Bell did in their manuals, and providing direct instruction about issues excluded from or made inaccessible to women riders in other manuals. Full-length manuals such as Maria E. Ward's *The Common Sense of Bicycling: Bicycling for Ladies* and Lillias Campbell Davidson's *Handbook for Lady Cyclists* position their authors as experts on whom the reader should rely, conveying technical information in a direct and detailed manner. Despite these differences in strategy, however, these instructional materials parallel Willard's and the *New York Times* author's writings in their emphasis on the difficulty of the task readers are undertaking in learning to bicycle, the need for patience, and the function of bicycle mastery as extending beyond leisure and toward demonstrating women's mechanical and physical abilities to the world. In doing so, these women enthusiast–authored instructional materials construct the same narrative, even though they differ in strategy; they both fill the informational gaps in materials such as Clyde's and Neeson's bicycle manuals and authorize women to take bicycling into their own hands, rather than accept the role of companion assigned them in these texts.

Indirect Strategies of Instruction: Willard and the *New York Times* Author

> Not a single friend encouraged me to ride except an active-minded young school-teacher, Miss Luther, of my hometown, who came several times with her wheel and gave me lessons. I also took a few lessons in a stuffy, semi-subterranean gallery in Chicago. But at fifty-three I was at more disadvantage

> than most people, for not only had I the impedimenta that result from the unnatural style of dress, but I also suffered from the sedentary habits of a lifetime. And then that small world . . . of those who loved me best, and who considered themselves largely responsible for my every-day methods of life, did not encourage me, but in their affectionate solicitude . . . thought I should "break my bones" and "spoil my future." (Willard 19–20)

Published in several editions by the F. H. Revell Company, Frances Willard's 1895 *A Wheel within a Wheel* articulates frankly the many obstacles that lie in the way of her efforts to learn to bicycle. Citing her age, her sedentary lifestyle, the inadequacy of the indoor riding hall for learning to ride, and the doubts of her loved ones, Willard portrays herself as a rider for whom the bicycle did not come easily. Serving as the president of the nationally active Woman's Christian Temperance Union, Willard was famous during her lifetime, a fact that differentiates her from many other riders who authored advice and instructional tracts. As Carol Mattingly notes, the charismatic and meticulously feminine Willard understood that "change for women would come only when large numbers of women demanded change and that those women would demand change only if convinced to do so by leaders whom they could safely and proudly emulate" (*Well-Tempered Women* 164).

A Wheel within a Wheel reflects this understanding, as Willard gives the details of her own difficult, year-long experience learning to bicycle in order to authorize and legitimize others' struggles and to insist that these obstacles were no excuse for failure. She affords women readers access to information not addressed by bicycle manufacturers and a level of personal ownership and reflection about bicycling that challenges the playful, effortless popular representations of young bicycle girls. Willard constitutes in *A Wheel within a Wheel* a public of women bicyclists of varying ages and ability levels, all riding together and supporting one another both for their own self-improvement and for the betterment of women in general. Throughout her text, she provides metaphors comparing her own struggles to learn to bicycle to other difficult but rewarding and necessary life challenges. This strategy of simultaneously limiting her topic to her own experiences and expanding it beyond bicycling through metaphor allows her to invite, without mandating, her readers to make the same connections, while at the same time legitimizing their inevitable self-doubt.

Early in her narrative, Willard proposes that "in many curious particulars, the bicycle is like the world" (22). Specifically, she sees the world as a place where a woman must constantly battle self-doubt in order to make her way, and where succumbing is not simply a biological imperative of one's sex but evidence of a weakness that can be overcome:

> That which caused the many failures I had in learning the bicycle had caused me failures in life; namely, a certain fearful looking for of judgment; a too vivid realization of the uncertainty of everything about me; and underlying doubt—at once, however . . . matched and overcome by the determination not to give in to it. (22)

In contrast to the comic depictions of inept women bicyclists paralyzed by fear but motivated by fashion to continue their bicycling lessons, Willard presents herself as a determined rider who does not downplay her struggles but translates them into metaphors for life. Whereas in many popular representations, fear of judgment and physical harm serves as evidence that women are ill suited for bicycling, Willard claims here that these are simply inevitable feelings that must be overcome—not only for success in bicycling but, by implication, for success in life. In her constant linkages between life experience and bicycle experience, Willard suggests that such realizations are her own but also provides openings for her readers to adapt these realizations for themselves—and thus to constitute the public she envisions for women bicyclists. Rather than explicitly urge readers to learn to ride, she guides them toward a linkage between bicycle mastery and life mastery. "I finally concluded that all failure was from a wobbling will rather than a wobbling wheel. I felt that indeed the will is the wheel of the mind" (26), she notes, reinforcing her indirect claim that women need only confidence and persistence to achieve personal or social success in life.

Similarly, Willard does not offer detailed instructions regarding the mechanics of bicycling, but instead models behaviors within the context of her narrative. She refers indirectly to her efforts to learn about "Gladys," the name she has given her bicycle:

> Gradually, item by item, I learned the location of every screw and spring, spoke and tire, and every beam and bearing that went to make up Gladys. This was not the lesson of a day, but of many days and weeks, and it had to be learned before we could get on well together. (25)

By referring to her need to identify "every screw and spring, spoke and tire" of her own machine, Willard models similar behavior for readers and contests both popular and manufacturer representations in which women waited for men to do bicycle maintenance. And by personifying her bicycle as she does, she implies that it is a creature not just to be ridden but also to be understood thoroughly and with significant effort.

Nonetheless, Willard does not neglect either the embodied instruction that riding requires or the mechanical components of the bicycle. Interspersed with her narrative are pointers to help smooth the way for readers, such as advice on mounting and steadying the bicycle and the following recommendation:

> Learn on a low machine, but "fly high" when once you have mastered it, as you have much more power over the wheels and can get up better speed with a less expenditure of force when you are above the instrument than when you are at the back of it. (21)

If Willard's metaphorical and narrative approach to bicycling created openings for readers to take ownership of their riding and link it to the advancement of women more broadly, the settings and actors within her anecdotes invite readers to imagine a broader range of contexts for riding than did manufacturer and popular representations. With the notable exception of an image of three young men assisting her in mounting the bicycle for the first time, few men appear in these anecdotes, which are peopled largely with women of varying ages, teaching and learning bicycling from one another. For instance, Willard writes of sharing a tricycle with her niece and another friend, taking turns racing it around the block together. She details her conversations and friendships with a series of female instructors. During one discussion with a fellow rider, she reports:

> We discoursed on the advantage to masculine character of comradeship with women who were as skilled and ingenious in the manipulation of the swift steed as they themselves. We contended that whatever diminishes the sense of superiority in men makes them more manly, brotherly, and pleasant to have about. (40–41)

Here Willard situates the bicycle not only as a means for women to gain confidence but also as an instrument that could change men's thinking. Within this narrative of the bicycle's impact on the gender order, women would learn to ride not to conform or adapt to men's need for companionship, as popular representations suggested, but to force men to abandon the sense of their own superiority.

Willard's riding is not all social or explicitly political, however; elsewhere, she indicates that riding is a pleasurable solitary pursuit—a claim often absent from popular representations of women's bicycling. She says that riding satisfied her "pure natural love of adventure . . . from a love of acquiring this new implement of power and literally putting it underfoot" (73), and she declares that her efforts to learn to ride were complete once she could mount and ride without anyone else present. Although she did not explicitly reference a broader class of riders than that described in most popular representations, neither did she assume a specific class for her readers by establishing a limited context within which they might ride.

In making clear the tenacity she needed to undertake the lengthy challenge of learning to ride, Willard certainly does not give the sense, as Bell's booklet does, that bicycling is simply an easy and fun undertaking for women. She demonstrates a keen awareness of the obstacles that some women riders experienced in riding, including their own self-doubt as well as the general criticism of the public. In writing these obstacles into a narrative of both personal and political triumph and introspection, rather than one that affirms the unsuitability of the bicycle for those who did not find it easy to master, she articulates the existence of a woman rider not present in popular and manufacturer representations of women on bicycles. Furthermore, in extending the range of contexts for women's bicycling beyond the romantic and adventurous activities implicit in these representations to include the solitary and the practical, she opens the machine up to a wider range of women than, for example, Bell's booklet acknowledges within its pages.

The anonymous 1895 *New York Times* article "Still the Wheelwoman" reads similarly to Willard's book in that it offers the author's experiences with candidness and humor, embedding only occasional direct instruction in a narrative that emphasizes not a single "correct" approach to bicycling, but the need for the rider to take ownership of her learning process. In contrast to Willard, the author uses a third-person voice and refers to herself as "our rider" or "our beginner" in a way that suggests that this protagonist could be any novice woman bicyclist, an "everywoman." In doing so, she manages to balance the particulars of her experience with generalizations about difficulties other women are likely to encounter. For example, she conveys to fellow riders the inadequacy of relying on instructors for support and advice, noting that for "our beginner," this was the source of many problems. "In four . . . lessons she had not learned the most important things, and had found her nervousness steadily increasing with each lesson," she explains, before shifting to a more direct address in urging readers to "make a change at once if they find their instructors incompetent or careless and inattentive" (21). This subtle weaving of personal experience and instructive generalization allows the reader both to position herself as a certain kind of beginner similar to the author and to reap the benefits of the author's experience.

Additionally, this questioning of the instructor's authority, in stark contrast to the trust placed in the instructor by most manuals, levels the hierarchy between learner and master, implying that struggling novices ought not to assume their difficulties are solely their own fault. It invests the novice with some level of embodied expertise, as the author recalls that only when she began to focus on her own balance (defying her instructor's advice to focus on the front wheel and push against it) did she begin to have success as a rider. Similarly, in discussing the always controversial issue of bicycle dress, the author urges readers to "improvise from materials at hand" when selecting appropriate clothing for bicycling, noting that she "found by experience and observation just what suited her best." Though the author does assert that women's bicycle dress should be "trim and inconspicuous," she does not provide specific directives about what it should involve, other than to describe her own preferences.

Like Willard, also, the *New York Times* author advocates a women's bicycling narrative that involves riders' mastery of all aspects of riding and mechanical knowledge. "It is quite worthwhile to spend a half hour alone some morning in mastering the art [of mounting the machine], for the woman who cannot mount can never ride alone" (21), she points out, advocating that women ought to become both solitary riders and self-teachers to be truly proficient and self-reliant. "In order to become complete mistress of her wheel, our beginner cleaned it herself, pumped up the tires, oiled it, and did everything necessary," even seeking help from her brother for tips about how to unscrew particularly difficult nuts (21). By admitting to a few failed attempts to pump up her tires, the author makes clear that mastering bicycle maintenance was not easy, but it was necessary regardless—thus supporting the narrative apparent in Willard's book regarding the difficulties and rewards of learning the bicycle.

Direct Strategies of Instruction: Ward and Brown

Not every women cyclist approached the task of communicating her knowledge so indirectly, however. Whereas Willard and the *New York Times* author both confined their advice-giving to their own experiences, shying away from directives, other writers took a more exhaustive, directive approach. Staten Island cycling enthusiast Maria E. Ward's popular 1896 book, *The Common Sense of Bicycling: Bicycling for Ladies*, is a good example of such a text. Although she possessed an encyclopedic knowledge of bicycling and assumed the role of the expert rider, Ward does not appear to have authored any other books.[2] Rather, she was a devoted member of the Staten Island Bicycle Club, an avid sportswoman, and an amateur who put her skills to use out of conviction and perhaps financial need.

Despite its direct approach, Ward's book helps construct a user narrative for her women readers similarly to Willard's book and the anonymous *Times* article for beginners. She situates her audience as a group of novices embarking on a challenging but necessary and rewarding endeavor that involves both physical skill and mechanical know-how. Like the indirect advice givers, Ward counsels that the truly competent female rider ought not to ride simply for enjoyment and health, in the company of her husband, father, or brother, but should become a self-sufficient student of the bicycle, capable of riding both alone and in the company of other women. She suggests that riders will be old as well as young and acknowledges that they may need to ride for practical purposes or even work transportation, as well as leisure. Like Willard and the *Times* author, Ward upsets the popular user narrative of the carefree bicycle girl and provides exhaustive instruction geared toward a user committed to making great efforts toward becoming a wholly self-sufficient bicyclist for her own sake.

Unlike the indirect advice givers, who use a strategy of playful self-deprecation to highlight their own struggles and put themselves on the same level as their readers, Ward distinguishes herself as an expert cyclist and takes a somewhat harsh tone with readers for their ignorance about what they are doing. Perhaps thinking of the many circulating parodies of inept bicycle novices at riding schools, she opens her preface with the following observation:

> I have found that in bicycling . . . women and girls bring upon themselves censure from many sources. I have also found that this censure, though

> almost invariably deserved, is called forth not so much by what they do as the way they do it. (ix)

Ward is not interested, as so many authors were, in defending women's *ability* or *right* to ride. Instead, she sees the problem as a matter of sustained effort and depth of knowledge, assuming that they are capable of riding, and seeks to draw from her own knowledge to educate women to ride well enough to avoid popular censure.

Although she differs from Willard and the *Times* author in the relationship she constructs with her readers, Ward's perspective emerges from skepticism about the traditional indoor riding-hall model of instruction that the most other manuals intimated were sufficient for women riders. Simply helping women pedal is not enough; rather, Ward asserts that bicycling entails not just riding but also "an intelligent comprehension of the bicycle as a machine, an appreciative knowledge of the human machine that propels it, and a realization of the fact that rider and bicycle should form one combined mechanism" (x). In educating readers about these issues, Ward's two-hundred-page book contains twenty-two chapters, including such topics as "What the Bicycle Does," "Helping and Teaching: What to Learn," "Women and Tools," and "Tires" (xiii–xiv).

Whereas Bell's booklet and the male-authored manuals indicate that learning to ride is an easy task, the thirteen-page "For Beginners" chapter of Ward's book indicates that riding was often a formidable one. Rather than provide any sense of the average amount of time it should take a woman to learn to ride, Ward emphasizes that learning difficulty varies widely from person to person: "The period of instruction may last for five minutes or six months" (23). In making this assertion, she authorizes the Miss Hopkinses of the world to persist in their efforts to learn to ride. Additionally, she offers direct advice about how to behave during a lesson, demonstrating the need for the rider's own attention to supplement the instructor's words. The beginner should "attend to the bicycle and to nothing else. Don't attempt to talk, and look well ahead of the machine. . . . Remember, the bicycle will go wherever the attention is directed" (23). Although Ward's direct, non-negotiable approach might have intimidated the would-be rider, it validates those who have found learning to ride difficult because it explains that the process is one that requires concentration and effort.

Ward does not talk about her own experiences in her manual, but she does embed her directive in contexts that parallel the settings for Willard's and the *Times* author's narratives. In doing so, she extends the narrative of the brave, determined woman rider whose riding is part of a network of female riders. Ward strays entirely from domestic or courtship scenes in describing contexts within which women might ride a bicycle, and she hints that the purview of the new technology might extend beyond the leisured classes by suggesting that not everyone will learn to bicycle in an indoor riding hall. In her "Helping and Teaching" chapter, for instance, Ward advises that "[a] trio of novices can form a very fair school. . . . If ladies are helping one another, the best way is for two to hold the bicycle, standing one on each side of the machine" (41). She even describes the likely scenario of the individual rider attempting to learn without assistance: the solo rider can "mount the bicycle in the gutter, and limp along. . . . Grasp a post firmly, and holding by it, try to mount; and study the tendencies and the balance of the bicycle without letting go the post" (45–46). Similarly to Willard's narrative, Ward's discussion of different means of learning to ride expands the range of social scenarios to include both female companionship and independent practice, rather than just male-chaperoned paid instruction or courtship excursions.

In addition to her thorough commitment to ensuring that riders learn to maneuver the bicycle, Ward seeks throughout her manual to help them become self-sufficient mechanics for the machine and understand how it works. Going beyond the approach of Willard and the *Times* author, who simply advise their readers to learn about the bicycle's mechanics, Ward dedicates several chapters to describing these mechanics and makes a serious plea for readers to attempt this work. For instance, on the first page of "Women and Tools," she repeatedly reassures readers that they are capable of mastering bicycle maintenance. "I hold that a woman who is able to use a needle or scissors can use other tools equally well" (112). On that same page, she breaks down gender binaries in relation to tool use, asserting that tools can be mastered by both sexes and that the skills required for doing so are not gendered:

> There are many capable people in the world, both men and women, who can comprehend at a glance the use or the application of an article or an idea—people who instinctively use their eyes and hands with ease and accuracy; there are others who learn more slowly to use their mechanical senses, and there are also those whose attention has never been called to certain simple mechanical facts and details that they are quite capable of understanding. To all the mastery of these facts means an expenditure of more or less time. (112)

This passage assures women readers that learning to use tools is not beyond their abilities, even as it acknowledges the added challenge that "those whose attention has never been called to . . . mechanical facts and details" faced in doing so.

Ward also acknowledges a wide range of reader positions (the talented and less talented, the experienced and inexperienced), not condescending to her readers by assuming their total ignorance but demonstrating that there is no place from which a learner cannot begin. As she recommends to the novice rider:

> The wheeler who desires to succeed cannot too soon begin to observe and take notes. Early learn to use the wrench yourself, and study how to apply that instrument properly. Study the different parts of the bicycle, and note how they are put together; and particularly observe each nut and screw, and determine its purpose. . . . Learn the names and uses of the different parts of the bicycle, and study their construction. (35–36)

This recommendation challenges readers to learn about the bicycle—a task that includes using tools and learning the names and functions of parts.

To these ends, in her "Tools and How to Use Them" chapter, Ward offers a series of simple definitions for items ranging from wrenches and screwdrivers to screws, bolts, and oilcans. She defines a nut, for instance, as "a piece of metal adapted to screw on the end of a bolt" (118). In addition, she encourages the reader to consider its identifying features and functions:

> Unscrew a nut gently and examine it. On the inside will be found a spiral groove and a spiral ridge or thread. Examine the bolt, and observe a similar spiral groove and thread. These, when screwed together, prevent slipping, and the nut cannot be pulled or pushed off. To remove a nut, it is necessary to turn it; and always turn one way, from left to right, if the nut lies uppermost. (119)

This description of the nut in form and function is representative of her descriptions of other items. Complementing the text is an image of a woman rider positioning the bicycle for proper maintenance (fig. 3.1). This image, along with some lengthy text about bicycle mechanics and maintenance, indicate the importance that Ward places on these skills to the self-sufficient woman rider's education.

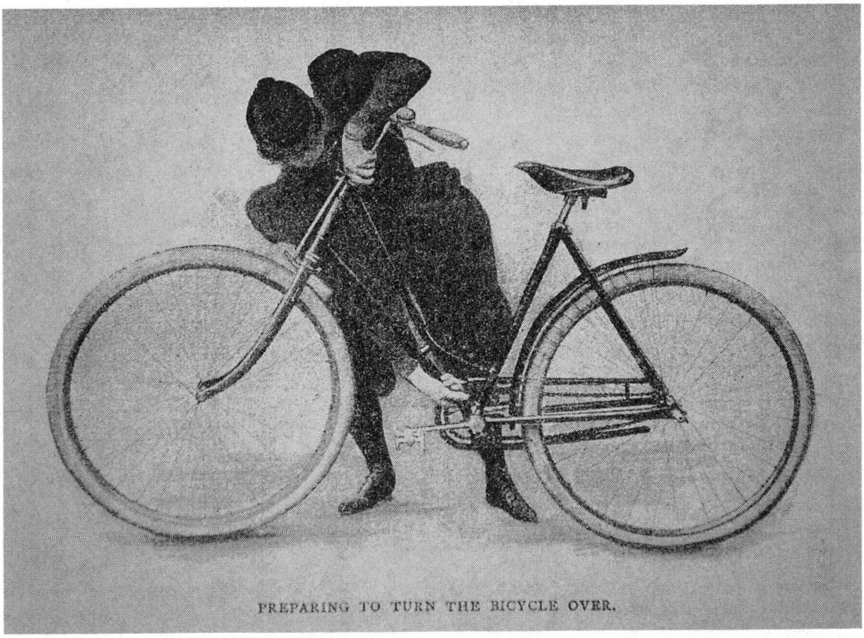

Figure 3.1. Woman positioning a bicycle for maintenance. Maria E. Ward, The Common Sense of Bicycling: Bicycling for Ladies.

Because Ward attributes prejudices against women to their own lack of thorough knowledge of the feats they attempt, she subtly discredits the bicycle girl of the popular magazine, who simply rides effortlessly without knowing how to maintain her own bicycle. Like Willard and the *Times* author, she champions self-sufficiency and suggests that its acquisition will extend to realms beyond that of the bicycle. For example, in her "Women and Tools" chapter, she notes:

> Women and girls are able to do good work, but they should not expect to accomplish such a result through ignorance or neglect. They must be willing to study and to give proper attention to important details and their knowledge of the subject must be sufficient to enable them to use judgment and discrimination. (114)

Ward envisions her women readers as capable of achievement through careful study beyond the superficial level of effort that bicycle manufacturers assumed was sufficient. Her manual, in its broad coverage of possible contexts for riding and information required for successful mastery, not only fills the voids left by manufacturers but also gestures toward the social transformation that women's self-sufficiency might bring about and encourages riders to see themselves as committed to a challenging but worthwhile enterprise.

Well-known British bicyclist Lillias Campbell Davidson takes a similarly direct and thorough approach in her 1896 *Handbook for Lady Cyclists.* Like Ward, Davidson acknowledges the role women play in perpetuating negative stereotypes about their riding abilities and sees her book as an expert's intervention to prevent this problem, explaining her perspective with gentle humor in her opening pages:

> It is a common thing to hear women who have been cycling for months to show the frankest ignorance about their mounts. . . . [T]hey ask, with an air of refreshing interest, "What is a crank?" and talk of "blowing up spokes" and I have had to restrain more than one energetic cycling lady from filling an oil well to overflowing with salad oil every time she starts out for a spin. A little practical advice will be of use to women who are about to take up the pastime for the first time, or who, though they have learnt to sit on a bicycle . . . have no friend more experienced or instructed than themselves to give them a few hints on the subject. (10–11)

Though Davidson's tone is gentler than Ward's, the two riders share a common assumption that they have expertise to dispense to their readers. Whereas Willard and the anonymous *Times* author position themselves as fellow novices, Davidson here clearly differentiates herself from the "energetic cycling lady" with the salad oil, describing herself as a "lady correspondent to more than one of the leading cycling papers" whose book is a response to "many hundreds of letters from cycling women and women who want to earn that adjective, in all parts of the world" (12). Davidson does not emphasize the need for the woman rider to trust her own instincts so much as the need to be thorough in her learning of the materials Davidson provides, "both for her own sake and for the sake of the pastime" (12). Regardless, Davidson does join the other authors in portraying a woman rider who is undertaking a challenging and potentially transformative endeavor, and who can then use her knowledge to assist others like her.

Davidson's twenty-five-chapter book features over 120 pages of advice on topics ranging from learning to ride to cleaning and care of a machine to country riding. Like Ward, she is direct and prescriptive in her prose, advocating particular maneuvers and discouraging those that might appear unfeminine. For instance, Davidson urges riders to avoid the "slipshod and slovenly" method of straddling the bike before taking off, promoting instead the "infinitely prettier and smarter" practice of springing onto the moving machine from behind (16). Elsewhere, she offers step-by-step instruction similar to that of Ward for maneuvers such as dismounting and riding on bumpy country roads.

Davidson's attention to bicycle care is perhaps more detailed even than Ward's. In addition to defining bicycle parts and describing procedures such as changing a tire, she recommends specific tools to readers. "Too long a crank throw is never to be commended. Better err on the side of too short cranks than too long ones," she advises. "From five and a half to six inches will suit the average rider though allowance must be made for extra height or lack of it" (40).

Although she describes tire repair as "fatiguing messy work" that most women would prefer not to undertake themselves, she also assumes that women will travel apart from male companions and will need to be prepared:

> A tyre repair kit should always be taken with one, and I advise every lady tourist to have a few lessons in tyre mending before she starts on a tour alone, or with a lady companion, no matter how much she may shrink from the mending of her tyres on ordinary occasions.

By assuming the relevance of this context in which the "lady tourist" will travel alone or with other women, rather than in mixed groups or with male companions, and by preparing women for their needs during this type of excursion, Davidson joins Ward in contesting manufacturer assumptions.

Additionally, Davidson does not limit her discussion to the leisurely riding undertaken by tourists, but spends some time addressing those women who may need to bicycle to work. In her chapter entitled "Cycling as Convenience," for instance, she commends the bicycle's role in improving the lives of the "vast army" of working women, spelling out with great detail the increased independence bicycling can bring to their daily lives:

> With a bicycle to bring her to and from her daily work, a woman can live farther away from it than would be possible if she had to depend on some less swift and independent means of transit. With a cycle she is unfettered

> in her choice of a locality for her house. She need not consult bus routes, tram lines, or railways. She is not tied to special times in the day, or in danger of finding all methods of transport crowded or disagreeable. She can start when she chooses, provided she arrives at a specified time, and she can regulate her pace to suit her own needs. She can choose her own road as a rule, and vary it to suit her own convenience. She has nothing to pay for getting in and out, and once her machine's initial cost is paid, she has not to add a season ticket to the lower price of house-rent or rooms she secures by living farther away from her daily occupation. (123)

Davidson's sustained observation expands the contexts for women's riding well beyond those delineated by Clyde, Neeson, and Bell, encouraging her readers to trace out the many ways bicycles might improve women's lives and especially suggesting its benefits for single and working women. For affluent readers who may not fully understand the potential significance of the bicycle for these groups, she breaks her explanation down in detail, not only making a glib reference to the machine's convenience but also providing concrete examples of the ways it frees a woman from public transportation and saves money, influencing her choices of both where to live and how to spend her time. In doing so, she unites her readers across classes and constitutes them as a more cohesive public, brought together by a well-developed vision of how the bicycle might improve all women's lives.

In general, women enthusiast–authored advice and instructional materials amended both the positive, romanticized and the negative, parodic characterizations of women bicyclists within popular magazines and newspapers. They filled the gaps left by other instructional materials, providing women with the support they needed not only to learn the steps of particular procedures but also to feel like they could and should continue the effort, despite the challenge of doing so. Additionally, women enthusiast–authored advice and instructional materials authorized riders to attempt bicycling in a wider range of contexts than many other materials: in all-female groups, alone, in transit to work, and in the explicit pursuit of personal autonomy. Above all, these materials helped a diverse range of women riders—old and young, single and married, urban and rural, expert and novice, leisure rider and working woman—to understand themselves as a group with overlapping interests, capable of both assisting and sharing experiences with one another in the pursuit of a challenging but rewarding activity.

Instructions for Change

Women-authored advice and instructional materials played a crucial role in encouraging reluctant riders to work through their fear of or difficulty in riding the bicycle. They also served as a response to the criticisms, both affectionate and otherwise, of women riders who did not fit the popular bicycle girl type advanced by manufacturers and articles in popular magazines. By encouraging women to think of bicycling not as an activity that ought to feel effortless from the start but as an important personal and even political challenge, these materials provided some incentive for struggling riders to persevere. Additionally, they sought to protect women riders from censure by helping them ride competently and irreproachably and by encouraging readers to think of their riding explicitly as a meaning-making activity capable of influencing public attitudes both about women on bicycles and about women's abilities more broadly. By demonstrating a thorough knowledge of the wheel and by gaining self-sufficiency, these enthusiasts believed, women could not only gain confidence in their own abilities but make others confident in these abilities as well.

Vitally, these authors collectively helped constitute their readership as a group of "wheel women," united in their efforts to convey to one another both the challenge and the significance of learning to bicycle. Just as contemporary political and social groups gain traction by naming themselves or by linking previously disparate attributes to form a new narrative, women bicycle enthusiasts generated in their instructional materials a way for readers to understand themselves as a group unified by self-sufficiency, introspection, and determination. Whereas women fiction writers, commentators, and travel writers all constructed an ethos for a particular figure or type of woman who possessed these qualities inherently, technical writers assured their readers that they, too, could come to possess these qualities through patient learning, even if they did not resemble the bicycle girl figure in the popular magazine. Varying in age, geography, class, and marital status, this figure was characterized by her willingness to assist other women cyclists, as well as by her consciousness that her efforts on the bicycle might have larger significance for women in other facets of life.

Traces of these women's collective activities remain, though they are not as plentiful as those that remain of the men's bicycle clubs of the day. Some of the women, such as Maria E. Ward, formed and were active in local women's bicycling groups and clubs, within which they circulated handbooks and even collectively owned bicycles to help women master riding. An 1897 *New York Times* article entitled "How to Choose a Wheel: Advice for Women Who Want to Ride Bicycles," for instance, summarizes a talk given to a group of women at Brooklyn's Hotel St. George by a Miss E. Marguerite Lindley. According to the article, Lindley's assistant, Miss Barrus, demonstrated how to sit on a bicycle while her friend spoke about topics ranging from proper saddle and handlebar height to anatomy (3). A picture of the "Hartford Ladies Bicycle Club," gathered at a park in that Connecticut city in the mid-1890s, portrays eight women with only four bicycles among them, suggesting that the group—like Willard and her friends—took turns learning to ride. And my own copy of Ward's book *The Common Sense of Bicycling: Bicycling for Ladies* features an inscription that indicates the book was given as a gift to its owner:

> 'Tis well to know your silent steed
> 'Tis well to know,
> Just how to go,
> That he may show
> His highest speed;
> 'Tis well to know
> Your silent steed

This message, dated August 1896, is evidence of both the camaraderie of riding and the emphasis riders placed on *knowing* about bicycling, as well as on participating in the popular activity. This emphasis emerged not from the popular magazines of the day, but from the efforts of women bicyclists themselves to help a broader range of prospective women riders navigate the physical and social challenges of learning to ride.

At the same time that women-authored instructional materials helped riders constitute themselves as a self-sufficient public, however, the agency that these materials exerted remained largely collected—geographically and temporally dispersed and indirect in its influence, not fully realized outside the embodied activities of women bicyclists that the materials were designed to promote. Technical communication—whether historical or contemporary—functions in this way, mediating, but not dictating, how individual users come to understand and enact the expectations for their behavior in relation to a particular technology. And though the embodied practices that technical communication supports in a single user are not significant in themselves, they accrete through repetition, becoming integral not only to the maintenance of a user narrative but also to the maintenance or dissolution of larger power relations, such as gender. The agency of such materials, furthermore, becomes greater when the circulation of the instructions is greater, whether through word of mouth or through publication and distribution—meaning that like the writers of popular magazines, writers of technical and instructional materials benefited from the burgeoning print culture of the late nineteenth century.

In general, enthusiast-authored instructional materials suggest something of the powerful role technical communication plays in mediating relationships between users and technologies such as the bicycle. As outsiders apart from processes of production or distribution, these writers could not directly influence the promotional or instructional efforts of bicycle companies. They did, however, influence riders by offering supplements to this material in which they helped riders envision themselves as capable, though popular representations did not always support this idea. Through their instructional and advice writing, these authors wielded significant power over the development of the bicycle, even if they never set foot in a bicycle manufacturer's headquarters.

Chapter Four

Women Bicyclists' Embodied Medical Authority

In his 1873 treatise *Sex in Education; or, A Fair Chance for Girls*, Dr. Edward H. Clarke of Harvard Medical School argues famously against coeducation on the grounds that subjecting girls to the same mental and physical exertion as boys would lead to their ruin. Citing symptoms as varied as atrophied uterus and ovaries, sterility, masculinization, and death, Dr. Clarke claims that women who pursue public and intellectual lives are sapping their bodies of energy intended for their reproductive functions; he recommends that girls' education, which he defines broadly as "the whole manner of life, physical and psychical, during the educational period" (4), be shaped around their gender-specific need for rest, especially during menstruation. As evidence of the danger of women's mental and physical exertion, Dr. Clarke gives examples of his own patients, including a Miss G——, whose early academic success led to her premature death and whose autopsy, he reports, revealed "commencing degeneration" (23) in her brain.

The central arguments underpinning Dr. Clarke's book were hardly novel; they merely affirmed the medical credibility of long-standing commonplaces about women's intellectual and physical limitations. Although scientific medicine, with its commitment to inductive reasoning and quantitative, experimental data, was eroding earlier notions of the human body as an economy within which "every part . . . was related inevitably and inextricably with every other" (Rosenberg 5; Wells 41), the assumption that women's bodies were naturally weak and incapable of physical and mental exertion persisted among both doctors and laypeople, many of whom continued to frame their arguments on the subject in these outdated economic terms (Vertinsky 7). Simply by diverting precious, limited energy to new activities, these skeptics worried, women could endanger their fitness for other biological and psychological activities, such as reproduction and parental nurturing.

This concern persisted into the 1890s and helped shape the arguments of women's bicycling opponents. Dr. Arabella Kenealy, for instance, worries within the pages of the British periodical *The Nineteenth Century* that one patient's bicycle rides had "altered the relation of her forces in such a manner as to increase the muscle-power at the expense of other qualities" and had worked to "destroy a complex, well-planned balance of faculties which had been Nature's scheme when Nature fashioned [the girl]" (638). Kenealy, a dedicated eugenicist, warns:

> Nature knows what are the faculties whence this new muscle-energy is born. She knows it is the birthright of the babies [these] athletes are squandering. She knows it is the laboriously evolved potentiality of the race they are expending on their muscles. (643)

Kenealy's dire predictions of the effects of bicycle riding on both the individual and "the race" indicate the power of the commonplace of the limited feminine bodily economy within both medical and popular culture.

Importantly, Clarke and, later, Kenealy had their critics among both doctors and feminists. Most notably, Dr. Mary Putnam Jacobi's 1877 *The Question of Rest during Menstruation* provides an influential medical counterargument to Clarke's *Sex in Education* based on the results of a massive survey revealing that there is no correlation between rest during menstruation and a woman's general health. Author and activist Julia Ward Howe, too, offers a public response to Clarke, featuring the testimony of physicians from both coeducational and women's colleges throughout the United States in her own book, *Sex and Education*. These medical experts argue that women students' health had benefited from, rather than been depleted by, both intellectual and physical activity at colleges such as Oberlin, Vassar, and Antioch. Similarly, British writer Laura Ormiston Chant responds to Kenealy's article, asserting a wide range of evidence of the health and vigor of educated women. In general, writers and doctors alike raised questions about the dire predictions that Clarke, Kenealy, and other skeptics of women's education and exertion advanced.

Despite these questions, commonplaces about women's inherent fragility persisted in reference to bicycles as well as other activities. Though Kenealy's wholesale denunciation of bicycling for women was unusual among doctors during the 1890s, most practitioners' endorsements of the new activity were accompanied by cautionary statements that reveal their continued belief that excessive physical activity would sap needed energy from women's reproductive function. Influenced by scientific medicine's attention to experimental method as a means to objectivity, they reframed Kenealy's dire warnings as recommendations for caution, endorsing the bicycle for women's use as a therapeutic or preventive regime to be used in strict moderation, with medical monitoring. For instance, Dr. J. West Roosevelt advises readers of *Scribner's Magazine*:

> There is no reason to think that a healthy woman can be injured by using the wheel, *provided she does not over-exert herself by riding too long a time, or too fast, or up too steep hills; and provided she does not ride when common sense and physiology alike forbid any needless exertion.* (712; emphasis in original)

Roosevelt's concern that women might suffer as the result of "needless exertion," as well as his veiled allusion to women's special need for rest during menstruation, parallels Clarke's warnings about women depriving their reproductive systems of needed energy even as it encourages women to ride in moderation.

Similarly, in "A Plea for the New Woman and the Bicycle," an 1895 speech delivered before the Washington Obstetrical and Gynecological Society and later published in the *American Journal of Obstetrics and Diseases of Women and Children*, Dr. Francis Nash provides a mixed endorsement of bicycling for women, promising that the bicycle will bring "grand results" (556) to women riders seeking relief from a wide variety of ailments, but adding the following warning: "A woman should not take 'century runs,' nor assume the position of a 'scorcher,' nor attempt high speeds or difficult hills. When it is necessary for her to breathe through her mouth she should dismount and walk" (558). Whether writing in popular magazines like *Scribner's* or offering recommendations before an audience of their peers, doctors all over the country tacitly affirmed the commonplace notions of women's bodily weakness that Clarke had helped legitimize two decades earlier, emphasizing the therapeutic value of the new machine for women but also radically circumscribing the range of its recommended uses.

Such cautious recommendations had an impact not only on women's mobility but also on the ways women riders might understand their own bodies' reactions to physical exercise aboard the wheel. Whereas, for example, a woman bicyclist might understand minor shortness of breath as evidence of grave danger due to her limited energies, a man might experience the same sensation as the healthy result of vigorous, manly exercise. Doctors' mixed prescriptions for women bicyclists, then, were instrumental in perpetuating—as well as reflecting—existing commonplaces about women's physical weakness. And in doing so, they helped exaggerate both physical and psychological differences between women and men, naturalizing differences that were cultural in origin.

In the discussion that follows, I first consider in more detail the role that doctors played in upholding gendered commonplaces about women's physical and mental capacities. I suggest that because of the nascent scientific medical establishment's efforts to police its ranks for evidence of rigor and orthodoxy, doctors—whether male or female—were poorly positioned to call these commonplaces into question, even when they did offer cautious endorsements of bicycling. However, women writers and bicyclists acting outside the medical establishment challenged commonplaces about their special fragility, positing with their pens as well as their bodies a feminine capacity for energy renewal through exercise and a wider range of ends to which their energies could be put. The remainder of this chapter thus considers the ways these non–medically trained women eroded the commonplace of women's limited energies and troubled the socially constructed boundaries between masculinity and femininity that medical discourse helped sustain. Examining their rhetorical work alongside that of doctors demonstrates the extent to which even authoritative channels can be vulnerable to the efforts of otherwise disenfranchised groups and individuals, such as women bicyclists, who are able to draw from a wider range of rhetorical resources *because* of, rather than in spite of, their marginal position.

Drawing from their own embodied experience aboard the wheel, non–medically trained women writers authored testimonials that reframed their exertions as evidence of good health rather than exhaustion. Because, in part, these rhetors did not need to abide by the methodological constraints of scientific medicine, they were able to offer a new and compelling metaphor for women's physical and intellectual energies that reflected their inherent strength and vitality and often contested doctors' insistence that women bicyclists required medical monitoring. Though these writers sustained the notion that women ought to ride bicycles specifically in order to protect and improve their health, they often couched their arguments in terms that rejected the notion that women's health was fragile or in need of special surveillance from doctors.

Additionally, women bicyclists' embodied acts of strength, endurance, and speed afforded a more radical rhetorical response to doctors' precautions, materializing the renewability and adaptability of the female body about which women commentators wrote and advancing a far wider range of contexts in which women might ride. Whereas women commentary writers retained doctors' commitment to the bicycle as an instrument of health, these riders—often young immigrants who raced for money and undertook epic rides requiring them to endure great hardship—gave visibility to their own appropriation of the "masculine" traits of strength, resilience, and competitiveness.

As rhetorician Celeste Condit has noted, public discourses affect scientific conversations "every bit as much as the reverse" (12), so that by generating commonplaces within broad public forums, they put pressure on the sorts of arguments possible among doctors themselves. Similarly, Greg Myers argues that "members of the public have their own persuasive resources, because they can connect the abstractions of scientific knowledge to lived experience, and public debates provide their own sorts of challenges to arguments" (269). Acting outside the medical establishment, women commentators and bicyclists drew from persuasive resources put in place by the rhetorical-material network surrounding women's bicycling—including the inventions, manuals, and physical spaces that made their feats possible—in denaturalizing a version of femininity that rested on women's inherent weakness and fragility. Though they did not meet with unmitigated success in toppling old commonplaces about women's bodies, they did much to relocate these commonplaces as cultural rather than biological, thus helping women at the turn of the century lay claim to a far greater range of activities than just bicycling.

The Bicycle and the Rise of Scientific Medicine

> [Bicycling] will bring great benefit to women in simple degenerated conditions of the heart, in dilated heart . . . in varicose veins and hemorrhoids, in almost all pulmonary affections except advanced tuberculosis; in various nervous diseases . . . paralysis, neurasthenia, and hysteria, migraine and the neuralgias; in anemia, chlorosis, amenorrhea, dysmenorrhea; in uterine and ovarian congestion and in chronic painless lesions without fever . . .

in dyspepsias, constipation, obesity, torpid liver, gout, diabetes mellitus; in spinal curvatures, weak and partially ankylosed joints. (Nash 560)

In this lengthy description of the benefits of bicycling for women, Dr. Francis Nash delineates an almost comically lengthy list of diseases that the new activity will help cure, as he makes his "plea" to doctors who, like Kenealy, worried that women's bodies would suffer from the exertion of bicycling. Though he offers a solid endorsement, the language in which he makes his argument reveals the extent to which he sought to medicalize women's bicycling on the grounds that their health was in crisis. Furthermore, his use of precise clinical terms such as "diabetes mellitus" and "ankylosed joints" demonstrates his alliance with the newly emergent field of scientific medicine, which by the 1890s had become the gold standard for practice throughout Britain and America.

The notion, now nearly inextricable from our conception of medicine, that doctors should undergo rigorous scientific training above the level of the bachelor's degree was a new one in the 1890s, when only a few American medical schools required more than two years of study and often included no laboratory component to their classes. Throughout the nineteenth century, doctors had employed a wide variety of approaches to their practice, and governance over their methods scarcely existed. By the last two decades of the century, however, the American Medical Association was working hard to enforce more rigorous standardized training, practice, and research—all associated with the new medical practices that had emerged in the universities of Europe. This approach emphasized scientific principles, inductive thinking, empirical methods, and precision in terminology. It shifted doctors' attention away from the whole "system," about which Clarke had written in the 1870s, toward discrete body parts susceptible to diseases with transferable symptoms and precise causes. It replaced lengthy narratives about individual patients with short, sparse descriptions of "cases" that used precise scientific terminology and situated observations in relation to previous research, demanding that credible practitioners demonstrate their strict adherence to its methods and conventions.

Within this increasingly rigid professional atmosphere, practicing doctors scrambled to demonstrate their allegiance to the ethos of scientific medicine. They did so by presenting papers at professional conferences that, as Carolyn Skinner has noted, served as sites where participants were called on "to demonstrate their medical orthodoxy and scientific rigor" (312) before their peers. Listeners were tasked with responding in ways that would encourage methodological improvement, and presentations were published in medical journals where they could be further scrutinized.

Within this rigorous evaluative environment, doctors were constrained from deviating from scientific orthodoxy. Like modern practitioners, they grounded their work in existing conversations about issues—such as women's perceived physical weakness—that animated the field at that time, and their presentation of cases followed an increasingly standardized format: physicians would describe previous studies on similar topics and then describe their own patients' initial symptoms, the progression of those symptoms, the treatments provided, and the patients' final outcome. In order to ensure the validity of their findings, doctors often sought second opinions regarding the treatments they provided (Skinner 311). In general, doctors at the turn of the century found themselves, in their professional presentations and papers, subject to the limits of what Risa Applegarth has described as *rhetorical scarcity*: "a manufactured situation of intense and increasing constraint . . . that significantly restricts rhetors' access to key rhetorical resources" ("Rhetorical Scarcity" 455).

As a result of their reliance on one another for validation and the conformity that belonging in the increasingly constrained field of medicine required, doctors often did not question shared fundamental assumptions about patients, diseases, and treatments. Most medical doctors did not debate, for instance, whether women's bodies were inherently weaker than men's; they shared the common assumption that this was the case but instead addressed the nature, sources, and potential treatments of women's weakness in clinical terms, substantiated with case studies in which they detailed the symptoms related to specific body parts. Tellingly, they did not contradict one another readily, favoring instead reserved judgments that would not signal outsider status. Their assessments of bicycling for women, then, were encouraging but tentative, tacitly affirming existing commonplaces about women's inherent weakness by urging them to take special caution—a prescription that predictably served to affirm doctors' own intervention and authority.

Within professional journals, scientific-leaning doctors often collected professional opinions from fellow practitioners through surveys. This approach allowed them to demonstrate their commitment to seeking peer opinions and to compiling many "cases," rather than relying on one extended narrative, before making a judgment on a particular issue. In talks that were later published as articles in medical journals, doctors reported distributing surveys asking such questions as "Have you seen any harm from [bicycling]?" or "Would you advise it in any form of uterine disorder?" (Townsend 593). In a survey of twenty-five doctors that appears in the *American Journal of Obstetrics and Diseases of Women and Children*, for instance, Dr. James Prendergast reports that in response to his query about symptoms related to bicycling, he received the following information from fellow doctors:

> One reports two cases of aggravated leucorrhea and one case of aggravated functional heart disturbance. Another reports a case of acute ovaritis.... Another states that he had seen bad effects in women with weak hearts or pelvic disease. (248)

The passage demonstrates Prendergast's commitment to clinical terminology and to capturing with precision a range of responses from his peers, as well as his caution in recommending the bicycle to women. Similarly, Dr. Charles W. Townsend's 1895 survey in the *Boston Medical and Surgical Journal* offers a range of restrictions couched in clinical terms. He reports that doctors responded to his query with the following observations:

> Four . . . had seen harm only from excessive use in the form of general fatigue. . . . One reports severe pain in the head in a stout woman of forty following excessive strain in climbing a steep hill. . . . Another has seen serious ovarian trouble directly due to riding long distances or during or near the menstrual period. (593)

It is of note that Prendergast cites Townsend in his study, demonstrating the extent to which the medical community at this time was taking on its modern characteristics, engaging in closed and careful conversations from which sharply deviant views were unlikely to emerge.

Revealingly, even as the use of clinical terminology distinguishes both Prendergast's and Townsend's statuses as scientific-leaning doctors, the emphasis on the link between women's bicycling and significant exertion—articulated in terms of "long distances," "excessive use," and "excessive strain" and linked to the menstrual period—reframes, but does not wholly abandon, the arguments implicit in Clarke and Kenealy's writings. Though these doctors' warnings are couched as restrictions, rather than wholesale rejections of women's bicycling, and though the highly individualized, literary examples like Clarke's Miss G—— have been replaced by the clinically worded array of "cases" reported by many different people, scientific-leaning doctors retained the notion that women's limited physical energies might be drained by excessive exertion if they were not careful.

Women doctors, whose numbers were plentiful at the turn of the century, generally spoke of the bicycle along similar lines. Though they did not publish their findings as widely as men, these doctors did describe their handling of cases in the *Woman's Medical Journal*, one of the few professional venues for publication available to them. Their descriptions of the cases they encountered are thoroughly orthodox, indicating the extent to which, during the 1890s, women practitioners were striving to achieve scientific legitimacy alongside their male peers. For example, Dr. Ida C. Barnes's "Morbid Conditions Complicating Menopause," which appeared in the *Woman's Medical Journal* in 1897, demonstrates both her commitment to precise terminology and the breadth of ailments for which doctors recommended the bicycle: "A young lady, a school teacher, inclined to obesity . . . ceased to menstruate for two years, at twenty-three . . . began to bicycle and the menses have returned with commendable regularity" (342). In considering the links between menopause and obesity, Barnes posits the bicycle as a solution. Similarly, Dr. E. M. Roys-Gavitt advocates bicycling in another article in the same issue, titled "Acute Miliary Tuberculosis," offering the case of a "young woman employed in store," which she describes as follows:

> Anemic . . . no perceptible cough or night sweats. . . . I . . . suggested a bicycle, and that she use it only to and from her business at first. . . . Since then she has not called, evidently satisfied with her condition. (324)

Roys-Gavitt's use of the bicycle as a therapeutic device for a specific ailment (anemia), as well as her curt description of the patient's symptoms, suggests her commitment to the language of scientific medicine. In general, these brief reports—published in a journal that circulated among women doctors around the country—indicate the ubiquity of their conception of the bicycle as a treatment and a cure, even as individual practitioners confined their descriptions to particular ailments. Such descriptions also confirm the degree to which women doctors, as well as men doctors, saw the bicycle as an explicitly medical, rather than recreational, technology.

Importantly, a few women doctors had opportunities to publish their medical opinions of bicycling outside professional venues, as bicycle manufacturers called on them to reassure the public of the safety of women's riding. Unsurprisingly, their recommendations took on a more accessible, encouraging tone in these publications, and in many cases they dispensed with the question of women's weakness altogether. In a Pope Manufacturing Company pamphlet entitled *The Bicycle in Relation to Health*, for instance, Dr. Marie Zakrzewski registers no reservations about bicycling, noting only that she "frequently recommend[s] bicycling to young ladies as a means of strengthening the body, . . . by its demand for active muscular exertion" (5). In the same pamphlet, Dr. Luzerne Coville indicates that "[e]asy riding over level roads gives one of our best passive exercises; scorching, hill climbing, and cross-country century trips are the best of active exercise" (28). Similarly, in an essay published by the Overman Wheel Company entitled *Bicycling and Health for Women*, Dr. Lucy Hall proclaims that she has "permitted the cycle to women to whom walking was markedly injurious, and [has] never had reason to regret [her] action" (6). Unlike doctors writing for an audience of peers, these physicians give no explicit restrictions or warnings about women's bicycling. Rather, they maintain that vigorous exertion will renew women's energies and not deplete them or cause bodily harm. Hall suggests:

> The respiratory system gives free play to expanding lungs, the heart's action is accelerated, the circulation stimulated, the worn-out debris of the system . . . is swept into the briskly moving current and onward to the organs of elimination. Sparkling oxygen takes the place of sense-dulling poison carbon dioxide, and every life force responds to the healthful impetus. (6)

Such a description employs the language of Clarke and Kenealy in its positing of a "system" rather than individual parts—perhaps reflecting the fact that most readers would have been more familiar with this older metaphor. However, in place of the systemic destruction that Kenealy indicates will result from bicycling, Hall offers a renewable feminine bodily economy—one that will only be strengthened through a new activity. As I discuss in the next section, non–medically trained bicycle enthusiasts took up similar arguments in their efforts to advocate women's bicycling.

In general, however, scientific-leaning American medical discourse situated women's bicycling in particular ways during the 1890s, ensuring that the activity was understood as a primarily therapeutic activity that, while beneficial, required doctor supervision and patient restraint. The professional constraints of the newly emerging field of scientific medicine—its commitment to increasingly precise terminology and empirical methods, for instance, and its mechanisms for peer evaluation through professional conferences and journals—encouraged consensus among both male and female practitioners, regardless of their own personal enjoyment of bicycling. As a result, medical discourse about bicycling at this time sustained existing narratives about women's inherent weakness, helping magnify physical and physiological differences between men's and women's bodies even as it encouraged women to ride to manage their health.

Women Commentators and the Strong, Renewable Bodily Economy

Significantly, doctors were not alone in their efforts to promote bicycling as a potential savior of women's health. Other women who lacked access to professional medical conversations—reporters, non-medically trained journalists, and bicycle enthusiasts—also offered their perspectives on the impact of bicycling on women's health in framing their more general arguments in support of the new activity. They did so in popular magazines and newspapers, speaking to a broad public that did not enforce the same level of rhetorical scarcity as did the boundary-maintaining medical profession. In substantiating their claims, they drew from their own embodied experiences and observations, asserting the resilience of women's minds and bodies more emphatically and less cautiously than doctors were often able to do, and speaking directly toward women in their efforts to persuade them to take up the bicycle.

Because, as rhetorician Jeanne Fahnestock has noted, appealing to broad audiences about medicine or science requires not only a confident restatement of information as factual and celebratory but also "the adjustment of new information to an audience's already held values and assumptions" (279), these commentators drew from the familiar but outdated bodily economy metaphor in framing their arguments in favor of women's bicycling. Similarly to Dr. Lucy Hall in her pamphlet for the Overman Wheel Company, they situated their claims not in conversation with scientific medicine but with their late nineteenth-century audience's existing values. They did so perhaps in part because they shared this older understanding of the human body, even as they revised this understanding by emphasizing the feminine bodily economy's infinite renewability. Whereas scientific medicine eroded the limited economy commonplace by situating women's physical limitations within particular body parts or ailments rather than a whole system in which medicine and morality were intertwined, these rhetors reasserted a link between the bicycle and the body's economic system but posited its infinite renewability. Within this framework, they denaturalized older commonplaces without seeming to do so, sharing in—and modeling—the readers' surprise at the capabilities of the modern bicycling woman.

Historians of science Roger Cooter and Stephen Pumfrey have outlined various ways in which scientific commonplaces, such as the limited bodily economy metaphor, evolve. They assert that science (and by extension, medicine) moves between and among elite circles and various publics, not only emanating outward from science to popular texts, and morphing along the way, but also moving from popular texts to scientific ones. Because conservative medical knowledge about women's bodies did not always reflect bicyclists' embodied encounters with the new technology of the bicycle, riders drew from their experiences in order to call this knowledge into question. And because non-medically trained commentators enjoyed both a wider audience for their writing and fewer rhetorical constraints than doctors, they could more directly complicate the commonplaces that undergirded medical opinions. Several representative examples of non-medically trained women's interventions in popular venues on the topic of women's bicycling illustrate the ways in which these texts asserted women's capacity for strength and vitality in making their claims.

Emma Moffett Tyng's 1890 article in *Harper's Bazaar* entitled "Exercise for Women: Tricycle and Bicycle" offers one such illustration. Tyng, a southerner who lived as an adult in New York, wrote consistently for *Harper's Bazaar*, authoring a series of articles promoting women's exercise, as well as articles on art and dress. In her bicycling article, she admits that when she first encountered a woman tricyclist in Great Britain while on vacation seven years earlier, she had predicted that "as a form of exercise for women [cycling] would remain forever in England" (614). However, in the intervening time she had been proven wrong: "[S]even years . . . brings about a complete reorganization of the man physical, and doubtless the man mental sympathizes to the change and the uproot of old lines" (614). This sense of surprise at the capacity for "the reorganization of the man physical" as well as mental situates Tyng as an initial disbeliever alongside the reader—one who has now noted women's capacity for both exercise and social transformation.

Tyng encourages readers to understand the motions and sensations of the bicyclist as therapeutic in nature, and she points to specific physiological benefits of riding:

> The exhilaration, the sense of action and aliveness, the increase of strength, endurance, and steadiness from week to week, these cannot be put in the scale with the things that might be had for one's good or gratification by mere right or purchase. (614)

Her emphasis on increases in women's abilities here contests the notion of women's limited energies that persisted in the popular imagination, offering instead the sense that exercise will yield continued benefits far surpassing those that can merely be bought.

In order to illustrate her points, Tyng describes the experiences of an individual, a "prominent literary woman" who used the bicycle to alleviate her "congestion of the brain" and found it beneficial for all of her ailments. The benefits of riding for the patient's specific body parts are numerous, as Tyng explains; the literary woman benefited from bicycling because "[t]he slight balancing of the body . . . trains the encircling muscles of the torso, while arms, wrists, and fingers are strengthened by the handwork in guiding" (614). The emphasis on exhilaration and experience, on rehabilitation, counters doctors' warnings of the potential for harm from excessive exertion, emphasizing a woman's capacity to "train" herself to develop stamina and strength.

In general, Tyng's series on exercise for women in *Harper's Bazaar* stresses the need for women to take control of their own health as a means of preventing illnesses that will require a doctor's care. As she notes in another article, "Exercise for Women: Walking":

> While many women still follow the traditions of delicacy and helplessness that have for so many years enfeebled their sex . . . they have come to understand . . . that a poor physique puts a woman at odds, and at the mercy of others when the stress of life comes. (546)

Not only does Tyng distance "modern" women from the "traditions of delicacy and helplessness" that have hampered previous generations, but she also asserts that women's efforts to renew their energies will make them independent, freeing them from being "at the mercy of others," such as doctors. At a time when many doctors offered prescriptions that further constrained women's mental and physical activities, this advice is significant. So great, in fact, is Tyng's commitment to physical exercise as a way for women to shed weaknesses that in her *Harper's* article about walking, she predicts that "[i]n the new creed to which women are giving allegiance . . . it will come to be . . . that weakness, unless inherited, is sin" (546). Tyng's example suggests the renewability of women's health through exercise, encouraging women to understand bicycling as a personally empowering, therapeutic activity.

An article appearing in *Outing* magazine in October 1891, Grace Denison's "How We Ride Our Wheels," argues in favor of riding along similar lines. Denison was a frequent contributor to *Outing*, authoring a series of articles reporting on her cycling trip to Ireland in 1893, as well as several accounts of her adventures riding near home. "How We Ride Our Wheels" begins with the assertion that the bicycle saves women "money, time, and strength"—a concise statement of three general topics that were to emerge consistently in the next decade as defenses of women's participation in the new activity. Like Tyng, Denison emphasizes the vitality that bicycling will bring women, not draining their energy as skeptics warned, but actually replenishing it. She promises that "the motion, once a timid rider has mastered the fear of balancing herself gracefully, is rather restful than tiring, and the muscles it develops are mines of strength and comfort." Over time, she says, "the delight of cycling makes the rider forget all the weariness, the strained muscles and the sense of anxiety and impotency which overcame her on her first uncertain and unfortunate attempts." Denison's emphasis on development and mastery situates the woman rider as an adaptable creature, attributing any physical weakness she may possess to a lack of practice rather than biology. In making these claims, Denison not only counters a major objection to women's bicycling but also encourages riders to interpret their own bodies anew and to focus not on avoiding exertion in the short term, but on embracing it as a means of bringing long-term health benefits. Whereas medical discourse encouraged women to read their bodies' abilities within the context of a single ride, Denison suggests that they interpret early symptoms not as evidence of their inherent limitations, but as evidence of their progress.

A similar example, taken from a single 1893 *Harper's Bazaar* article and syndicated in smaller papers across the country, parallels the arguments advanced by Tyng and Denison. Like these writers, Philadelphia writer Edith Townsend Everett proclaims the renewability of the feminine bodily economy. She situates the bicycle—"the best medicine ever provided"—as a means for women to rely on themselves, rather than on doctors, to prevent and treat their physical ailments. Urging readers to "lock up the medicine cabinets, throw away the keys, and drink in great, pure, invigorating draughts of country air, doled out . . . in daily doses by enjoyable rides on the trusty wheel" (485), Everett positions readers as self-reliant, and she maintains that their own intuition regarding their bodies' capacities is superior to doctors' medicines or advice.

Like Denison, Everett underscores the woman rider's capacity for improvement over time. She notes that although "many beginners are apt to make the mistake of undertaking too long runs at the outset," their difficulties are not permanent. In contrast to doctors who warned women of the evils of overexertion, Everett reassures that "little by little fatigue is overcome, and greater distances can be traversed as you gain in strength and acquire the necessary skill" (485). By providing this advice, Everett implies that the female body is not simply unable to endure physical challenges, but that it must—like the masculine body—train in order to be successful. In doing so, she collapses a rhetorically maintained boundary between male and female bodies, situating women alongside men in their capacity for growth through adversity.

Authoring exercise-related articles in magazines ranging from *Harper's Bazaar* to *Good Housekeeping* and later serving as editor of the *Wheelwoman*, a short-lived magazine devoted entirely to women's bicycling, Mary Sargent Hopkins affords perhaps the most extensive example of a woman who tirelessly voiced her commitment to promoting women's health through fitness. Like Tyng, Denison, Everett, and others, Hopkins—who often wrote under the pen name "Merrie Wheeler"—emphasizes women's capacities for increasing strength and endurance and encourages women to trust their own judgment regarding their bodies' capabilities. However, she situates these capacities within her own theory of health, advancing not just the improvements she had observed in the poor health of her fellow bicyclists but also a broader sense of the significance of physical activity in utterly transforming women's lives.

Like other commentators, Hopkins shifts the origin of the women's weakness commonplace from nature to culture and encourages women to take control of their own health rather than rely on doctors. In an article titled "Out-of-Doors M.D.," for example, she declares:

> The delicate and languid woman has gone out of fashion; and no influence has been so active in bringing out this desirable result as . . . Mother Nature, sunlight and fresh air, which are only other names for the Out-of-Doors M.D. (127–28)

Hopkins's insistence that women's delicacy was a matter of outdated fashion, as well as her replacement of an actual, human doctor with the "Out-of-Doors M.D.," echoes Tyng, Denison, and Everett in its signaling of the inadequacy both of old commonplaces about women's weakness and of women's reliance on doctors for advice. Hopkins replaces medicine with the bicycle as a means of ministering to one's own health, arguing that "the bicycle . . . has been a decided lever in overturning old-fashioned conventionalities which hampered womankind and made of her a being too fragile for life and all that it implies for a woman" (128). She urges readers to buy a wheel and to get a "daily dose," promising women that "if taken regularly, [it] will surely steady your nerves, strengthen your arms, brighten your cheeks and eyes, and expand your heart" (129). Elsewhere, she points to women's new "clearness of glance and of skin," and "roundness of curves which can be obtained by no artificial means" ("How the Bicycle" 244) as evidence of the bicycle's observable positive effects; her characterizations encourage riders to think of their bodies as renewable through exercise in visually discernible ways.

Significantly, Hopkins likens exercise to a theory for living or even a religion, writing in a *Frank Leslie's Popular Monthly* article entitled "The Outdoor Woman: The American Woman in Action" about "the religion of out-of-doors," which "works an entire change in [women's] manner of living" (314) and lifts them "from inertia of body and stagnation of mind to a higher life physically, mentally and morally" (315). She confides in her readers: "You see I put the physical first, for I believe that a normal physical condition is the foundation for all that is healthy in mind and morals" (315). This assertion of her own authority—of the ordering of the world that she believes is appropriate, despite her lack of formal medical training—tacitly encourages readers to take similar ownership of their experiences, to develop their own theories about women's health. In addition, she asserts the centrality of physical exertion to women's advancement, countering the contemporary notion that it might interfere with their intellectual and moral development. As she puts it, physical exercise will prepare women for any task they pursue, whether it be "to teach the lesson of life from the stage; to argue for the right in court;

to run a stock farm out West; [or] to seek out the forgotten poor in the city's slums" (316). In general, Hopkins suggests that in quickly changing times, women ought to dismiss old ideas about their frailty and limitations, look to their own experiences as evidence of their capacities, and embrace new possibilities for their renewable good health and participation in society.

Finally, in a *New England Kitchen* magazine article entitled "Bicycling for Girls: A Word to Mothers," Hopkins addresses her readers as mothers in an attempt to advocate directly for a change in their attitudes toward women's health: "Mother, your girl does not need stays, braces, or medicine, but good, wholesome, hearty, outdoor life, that will give her an appetite for food, and healthy sleep." Similarly, she indicates that girls are already intuitively aware of this need:

> [They] are eager to seize upon anything which will benefit them physically. . . . There is a reaching out for those forms of exercise that will be most valuable in building up the constitution—the constitution which partakes of the enervation of a generation ago. (142)

In her efforts to intervene between daughters and their mothers—who, Hopkins implies, belong to a generation in which girls were expected to be "'ladylike' even at the expense of 'rosy cheeks and bright eyes'"—Hopkins emphasizes the need for "building up the constitution" and expanding the body's energies through exercise. Because this is what girls "are eager" to do, she advises that girls and women should be invested in the maintenance and improvement of their own health, rather than entrust their care to doctors. Nonetheless, she offers mothers discretion in monitoring their daughters' riding, urging them, "See to it . . . that [your daughter] rides neither fast nor far, until she has become accustomed, and in a degree hardened to the exercise" (143). Even as Hopkins encourages parental monitoring of girls' riding, her indication that eventually daughters *will* be able to ride fast and far—that they will become "in a degree hardened"—indicates her belief in girls' innate capacity to increase their strength and energy.

In general, Hopkins's allegiance to the "religion" of the out-of-doors—as well as her insistence on its novelty for women—enables her to recommend that readers ought to undergo a total transformation in their thinking about their own health. By exercising outdoors and, more specifically, by engaging in the "Merrie Wheeler's" own favorite exercise, women will gain strength they never realized they had before—strength that doctors had not detected that they possess. Note, however, that Hopkins offers throughout her many writings a conservative view of the social impact of women's exercise, positing that better health will enable women to become better wives and homemakers. She insists that she hates "a masculine woman" ("Woman's Wheeling Dress" 21), urging riders not to wear bloomers or ride recklessly and suggesting that riding should enhance their feminine appeal. Nonetheless, her writings about health and bicycling implicitly suggest that women should take a stance with respect to their own health and their relationship to doctors.

Tyng, Denison, Everett, and Hopkins constitute a representative sample of the sorts of interventions that non-medically trained bicycle commentators made in advocating the new machine as a specifically therapeutic, health-bringing machine for women. Writing in popular venues, these rhetors indirectly challenged old commonplaces about women's bodies in ways that doctors writing in professional venues did not. They did so by situating the bicycle in opposition to doctors and medicine and women's weakness as an outdated "fashion" rather than a biological fact, and they encouraged women to experience the aches, pains, and physiological responses of their own bodies differently than they had previously done. These rhetors enjoyed greater flexibility in their methods and arguments than did medical doctors writing for peer audiences, who were compelled to demonstrate their adherence to the increasingly closed field of scientific medicine. Because their arguments appeared in popular, mass-distributed venues, they circulated widely—counteracting the caution that doctors recommended women exercise when bicycling and, more significantly, the old commonplace that women were subject to biological weaknesses that men lacked. In their figuring, the weak, limited feminine bodily economy became not merely less sensitive to disturbance, but infinitely renewable, energized, and strengthened with sufficient practice.

Embodied Arguments

Despite the important refiguring of women's biological capabilities by women's bicycling commentators, their arguments shared in common with doctors the assumption that women would ride the bicycle for healthy recreation. That is, they sustained the notion that women would ride to prevent physical illness, recuperate the body, or unburden their minds of daily drudgery so that they could strengthen their commitments to home and family.

Whereas men might put the bicycle to a near infinite range of competitive, occupational, and recreational uses, women's riding remained comparatively circumscribed. This tacit difference in the appropriate use of a single—or minimally adapted—machine thus served to bolster existing conceptions of gender difference. If, as Judith Butler and many others have posited, gender constructs are sustained, complicated, and challenged through performance, then the embodied activities of women bicyclists themselves become critical locations from which to understand how late nineteenth-century cultural commonplaces about women's biological and psychological characteristics were called into question. Though many women bicyclists enacted an emerging dominant cultural script for appropriate performances aboard the bicycle, many did not, and in this section I consider how a small number of racers and endurance riders not only materialized commentators' claims about the strength and renewability of the female body but also denaturalized other gender differences that their contemporaries perceived as biological.

These riders paid no heed to and, in the case of endurance riders, were sometimes openly critical of doctor recommendations. Their efforts were often highly visible, witnessed by hundreds or even thousands of spectators and reported widely in newspapers. Notably, their appropriation of such masculine qualities as competitiveness, resilience, and ambition represented for those who saw and heard of their efforts what Kenneth Burke might describe as perspective by incongruity (*Permanence*): the pairing of seeming opposites for the purpose of demonstrating that they are not actually opposed. In this case, the pairing of masculine endeavors and qualities with female bodies helped denaturalize gendered oppositions.

These women were not always well received in the popular press, but the influence they did exert is suggested by both the persistence of their performances and the changing tone of newspaper reports of their doings by the end of the 1890s. Just as women's health commentators took advantage of such material nodes as the mass-distributed magazines discussed in chapter 2, women racers' and endurance riders' performances were enabled by the already strong network of physical and textual spaces within which such embodied practices were already taking place, largely among men: the racetrack and its managers, the road, and the bicycling guidebook, for instance.

Though Burke's conception of perspective by incongruity refers primarily to words, such as the pairing of "decadent athleticism" (*Permanence* 90) to describe as self-indulgent the early twentieth-century movement toward college athletics, his commitment to a broader notion of language as consisting of all symbolic action accords well with the meaning-making capacities of these women riders' embodied performances. As posthumanist philosopher Karen Barad has pointed out, the material and the discursive are inextricable from one another as new meanings are conveyed, contested, and complicated through performances. Barad notes that, in a performative vein, "the primary semantic units are not 'words' but material-discursive practices through which boundaries are constituted" (818). In the case of racers and endurance riders, women's "masculine" embodied practices constituted the sort of dissolution of oppositions to which Burke refers in his many discussions of perspective by incongruity. In doing so, these women upset boundaries distinguishing men's and women's natural or biological abilities, proclivities, and relationships with objects and people in their environment. Women bicyclists who rode for speed, endurance, and money challenged a delicate cultural construction of femininity that hinged not only on women's inherent biological weaknesses and limited energies but also on their psychological characteristics.

In this section, I examine riders who denaturalized contemporary constructions of femininity by performing feats of speed, strength, and endurance not endorsed or acknowledged by even the most supportive medical authorities on bicycling. Whereas, as I have demonstrated, doctors and bicycling commentators framed bicycling as a specifically therapeutic exercise, these riders enacted other rhetorics through their embodied performances of often grueling bicycling undertaken for money or public recognition. Traces of the reception these women received for their embodied endeavors survive in newspaper accounts of races and endurance efforts, affording a glimpse into the complex and often contradictory responses these women competitors invited. Additionally, shifts in the framing of their performances in these articles provide some indication of the public's increasing familiarity with and enthusiasm for their efforts. Though they did not set out intentionally to denaturalize physical and psychological constructions of femininity and masculinity, and though their efforts did not wholly eliminate these constructions from cultural circulation, the collective weight of their efforts did call these constructions into question.

Women's bicycle racing offered one important and increasingly visible avenue through which riders demonstrated both their physical strength and their taste for public competition and recognition. Although during the late 1880s, a few female racers had gained notoriety racing aboard high-wheeled bicycles alongside male racers and even horses, the publicity surrounding their participation was limited, as most of the spectators were wheelmen. Louise Armaindo of Montreal, for instance, was known for racing male opponents for money, often defeating them with a head start and earning the title of "the champion long distance lady rider of the world" ("A Bevy of Cycling Girls" 2), according to one 1889 article in the *New York Evening World*. A rival, Elsa von Blumen of New York, refused money for racing but was described in the *Evening World* as "a spirited and young dashing rider of the wheel" and a "stayer" for her ability to continue competing even when injured or exhausted ("Hattie Is a Winner"). Women like Armaindo and von Blumen violated explicitly dominant notions of women's bodily limitations, but perhaps because they were so few in number, their activities did not attract significant attention outside of the cycling press. Brief descriptions of their racing activities appeared, almost without comment regarding their gender, in newspapers and magazines such as *Outing* and *Sporting Life*, and—because few women had taken up bicycling during the 1880s—they raced before primarily male audiences.

By the mid-1890s, however, women's bicycling had become more popular in general, particularly among young immigrant women in larger cities, who rode for prize purses upward of several hundred dollars. As a result, they attracted greater notice as the decade wore on from both spectators and newspapers, which published accounts of their exploits that often far exceeded in detail the reports on men's races. The outcomes of several ladies' Safety bicycle races from 1896, for instance, were described in great detail in large city newspapers such as the *New York Times* and syndicated around the country in smaller papers, so that a broader audience had access to the events. These articles reveal a lingering sense of novelty for women's bicycle racing. They attend to the spectacle of the women's exertions as much as the competition of the races themselves.

For example, one *New York Times* article about a Brooklyn sprint race in the summer of 1896 features the headline "She Won and Fainted: Miss Roos, a Long Branch Belle, Insensible for Hours." After describing the awards and noting that "a large crowd had gathered" for the 1.75-mile race, the article goes on to say that several of the riders scratched their entries and failed to show up at the start—a point that suggests both the possible stigma of racing and the author's sense that women are naturally shy of competition. Additionally, the author attends to the exertion of the riders as much as he does to the competition itself, as the headline implies. Jeannette Well, who won the race, receives little attention other than the description that she was "the youngest and smallest" among the racers; the third-place finisher, Miss Roos, gains the headline as well as the following lengthy description:

> The sun was beating down hot upon the avenue, and the riders in the race suffered intensely, so much so that several of them were almost exhausted at the finish. Before Miss Roos could dismount from her wheel she fell headlong off it upon the hotel lawn and fainted. A doctor came. It was feared that the girl was dying. She remained insensible for several hours. (2)

This telling differs from the coverage a similar event involving male riders might receive in newspapers, as race descriptions usually primarily included prizes and the battle among the leaders. Nonetheless, the article describes the event in terms that emphasize the athleticism of the riders and the drama of the competition, even as it reveals the crowd's complicated reaction to their effort:

> A good start was made . . . with Miss Roos in the lead, followed by Miss Jeanette Well in second, with Miss Hammerstein third . . . and the unknown last. All rode under difficulties, as the avenue had many vehicles and other bike riders upon it the whole length of the route, and it caused the girls considerable annoyance, as they had to go around those they met. (2)

The "unknown," the article reports, broke into the ranks of the eleven named "girls" and sprinted to victory before officials discovered the "joker" was a young man named Willie Friedman, who was disqualified when his identity was revealed. The article's casual mention of "the unknown" Friedman suggests that racing women's endurance of such mockery was not unusual; nonetheless, the effort the writer makes to describe the racing conditions offers a sense that the competition itself drew some genuine interest.

Some women riders went beyond the short distances, participating in the six-day races that were popular with male riders by the century's end. These events were held in indoor venues, and racers would compete for nearly a week with only minimal rest, vying to cover as much distance as possible in the time allotted them. Though one bicycle maker comments in the *New York Times* in 1900 that such "disgraceful, unmannerly, and reckless performances" were "directly responsible for the falling off in the use of the wheel" ("Heard about Town" 26), news of these events circulated widely in papers around the country. An early women's Safety race at Madison Square Garden apparently attracted fifteen hundred spectators, most of whom, the *New York Sun* reports, were men ("The Woman's Bicycle Race," image 9). The author notes that the women riders "reclined on couches" and "all chewed gum" while waiting to race, clad in "gay costumes in which bloomers were a feature" ("The Woman's Bicycle Race," image 9). This description highlights unladylike behaviors of the racers, evidence that the spectacle of these women's bodies extended even to the time they spent off the wheel. However, the very last sentence of the article reports that the women "rode like experts and made good time" ("The Woman's Bicycle Race," image 9)—a hint that the competition itself may have shifted the author's thinking.

A second report on the same race three days later indicates the author's evolving perspective. The article relates that the most recent crowd had grown to two thousand, with managers anticipating even larger crowds at the race's conclusion. The author seems conflicted about how to report this early six-day race, fluctuating between focusing on the competition and considering the spectacle of the women riders. Though the headline, "Nelson and Baldwin Lead," emphasizes the competition among the two front-runners, the author devotes little time to describing their race. After mentioning that Frankie Nelson and Helen Baldwin "were only a wheel's length apart last night . . . when they left the track at ten o'clock," the author continues to sketch out the individual personalities of the remaining racers: "Kittie Staples, who fainted on Tuesday night, was the centre of the attraction." Her fainting, the author observes, has become "monotonous," leading some to speculate that she is "faking"—perhaps for notoriety (4). Another racer, "Ruth Dennis, the pretty 17-year old girl from Somerville, New Jersey," confesses that she will not win but will keep riding anyway in the hope of earning the $20 awarded to each rider completing two hundred miles (4). And another rider, "Catharine Flanagan, the Irish girl," the article reports, "was taken in by Billy Murphy, the well-known rider, and she improved at once," making her "easily the favorite of the second squad" (4). These descriptions of individual riders, each with their own identity markers, hint at the author's increasing investment in the event, if not fully in the competition. Whereas the report of the first night suggests that the women racers are all the same—they all chewed gum, wore bloomers, and "rode like experts"—by the third night, they have become individuals in whom the crowd has become invested.

Two days later, in the January 10 report of the race, the author's focus on the race leaders has increased, as the article elaborates further on Baldwin and Nelson. Both, the author indicates, "are well-trained and handled, and use the best of judgment in riding"; as a result, the author admits, "the struggle between them is a pretty one" ("Still a Wheel's Length Apart," image 4). Tellingly, however, the two are contrasted in appearance: the author reports that "Miss Baldwin's attire is particularly neat," as she wears "a yellow shirt waist and a big white linen collar," with her hair "crimped and curled." While Baldwin's "general appearance was applauded on all sides," the author reports that "Frankie Nelson, her rival, was not so dressy. She wore black knickerbockers and a loose black jacket with a green belt." This focus on the apparel of the riders indicates a lingering fascination with women racers who violated standards of decorum, even as the article betrays some affection for the competitors, who have now become individuals. Catharine Flanagan, the author reports, continues to please the crowd, even receiving love letters in the dressing room "that she said she would frame" and demonstrating her talent and skill under her new trainer. In the end, Nelson wins the race, along with $350 and a diamond medal, Baldwin finishes second with $100 and a medal, and awards are given out to riders in the categories of Most Graceful, Most Beautiful, and Best-Dressed. The event was a financial loss, according to the organizers, though eighteen hundred people gathered at Madison Square Garden to see the awards given. This early six-day women's Safety race demonstrates the way that racers—by demonstrating their competitiveness, their desire for glory, and their exertion—embodied a perspective by incongruity, often mingling culturally endorsed traits of femininity, such as wearing fashionable attire or cherishing love letters, with these traditionally masculine qualities. In doing so, they chipped away at commonplaces about women's weakness and natural proclivities.

Although the League of American Wheelmen, the largest bicycling organization in the United States, officially barred African American men and women from its competitions beginning in 1894, some African American women riders excelled at racing and drew similarly from this form of perspective by incongruity, blending their concerns about both femininity and race in their attire and their racing performances. Twenty-one-year-old Kittie Knox, of Boston's all-black Riverside Cycling Club, participated in League of American Wheelmen (LAW) meets as a member and completed several century runs during the early 1890s, including one in which she finished twelfth out of fifty racers, male and female (Adams). Described consistently as "an extremely comely colored girl," Knox won a widely reported bicycle apparel contest for "wearing the most tasteful and artistic women's wheeling garb" at an 1895 Malden, Massachusetts, parade ("Color Line Drawn" 2). When the widely celebrated rider was denied entry to a major LAW meet at New Jersey's Asbury Park because of the recent addition of the word "white" in the league's bylaws, both the cyclists and mainstream press expressed anger. The *San Francisco Call* reports, "[N]inety-nine out of every hundred members express the heartiest sympathy for her and condemnation of the hasty action of the badge committee" ("Color Line Drawn" 2). Knox blended a careful adherence to appropriate standards of femininity with racing practices rarely associated with her race and gender in order to win much of the white racing community's sympathies. In doing so, she embodied new arguments both about femininity and about race relations in general.[1]

Just three years after its exclusion of African American racers, the league included in its 1897 bylaws a provision preventing any LAW-sanctioned race event from including a women's race on its schedule (Macy 73). Nonetheless, white women racers fared better than their African American sisters, as women's racing continued to gain publicity outside of the league's purview. Track managers saw that these races were lucrative and often attracted large audiences. As one writer puts it in the *Washington Times*, "[I]f the League of American Wheelmen attempts to blacklist the tracks on which the . . . [races] will be run, they may find themselves minus a number of the best American tracks before the season is over" ("Miss Lissette in America" 6). The reporting for these races betrays shifts in public attitudes about both racing women's propriety and their bodily capabilities, as the events became more commonplace. Headlines, for instance, focus on the competition among race leaders rather than on the spectacle of participants' health or exertion. One 1899 headline in the *St. Paul Daily Globe* reads, "Ladies Ride Neck and Neck," and the article reports with some excitement on the finish of an evening leg of a six-day race held in that city:

> Baldwin won the lead over Farnsworth in a wonderful burst of speed during the last three minutes riding. She had promised her friends to do it or never mount her wheel again, and when she took the lead and held it the 5000 people went wild. (5)

The author's use of last names for the riders, as well as the report of the spectators' "wild" response, suggests that the crowd must have at least partially embraced the women's competition, thus undermining the residual notion that women were fragile and competitiveness was an inherently masculine trait. In contrast to reports on the earlier races, this article nowhere indicates alarm over the riders' health or hints or comments on the racers' apparel.

Particularly in the later years of the bicycle craze, women riders began to undertake longer rides, outside of indoor arenas, through which they made displays that often overtly challenged doctors' prescriptions for women's bicycling. They participated in century runs—hundred-mile bicycle rides—as well as double and even triple centuries that were sanctioned by the Century Road Club of America, founded in 1891 in Chicago and soon opening chapters all over the country. These events attracted riders in much the same way as today's marathons, as completing a century was considered a difficult but achievable accomplishment. Finishers' names were published in official documents, and courses and times were carefully monitored by club members. Century riders who completed their efforts within a given amount of time could submit proof of their performances to the national club headquarters. Although the national century organization did not, as the League of American Wheelmen did, prevent women from joining the organization, public opinion about women's participation in the rides was mixed. The Associated Cycling Clubs of New York, for instance, barely defeated a series of resolutions to bar women from all century races. Despite their failure to garner sufficient support, these resolutions later appeared in syndication in newspapers around the country, having been revised as an anonymous commentary about the general issue of women's involvement in centuries:

> It is maintained that century runs have become athletic competitions, such as require the utmost physical endurance on the part of the riders, and that constitutionally a woman is not sufficiently strong for such a fatiguing test. Distinguished medical authorities pronounce the task of covering so great a distance as a hundred miles in a day awheel exceedingly harmful, on account of the prolonged nervous and physical strain involved, for which women rarely possess the requisite physique, and for other reasons that physicians only can properly appreciate. ("With the Return of the Cycling Season" 2)

The author's insistence on women's biological weakness is striking, as is his vague and liberal use of medical authority to support his claim. "If women lack the good sense and good taste to determine this matter for themselves, the men should determine it for them," the author goes on to declare—signaling at once his arguments that the New York clubs should discontinue women's racing and, more broadly, that other clubs around the country should prevent women from completing centuries.

A columnist writing in the *New York Sun* that same season takes a milder stance on the debate, professing that though "[he] would not take [his] wife or sister on a century run," he believes that women should not be officially excluded from participating because "it is not a subject for organized action." "I think gradually women will come to realize they have no place in them," he proclaims. Still another author in the *Washington DC, Evening Star* simply suggests the exceptionality of female endurance riders, admitting, "Some women ride centuries, it is true, but they are men in strength." Most women, he asserts, should limit their riding to one hour or less ("Limit to Women's Bicycle Rides" 8).

Despite these debates, many women did ride centuries alongside male riders. News of their feats was occasionally given special notice in newspapers and magazines, as when New Yorker Tillie Hummel completed three consecutive centuries in 1897. Newspapers around the country published her interview with an anonymous author the day following her ride. The author describes Hummel as "a young girl . . . frail and delicate, far from one's idea of a woman strong enough to even think of undertaking such a run." Though the interviewer admits to finding Hummel "perfectly fresh," "to [his or her] surprise," he or she also offers the following lament:

> It was hard to believe, despite her protestations, that such a terrible strain would not eventually tell on her constitution, and it was . . . a saddening sight—this young girl, not yet out of her teens, glorying in and proud of a feat which five years ago would have been considered degrading and unwomanly. ("Great Bicycle Feat" 6)

The author's skepticism about the impact of century riding on Hummel's health, as well as his or her apparent disgust with the bicyclist's pride at having accomplished such a "degrading and unwomanly" feat, demonstrates both the far-reaching impact of old medical commonplaces about women's weakness and the mingling of the moral and the medical in the late nineteenth-century public imagination.

Interestingly, however, Hummel's "protestations" about her health suggest that she hopes specifically to dispel these commonplaces. She assures the interviewer that she "felt equal to commencing the ride all over again that very day" and goes on to say, "Before undertaking this adventure I was in splendid condition physically, weighing 110 pounds, and I lost only two pounds on the run, contrary to medical opinion, as my appetite has increased favorably" ("Great Bicycle Feat" 6). This jab at "medical opinion" echoes the call among women commentators for bicyclists to trust their own embodied responses to the bicycle and counters the argument put forth by the Associated Cycling Clubs of New York. The bicyclist has precise evidence—the very slight changes in her weight—to dispel the fallacy that she might waste away as a result of her endurance riding. Additionally, she shifts attention away from her physical condition by noting that she undertook the triple century "to compete for a record and a medal, the former of which I gained and the latter I expect to obtain when finished" ("Great Bicycle Feat" 6). Hummel's deliberate efforts to allay public concerns regarding her health indicate the extent to which she understood her own body as evidence in an ongoing debate about women's physical and mental capacities.

By the late 1890s, the debate over women's century riding had receded, and women continued to ride centuries with less comment than earlier riders had received. An 1899 *New York Times* article, in which the author reports the increase in the popularity of century runs, announces that "[m]ore women have made records this season than ever before" ("Great Increase" 27). As women's participation in century rides became more common, several women pushed beyond even the century ride and bested each other by completing more miles in a given amount of time or by surpassing one another's maximum distance.

In May 1899, Irene Bush of Brooklyn completed four hundred miles of riding in just forty-eight hours—only to be surpassed by Jane Yatman, a young bookstore clerk from Manhattan. Yatman, who rode seven hundred miles consecutively, was then bested by Jane Lindsay for a record number of miles completed. Several *New York Times* articles about Lindsay's feats detailed her deteriorating physical condition as she challenged Yatman's record. For example, an October 17, 1899, write-up that was syndicated in other papers around the country reports that her wrists, eyes, and knees were all hurting her after five hundred miles of riding—a fact that apparently made it "doubtful if she will succeed" ("Mrs. Lindsay Has 500 Miles" 8). Nevertheless, Lindsay did succeed in surpassing Yatman's mileage, completing eight hundred miles to Yatman's seven hundred on October 19, 1899. The *New York Times* commentary reveals some disdain for her efforts and for the competition between Lindsay and Yatman:

> No pecuniary recompense whatever attaches to these useless and necessarily injurious trials of strength. Bitter rivalry, that characteristic feminine trait, and the determination to "get even," are seemingly the actuating motives. For this incredible physical torture, exhaustion so extreme that it causes the reason to reel and is destructive of good looks. ("Mrs. Lindsay's 800 Miles" 9)

Despite dismissing the athletic competition between Yatman and Lindsay as a petty demonstration of feminine rivalry, the author does admit to both Yatman's and Lindsay's "pluck and grit" and notes that Lindsay appears "little the worse for her journey" ("Mrs. Lindsay's 800 Miles" 9). The contradictory framing of their effort reflects the author's experience of the perspective by incongruity that women's endurance and competitiveness invited in spectators, who were forced to grapple with the disjunction between Lindsay's apparent good health as a woman and her enactment of behaviors assumed to be harmful to women's health and good looks.

In an even more spectacular exhibition of extreme endurance that received mixed responses from the media, Margaret Gast (fig. 4.1) sought in 1900 to surpass a women's distance record of forty-five hundred miles in thirty days. Gast rode along a stretch of coastline on Long Island for two hundred miles each day until a sheriff stopped her from continuing her demonstration of strength. A *New York Times* article reporting on her progress observes that during her ride,

> the dwellers along the . . . stretch of road which the young woman. . . . traverses eight times a day, are practically unanimous in their denunciation of the spectacle, [which has produced] an effect on the minds of the children who witness it. ("Miss Gast's Cycle Riding" 9)

The author's declaration of the universal "denunciation" of Gast's ride, like the commentary on Lindsay's ride, demonstrates the challenge that bicycling

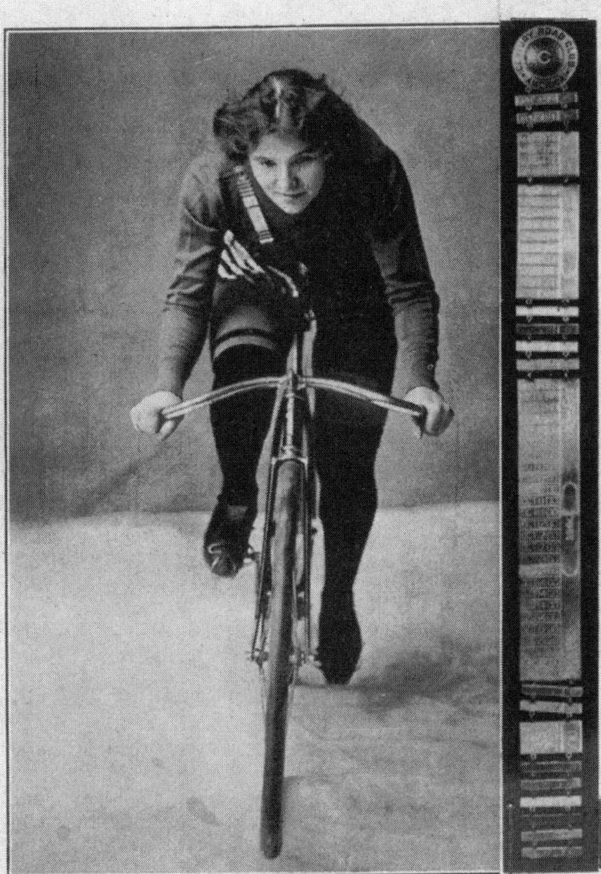

MARGARET GAST

Champion Cyclist and World Record Holder

MAY 1900

1,000 Miles — 120 Hours

OCTOBER 1900

500 Miles — 44 Hours, 45 Minutes

1000 Miles — 99 Hours, 55 Minutes

2000 Miles — 222 Hours, 5½ Minutes

2600 Miles — 295 Hours, 55 Minutes

Now Residing At Pawling, New York

October 1958 — 82 Years of Age

Figure 4.1. Margaret Gast's racing card. Image courtesy of Jack Nagengast.

women faced in testing—whether for themselves, their competitors, or others—their strength and endurance. Though nearly everyone was in favor of women's bicycling for the therapeutic purposes touted by doctors and commentators, a rider competing or deliberately pushing her body to its limits remained an ambiguous figure—one whose acts were so transgressive that she could even be accused of harming children simply by riding in public.

To justify the decision to prevent Gast from completing her ride, as well as to discourage women from making similar efforts in Long Island in the future, the Long Island district attorney apparently offered the following statement, published in the *New York Tribune*:

> Such a feat as that performed by Miss Gast only encourages others to try to repeat or excel it. If such performances were allowed to continue a lot of women would be competing with each other, and would so overtax themselves that they would be unfitted for anything else in after life. Some of them might possibly lose their lives as the result of their efforts. ("Miss Gast Stopped" 5)

These comments indicate the extent to which skeptics continued to register their disgust for women's performances of strength, speed, and endurance by invoking their concern for women's health, even as riders like Gast, Hummel, and Lindsay completed their rides unharmed. Tellingly, Gast says in an interview after her ride was stopped, "[T]here was nothing wrong with me when the ride ended, so I have nothing to complain of." She hoped only for "possible profit" and to "be known as the champion woman cyclist of America" (9). Her refusal to engage in medical discourse about her inevitable breakdown of energy, to reassure her audience in any definite way, is perhaps part of the reason behind the negative attention she received. Yet this refusal also highlights the extent to which Gast embodied a range of behaviors not traditionally labeled as feminine.

Women who used the bicycle for racing and for exhibitions of endurance, more so even than women commentators who argued that the bicycle would improve, rather than endanger, women's health, challenged medically authorized commonplaces regarding women's biological and psychological limitations. In making visible—both directly and through circulating newspaper accounts of their efforts—their exertions and competitive drive, they materialized a Burkean perspective by incongruity, pairing femininity with what audiences believed to be the most masculine of activities. By considering how their efforts were covered in newspaper articles, we can see that over time, racers' activities gained more credibility and acceptance, whereas endurance riders continued to elicit medically authorized criticism. Perhaps, as the response to Gast's ride suggests, this was because of the comparative visibility of endurance riding, which occurred on public roads rather than in a closed arena such as Madison Square Garden. Additionally, the *New York Times* account of Lindsay's ride expresses disgust with the lack of "pecuniary recompense" for endurance riders ("Mrs. Lindsay's 800 Miles" 9), a fact that points to their comparative wealth and class status, and thus to greater anxieties regarding the propriety of their behavior. Regardless, all of these racing and endurance riders embodied a femininity that violated both contemporary medical understandings of women's bodies and minds and late nineteenth-century gender ideals. The riders' efforts did not ultimately eradicate these understandings from cultural circulation, but they did help make such notions less persuasive.

Beyond Medical Discourse

Acting outside professionally authorized avenues of medical discourse, women bicyclists used different, historically emergent strategies to challenge long-standing commonplaces regarding women's biological weakness. Although the medical establishment had and still has tremendous power in both legitimizing and delegitimizing discourses about bodies, that power is not absolute and is often not very responsive to changing material landscapes outside its purview. In the case of women's bicycling, medical discourse continued to reflect older conceptions of women's bodies even as actual women's bodies increasingly evidenced the need for revision. The occasional denunciations and frequent warnings that doctors directed at women bicyclists reflected in part the increasing standardization and regulation of American medical schools, professional conferences, and journals—a situation that made it difficult for doctors to depart in their prescriptions from conventional warnings about women's bodies. That is, the developing field of medicine offered even its insiders a scarcity of rhetorical resources—rhetorical scarcity—for promoting radically new ideas about women's physical potentiality. Rather than open themselves to a broad range of conclusions regarding women's health, doctors engaged in ongoing professional conversations, one of which was the perceived "problem" of women's inherent biological weakness. As a result, even those most enthusiastic about the bicycle's appropriateness for women's use qualified their recommendations in such a way that they perpetuated this commonplace.

In contrast, women whose rhetorical agency was not circumscribed by professional constraints constructed and enacted arguments that emphasized the renewability and adaptability, rather than the weakness, of women's bodies and minds. In widely distributed popular magazines, writers such as Emma Moffett Tyng, Grace Denison, Edith Townsend Everett, and Mary Sargent Hopkins weave into their endorsements of the bicycle a narrative about women's health that dispenses with medical caution. These writers suggest instead that weakness in women had been the product of "fashion," rather than biology, and that women who rode the bicycle would find reserves of strength they had never before tapped. They encourage women to reinterpret their bodily reactions to exercise—shortness of breath and muscle tiredness, for instance—as evidence not of the need for caution, but of improving health. And, perhaps most significantly, they assert women's need for self-reliance in matters of preventive and therapeutic general health, discouraging doctor visits and downplaying medical authority. Nonetheless, their conception of bicycling retained, alongside professional medical discourse, the tacit assumption that women would ride primarily for health and mild recreation, as a way to improve their feminine commitment to the domestic realm in which they belonged.

In contrast, the embodied performances of women bicycle racers and endurance riders offered no such assessment. These riders materialized and often extended the arguments of women commentators; their spectacular demonstrations of strength were enacted in public venues and described in newspaper articles that circulated around the country. Whereas medical commentators sought to revise assumptions about women's bodies by working within, rather than outside, the long-held commonplace of the bodily economy, racers and endurance riders largely disregarded the assumptions of their audiences altogether. They performed unapologetically for money and glory, psychological qualities associated with masculinity. Though they sometimes provided direct assurances of their health through interviews, as in the case of triple-century rider Tillie Hummel, in general they distanced women's bicycling from the issue of health altogether, instead enacting uses of the bicycle identical to the uses to which men put the new machine. In doing so, they generated for both spectators and readers a Burkean perspective by incongruity, collapsing broad oppositions between masculinity and femininity through their embodied performances. Though contemporary access to these performances is constrained by their fleeting nature, newspaper reports suggest that spectators were grappling with the challenge these riders presented to their conceptions of gender differences.

To be sure, women commentators, racers, and endurance riders did not wholly unseat long-standing cultural commonplaces about women's inherent biological weakness. Opposition to women century riders continued, with skeptics often couching their arguments against women's athleticism in medical terms; as recently as the 1970s, women were barred from similarly strenuous athletic competition, such as long-distance running, on the grounds that their bodies could not withstand the strain. Nonetheless, we ought not to understand the efforts of non–medically trained women to erode these commonplaces as rhetorical failure. Rather, we should understand the challenge of transforming such profound cultural biases as complex and ongoing work, undertaken over time through the not necessarily coordinated efforts of a variety of rhetors and rhetorical strategies. In doing so, we make visible rhetorical agents who might otherwise be overlooked, and we gain access to a more robust account of how social change occurs.

Accessing this robust account is fundamental, too, to the ongoing feminist rhetorical project of uncovering the role that rhetorical constructions of gender difference play in maintaining inequalities between men and women. Such differences justify and naturalize the closing off of opportunities for both sexes; they prevent us from being fully human. The rhetorical work of relocating these differences from nature to culture—of challenging the biological basis of culturally agreed assessments of gendered bodies—is complex and difficult to trace. Yet if we are able to gain access to the wide-ranging means by which rhetors, with or without authorial intention, have accomplished this collective undertaking, we will gain access to a wider range of strategies by which to make contemporary interventions in this important area.

In this chapter, I have suggested the role that individual women, from Dr. Lucy Hall to Mary Sargent Hopkins to Margaret Gast, played in challenging late nineteenth-century constructions of gender difference. However, I have not meant to imply that these women necessarily acted consciously to bring about change or that they did so alone. Rather, I offer these rhetors as representative of a wide range of women whose actions contributed to these changes. Not only commentators and competitive athletes, but also ordinary women who took up the bicycle surely exceeded both their own and others' expectations for their strength and speed. Such women may have, as commentators often remarked, begun bicycling as a medical prescription or preventive and surprised themselves by eventually completing a century ride—a highly public undertaking that sent ripples through the networks to which these women belonged. The rhetorical force of such imagined performances can scarcely be measured, which is perhaps why, as rhetoricians, we have often failed to acknowledge the extent to which, as Nathan Stormer has argued, we ought to "understand rhetoric as a historical product of practices" (258) rather than the reverse. The practices of bicycling women—enabled by both the verbal encouragement of commentators and the examples of competitive bicyclists—enable a new rhetorical construction of gender relations, even as they help topple the old.

Critically, the agency exercised by the rhetors both named and imagined in this chapter emerged within much more extensive, historically contingent networks that included not only human actors but also physical spaces, temporal relations, and material objects. Without racing organization officials, indoor racetracks, and public interest afforded in part by the bicycle club movement of the 1880s, women six-day racers would not have been able to perform perspective by incongruity as they did. And without the formalization of medical training and values, as well as the material affordances of the medical journal, doctors could not likely have exerted as much influence on the promotion of bicycling; they could not have obtained a near consensus on the role bicycling ought to play in women's lives. Such examples demonstrate the degree to which agency circulates through large, diverse networks, both formal and informal, as well as the impact that agents—such as female bicycle racers—have on the networks in which they are enmeshed. They demonstrate, above all, the complexity and contingency of rhetorical agency, as it is shaped by a wide and constantly shifting array of material and rhetorical constraints.

Conclusion

Toward a Technofeminist Rhetorical Agency

Signs that the bicycle craze was receding appeared as early as the fall of 1897, when Albert Pope's powerful rival, A. H. Overman, announced he was shutting his company's doors. Despite astounding success during the previous cycling season, the 1897 season had brought the Overman Wheel Company severe losses from which it never recovered (Herlihy, *Bicycle* 285). Though recreational and practical bicycling remained popular among more and more diverse groups of Americans, new companies had saturated the market, causing both the quality and the price of new bicycles to plummet. In 1897, even the formidable Albert Pope was forced to lower the price of his premier line of bicycles from $100 to $75 (Epperson 313); two years later, he joined the owners of forty-four other bicycle companies in selling his factories to the American Bicycle Company, a new bicycle trust that sought to salvage through consolidation what was left of the floundering industry. By 1902, even the trust had entered into receivership (Epperson 319), and by 1908, when Henry Ford introduced his moderately priced Model T, Americans had shifted their attention to an entirely different machine: the automobile.

Despite the brevity of the bicycle craze and the speed with which optimistic projections of its centrality to twentieth-century American life were disproven, the machine that attracted so many followers did make a significant impact on the material and rhetorical landscapes of the United States. Materially, it prompted the development of the very streets and highways that the automobile came to dominate, as League of American Wheelmen members were among the first to lobby extensively for the use of public money to pave American roads. Cycling tourists, too, assisted in the development of roadside restaurants, hotels, and businesses geared toward travelers who would later drive cars. And early racers helped generate a cultural climate for athletic spectating, which carried over seamlessly into other professional sports, such as baseball and basketball.

In addition to paving the way—both literally and metaphorically—for roads, automobile travel and tourism, and sports, the bicycle craze left behind a lasting legacy for American women at the end of the nineteenth century. To be sure, Susan B. Anthony's proclamation that the bicycle had "done more for the emancipation of women than anything else in the world" (Bly 9) seems less hyperbolic when one considers women bicyclists' increased mobility and independence aboard the bicycle, their improved health and physical confidence, and the opportunities bicycling afforded women and men to merge the "separate spheres" of the nineteenth century.

In this book, however, I have attempted to highlight not just what the bicycle did for women but also what women did for the bicycle to *enable it to become* the emancipatory machine that Anthony celebrated—and to enable 1890s bicycle culture to unfold as it did. In this sense, the bicycle's legacy is one not of emancipation, but of self-education and community building. The bicycle craze, which prompted so many late nineteenth-century commentators to marvel at the rapidity of social change, demonstrated to women the fragility and contingency of social relations that had once seemed so permanent. As the rhetorical-material network of 1890s bicycle culture—with its range of new identities, accoutrements, available physical spaces, garments, and the like—expanded, so too did the grid of possibility on which riders plotted their performances of gender. And as it did, these women came to understand themselves as potential agents of cultural change.

Technologies, as Judy Wajcman has noted, are often viewed through either utopian or dystopian lenses but in actuality cannot be reduced to inherent "good" and "bad" qualities (*Technofeminism* 6). Rather, technologies' legacies are written through use, and use is mediated by rhetoric, including the sorts of rhetorical activities in which American women bicyclists engaged during the 1890s. From authoring instructions and advice to producing new narratives about who the women bicyclist might be, these rhetors not only encouraged women to overcome social reservations in order *to take up* the bicycle but also invented new contexts for the machine's use that would enable women to do so. More specifically, individual bicycling women whose words were published across the nation in mass-distributed popular magazines and syndicated newspapers negotiated with other bicycle users and with manufacturers in expanding popular notions of who should ride, how and with whom they should ride, and under what conditions riding was appropriate for women. In doing so, they helped make bicycling physically and socially more comfortable for women, thus increasing the number and visibility of female riders in life, as well as in print.

In the preceding chapters, I have described nineteenth-century women bicyclists' wide-ranging rhetorical and embodied activities, demonstrating how, collectively, their efforts contributed to a broader instantiation of social and technological change. Early tricyclists entered and transformed the masculine space of the bicycle club in the late 1880s, helping render the high-wheeled Ordinary obsolete because its features no longer matched the recreational uses to which riders, both male and female, most wanted to put their machines. Despite its suitability for touring and courtship, however, the Safety bicycle still required both material and rhetorical adjustments to appeal to broader groups of women interested in bicycling in contexts beyond the recreational field of the bicycle club. Women rhetors worked in various ways to provide these adjustments. Over the 1890s, inventors tinkered with the bicycle and its accoutrements, adapting the machine to its female riders through both patented and marketed inventions and more tactical unpatented innovations. Meanwhile, fiction and travel writers produced narratives about the woman bicyclist that simultaneously wrote the new machine into familiar contemporary scripts of femininity and masculinity and played with those scripts, creating room for new identities for women that were further articulated in riders' personal commentaries about bicycling. These varied writings circulated widely within the new venue of the popular magazine, aligning the so-called bicycle girl with a vibrant and robust ethos that helped promote the new machine's widespread use among women.

Within instructional handbooks and advice columns, however, some women writers further complicated the bicycle girl ethos, reaching out to a more diverse group of prospective riders and constituting this group as a discrete community of wheelwomen, whose needs for both practical advice and encouragement could be met by peers with shared concerns. Finally, women riders spoke back to medical authorities through both written and embodied rhetorical acts, qualifying, redirecting, or outright rejecting age-old commonplaces about their physical weakness that had previously contributed to the maintenance of gender differences. By relocating notions of femininity long understood to be rooted in biology within the more permeable realm of culture, women's health advocates, racers, and endurance riders denaturalized not only doctors' restrictions for women aboard the bicycle but also broader medical and cultural restrictions on their other physical and intellectual pursuits.

Significantly, women bicyclists were wide-ranging not only in their rhetorical strategies and in the contexts for which they wrote but also often in their alliances, geographic locations, and even their ultimate ideas about what bicycling ought to become. Though some women's bicycle clubs did exist and undoubtedly served as invaluable resources for members, the women about whom I have written in this book did not consciously engage in a collective rhetorical enterprise. Although in some contexts, such as in handbooks and advice columns, they constituted themselves as a distinctive public, in general they were not deliberately cooperative in positioning the bicycle to produce social change. Rather, as I have suggested, their rhetorical activities might be described as "collected"—minimally orchestrated and accumulated through repetition, distribution, and syndication—and, perhaps most important, as helping to mediate the relationship between the new technology of the bicycle and its female users.

Although such "collected" rhetorical activities have not received particular notice among feminist rhetoricians because of their invisibility relative to the efforts of discrete organizations and collectives, the accumulated impact of these activities contributes to social change, often preceding and exceeding the activities of discrete entities like clubs and organizations. If we seek to understand something as broad and complex as the means by which a technology becomes woven into the fabric of a cultural moment, we ought to take this accumulation seriously, looking not only at collectives or organizations as sources of women's rhetorical agency but also at the ways individuals produce rhetoric that "collects" through repetitions accomplished within historically available material channels of distribution—and that continually transforms those channels in the process. For late nineteenth-century rhetors, these channels included the popular magazines and newspapers of a burgeoning print culture; for rhetors today, they might involve the various affordances of the Internet, which allow individual people widely distant in space to form loose communities and alliances, engage in self-education, and bring together financial, material, and intellectual resources.

While the work of collected rhetoric goes on whether we name and acknowledge it or not, *Claiming the Bicycle* suggests that its successful coordination can be bolstered, if not by our total awareness of our role as individuals in larger forces of social change, then at least by our individual belief that we might make some sort of difference as rhetorical agents—that we *can* intervene productively. It is this belief that waned throughout the twentieth century, as people—technology users, individuals immediately disconnected from processes of production and distribution of technology—lost sight of what Robert R. Johnson describes as "the arts of know-how" (5) which are derived from direct experience rather than particular training, education, and acknowledged expertise. As information and resources were consolidated into the hands of experts working inside corporations, the potential innovations and contributions of technology users became "a type of knowledge that has been stripped of its ability to consciously voice its purpose, power, and means by which it can make its knowledge visible" (5). In other words, in becoming strictly consumers rather than producers, we lost touch with our ability, as individuals and as technology users, to speak back to technology even from positions far removed from the engineering firm or manufacturing plant.

Fortunately, in recent years, technology users have begun to regain a sense of their own "know-how," and now, as in the 1890s, new historically situated opportunities to engage critically with technology have emerged. Just as the widely distributed, inexpensive, playful popular magazine provided an important venue for late nineteenth-century women writers to give symbolic shape to the bicycle, today the Internet offers a similarly accessible venue through which individuals can resist, reshape, and appropriate technologies in ways that designers, manufacturers, and advertisers may not have anticipated. Users can post and view instructional YouTube videos to educate themselves and others on topics as diverse as making biodiesel fuel and playing musical instruments. They create websites and online communities to provide advice and support for dispersed, "collected" communities, not unlike the women bicyclists of the 1890s, and they make use of existing websites like Change.org and Kickstarter to promote their own material and rhetorical goals. In this era of intense skepticism about the very big businesses that consolidated innovation during the mid-twentieth century, DIY instruction and culture are burgeoning, offering new narratives about technology and users that reclaim some of the optimistic, pragmatic engagement that characterized women's involvement in the bicycle craze of the 1890s.

Women have played a significant role in these initiatives, and in the process, they have shifted the relationship between gender and technology and reshaped the broader network within which gender and power relationships develop, become naturalized, and are challenged. They have authored instructional videos, circulated online petitions to protest advertising and design practices offensive to women, and blogged humorously and honestly, in ways reminiscent of Frances Willard's *A Wheel within a Wheel*, about their experiences with technology-related ventures ranging from home remodeling to competitive sailing. These dispersed interventions in technological use and development have not necessarily been conceived specifically as feminist social action, but they nevertheless possess the power to accumulate—through views, links, Facebook likes, petition signatures accrued, repeated arguments, memes, and other rhetorical micropractices—and accomplish feminist goals in relation to the technologies and technological practices they consider.

Though exciting feminist user engagement is obviously well under way, I argue that feminist rhetoricians—historians of rhetoric, technical communicators, and rhetorical theorists—might play a role in making this work more visible and self-conscious by advocating what I describe here as a "technofeminist rhetorical agency." While not disregarding the need for women to intervene within engineering or manufacturing contexts, this concept reminds us that even users, though relatively marginalized from processes of design and manufacture, possess rhetorical resources for mediating the material and symbolic shape technologies take. Building on recent scholarship that describes rhetorical agency as materially and historically situated (Herndl and Licona), emergent (Cooper), protean (Campbell "Agency"), and partially reliant on—rather than resistant to—the very authoritative forces it seeks to transform (Winsor), I offer a few productive generalizations about what sort of technofeminist rhetorical activity might constitute an agential, rather than a passive, user orientation to technology.

In particular, three such generalizations strike me as useful in guiding contemporary feminist scholars and technology users toward an agential orientation. *First, a technofeminist rhetorical agent rejects the notion that technologies come to her in finished form or that her relations to technologies are fixed or determined by forces beyond her control.* She rejects the notion that technologies are inherently masculine or that men objectively possess superior aptitude with technology, and she uncovers the rhetorical means by which this illusion of a static orientation is accomplished. She considers the rhetorical framing of a new device through advertising, instructional material, and even fictional representation as constitutive of the device itself. *Second, a technofeminist rhetorical agent understands her interactions with technology as helping maintain, complicate, or contest dominant social norms, gendered and otherwise, and she sees potential avenues for social change in both technology use and technical writing.* Far from embracing all technologies as inherently productive or denouncing technology from afar, she turns a critical eye to new applications, taking note of what affordances they provide, to whom, and under what circumstances. She critiques monolithic characterizations of "the user" as a universal or representative type to whose interests manufacturer-produced instructional and advertising materials are directed. Rather than expecting simply to adapt to existing technologies, she seeks out ways those technologies might be accommodated to her or to other new users. *Finally, a technofeminist rhetorical agent strives to be a tinkerer, in its broadest sense.* Through use, she understands, emerge inventions both rhetorical and material. She envisions her environment as dynamic and strives to marshal, rather than be marshaled by, the technologies with which she interacts, and she understands the material channels through which she might communicate the results of her tinkering with others.

In advocating this sort of orientation, I do not want to overstate users' capacity for agency over technology development or disregard the hold that large-scale manufacturers and business interests have on innovation. Neither do I want to disregard the need for rhetoricians—and feminists of all stripes—to continue to fight for women's access to these highly influential spaces. Nonetheless, a single-minded focus on *access* perpetuates the problematic notion that women are, and have been, passive consumers of or recipients of technology—that agency is available only to those who occupy "insider" roles in technological innovation. Such a focus squanders valuable "outsider" rhetorical resources that are, via historically contingent avenues and to varying degrees, always available, and it tacitly instrumentalizes technical communication, elevating technology itself as "the" solution to social problems, feminist and otherwise.

The women about whom I have written in this book were not remarkable, other than in that they understood themselves as rhetorical agents in a way that most technology users, or consumers, do not today. Whereas, for instance, Lena Sittig went to work creating and patenting women's bicycle clothing and Maria Ward authored her extensive bicycle handbook because both were sincerely confident in their ability to aid their fellow bicyclists, contemporary women have often fallaciously absorbed the lessons that technology is neutral, that they should follow the instructions and "use as indicated," and that their ability to do so successfully is a reflection of their own (gendered) aptitude rather than of the necessity of having support systems to assist them. Sittig, Ward, and others assumed it was *their responsibility* to adjust the bicycle to women's use; modern feminist technology users have the opportunity to regain that sense of responsibility. In doing so, we will regain some power in shaping the direction a new technology takes. When we do not write our own stories, when we accept the dominant cultural narratives that emerge about people and machines, when we do not think of ourselves as potential innovators of the mundane objects with which we interact, we become complicit in the maintenance of hegemonic power relations, gendered and otherwise.

While the wide range of feminist rhetorical interventions in technological development demonstrates the productive work that scholars are already undertaking to transform the contemporary landscape of gender and technology, I would argue that as feminist teachers of both rhetoric and composition and technical communication, we are especially well positioned to contribute productively to restoring our students' sense of their agency as users. As teachers, we possess the power to disabuse within our students the false notion that writing—whether technical, personal, fictional, or otherwise—is *peripheral to*, rather than *constitutive of*, a technical object itself and is thus not a transparently or neutrally written directive, but a rhetorically crafted, ideologically significant mediator of material realities. Whether or not they intend to become professional technical writers or engineers, students ought to understand writing and the material world from which it emerges as mutually constructed, mutually emergent. Students need to look beyond the limited artificial categories of "users" and "producers" of texts, technologies, and social realities, as well as to see themselves as already always complicit in the production and transformation of gender and power norms. They should see their writing not just as classroom exercises or workplace preparation, but as interventions that exceed these boundaries—that intervene in their construction. By doing so, contemporary students might recover the agency that characterized nineteenth-century women's interactions with the bicycle and allowed that machine to exceed the expectations of designers, advertisers, and manufacturers.

Importantly, however, making students' interventions in the technological realm productive will involve more than just helping them *see themselves* as potential agents of change. This work will also by necessity engage with broader questions about the circulation of their rhetorical practices—the constantly shifting, historically contingent material means by which they will ensure their voices are heard widely. As Paula Mathieu and Diana George have argued recently, composition and technical communication teachers must convey in their teaching not only "the language used, the way the argument is made, and the author's bio" but also the role "a piece of communication plays, can play, or has played in the world outside as well as inside our classrooms" (146). Doing so involves being aware of how messages rely on authors' ability to select and take advantage of effective "delivery systems" that will increase the visibility and impact of their efforts. Whereas in the nineteenth century, these "delivery systems" included newspaper columns, popular magazines, and other print means, today they include digital and social media as well. I am scarcely the first person to advance this project; Stuart Selber, Johndan Johnson-Eilola, J. Blake Scott, and many others have already argued for cultural studies–inspired pedagogical models of both composition and technical communication that honor the larger systems in which discourse intervenes. Nevertheless, feminist teachers of both technical communication and composition have yet to fully articulate the stakes of such pedagogy for their work, and it is my hope that *Claiming the Bicycle* addresses this gap.

This book began by detailing Annie "Londonderry" Kopchovsky's sensational round-the-world bicycle journey, a story that has recently gained popular attention. To be sure, Londonderry's willingness to leave her family for more than a year, change her name, travel largely unaccompanied while promoting her public appearances, and blur fiction with fact in telling her story all testify to the determination—or possibly desperation—of this complex and intriguing heroine. However, Londonderry's story is compelling not only for the particulars of her case but also because it demonstrates so succinctly the extent to which women in her day situated the bicycle as a means of both rhetorical and material change. Though few other individual women made statements as public, or as precarious, as Londonderry's, many women understood the bicycle as a means of enacting social change. Through many small rhetorical acts, these women helped *make it so*, and I hope that their collected efforts testify to the sort of work contemporary technology users can do to wield influence of their own. If anything, Londonderry's story and the stories of beautiful Belva the tricyclist, Mary Sargent Hopkins, Maria E. Ward, and others might remind us that the agency of users is not a utopian dream but a lost heritage.

Notes

Works Cited

Index

Notes

Preface: Considering Women, Rhetoric, and Technology

1. Nellie Bly's sensational tales of her experiences posing as an inmate in a madhouse and racing around the world had made her a household name by the early 1890s. In part because of Bly's success, Jean Marie Lutes has noted, stunt reporting "became a national phenomenon" during the 1880s and 1890s ("Into the Madhouse" 218), often allowing young women to overcome a lack of professional credentials by engaging in outrageous acts and then writing about them for newspapers. Such work satisfied Americans' increasing desire for sensational stories in an increasingly literate, entertainment-hungry society.

2. Londonderry's choice of a bicycle journey was not unprecedented, as Ordinary rider Thomas Stevens had received acclaim for his round-the-world trip in the mid-1880s, reporting his journey as a correspondent to *Outing* magazine. Other riders followed, including Frank Lenz, whose mysterious disappearance in Turkey in May 1894 became a topic of great concern during Londonderry's journey. Lenz was later found to have been murdered by a band of Kurdish bandits (Herlihy, *Lost Cyclist* 212).

3. The Safety is essentially the standard bicycle model we have today, with equal-sized wheels and a chain mechanism for locomotion. The Ordinary, in contrast, featured small back wheels and front wheels upward of five feet in height. Ordinaries were extremely popular in the 1880s, though they were not referred to by that name at the time, but simply as "bicycles." When the Safety emerged, the high-wheeled machine became known as the Ordinary bicycle model.

4. This includes only the number of bicycles that were sold. There is no way to account for those that were sold but scarcely ridden, those that were sold to individual women but were shared and ridden in groups, or those that were simply rented for afternoon excursions in parks and resorts.

5. Peter Zheutlin's 2007 *Around the World on Two Wheels: Annie Londonderry's Extraordinary Ride* recounts the details of Londonderry's journey, as does a documentary directed by Gillian Klempner Willman titled *The New Woman—Annie "Londonderry" Kopchovsky* and Evalyn Parry's musical play, *SPIN*.

6. There were some women, however, who authored words sanctioned by bicycle manufacturers. For instance, as I discuss in chapters 3 and 4, respectively, Ida Trafford

Bell authored an instructional booklet for the Pope Manufacturing Company, and Dr. Lucy Hall authored a booklet for the Overman Wheel Company about bicycling for women.

7. See, for instance, Wiebe Bijker and Trevor Pinch. Among other examples of technological development, Bijker and Pinch offer the late nineteenth-century bicycle as an example of the "social construction of technology" (SCOT) model of technological change; they suggest that as male riders of the high-wheeled Ordinary became less interested in demonstrating their manliness through acts of courage and daring, they came to find that machine lacking—a sentiment that, articulated over time, exerted pressure on manufacturers to develop new designs. Though I agree that users influence the direction of technological development by articulating new purposes and contexts for use, I complicate Bijker and Pinch's emphasis on user discourse by suggesting that users not only *discussed* possible material and rhetorical changes but also *enacted* them through more formalized rhetorical activity: published articles, user instructions and advice, and patented accoutrements, for instance. Additionally, I emphasize women, whose "relevance" as bicycle users, in their figuring, is limited to an obvious dissatisfaction with the Ordinary but becomes more apparent when one expands the consideration of technological development beyond the phases of manufacturing and distribution.

Introduction: Regendering of the Bicycle during the 1880s

1. Throughout the early 1880s, the high-wheeled bicycle was referred to simply as the "bicycle." Only when alternative models began to appear at mid-decade did the machine earn the name Ordinary to describe its status as the ordinary or standard model. However, in order to distinguish it clearly from the other models I describe, I refer to the high-wheeled bicycle as the Ordinary throughout this and subsequent chapters.

2. Although individual clubs established their own standards, most had steep membership fees: initial joining fees of $10 to $15 (roughly $250 to $350 in today's currency) and monthly fees of $1 to $2 dollars ($25 to $50 today) (Connecticut Bicycle Club; Measuring Worth Inflation Calculator). Uniforms added significantly to the expense of membership; for example, the Capital Bicycle Club uniform cost $18. In addition, clubmen took new applications for membership seriously; as one Connecticut Bicycle Club membership pamphlet explains:

> Every candidate for membership must be at least twenty-one years of age and be recommended by two members of the club. All names shall be presented to the club committee and posted by them on the club bulletin for a period of not less than two weeks before action shall be taken by the committee on the application. Members shall have the privilege of presenting to the committee any objections to a candidate, such communications to be considered confidential. (18)

Members could be expelled or reprimanded for "objectionable" behavior and were required periodically to pay additional fees for special events, such as trips and banquets. Other clubs, such as the Mercer County Wheelmen of New Jersey, indicated explicitly in their bylaws that members must be "white" males; although by the 1890s a few African American bicycle clubs had emerged, during the early days of the sport this system of rules and expenses established a strong association between bicycling and a very specific form of classed and raced masculinity.

3. For instance, a toast to "Our Married Members," recounted in the program and attributed to Francis Bacon, reads as follows: "He that hath a wife and children hath given hostages to fortune; for they are impediments to great enterprises either of virtue or of mischief." A Spencerian toast that year, given to "Our Bachelor Members," said, "A bold, bold man."

4. Some clubmen did race tricycles on the racetrack. But women were not welcome to race at club races and thus, as Willard's story suggests, were forced to attempt racing in less ideal conditions—on tight, angular city blocks.

5. The basic design of the Safety bicycle had long been in place. European inventors had tinkered for decades with low-seated, two-wheeled "velocipedes," yielding a machine equipped with pedals and cranks by the 1860s (Herlihy, *Bicycle* 76). During the winter and spring of 1869, this machine had briefly attracted American attention. Within a few months, however, the velocipede was angering pedestrians, who felt endangered by its riders, and it proved expensive and uncomfortable because its low positioning ensured that riders absorbed the full shock of the roadways. In the late 1870s, British engineers Henry Lawson and James Starley had each renewed interest in a machine with smaller, equal-sized wheels. Lawson's 1879 "bicyclette" featured a chain drive, which should have made the machine both easier to maneuver and fast enough to compete on the racetrack with the Ordinary (Herlihy, *Bicycle* 216). The new technology did not catch on, however, though in 1885, European manufacturers embraced a similar machine, the British Rover. American manufacturers stubbornly resisted the design shift—likely in large part because they still saw their primary customer as the male bicycle club member concerned with skill and bravado. When touring a British factory where safeties were being produced, Pope declared in 1886, "One thing I am now satisfied, and that is that we in this country have nothing to learn from the Englishmen as to how to build a bicycle" (qtd. in Herlihy, *Bicycle* 241).

Chapter One. Women Riders and the Invention of the Modern Bicycle

1. As Carol Mattingly has noted, the emergence of the bloomer costume during the 1850s in association with women speakers attracted widespread criticism, even as it provided them with a costume that associated women with the public arena (*Appropriate[ing] Dress* 38).

2. According to historian Anne L. Macdonald, Sittig exhibited her garments on mannequins and live models at the local skating rink where novice bicyclists from

the prominent Cycle Club of Brooklyn learned to ride before attempting the roads. This allowed them to both study the clothing up close and see it in action (203).

Chapter Two. Popular Magazines and the Rise of the "Bicycle Girl"

1. S. S. McClure was editor of *Outing* in the late 1880s, when it was still owned by the bicycle maker Albert Pope. Subsequent editors of the magazine continued the practice into the 1890s, as evidenced by the content of the issues. Though McClure does not explicitly reference "wheelwomen," women did contribute pieces in increasing numbers from the late 1880s onward.

Chapter Three. Women's Written Instructions for Change

1. Though it is impossible to know what sort of training bicycle instructors had, in his autobiography, Samuel S. McClure describes being whisked to an indoor bicycle arena on his first day at the Pope Manufacturing Company, learning how to bicycle as he teaches (146).

2. In records kept at the Staten Island Historical Society, it appears from correspondence that Ward attempted to publish a sort of consumer guide reviewing bicycle equipment from many different companies.

Chapter Four. Women Bicyclists' Embodied Medical Authority

1. Though the league's ruling stood, Knox's exclusion proved divisive within the organization and helped spark activism among the growing African American cycling community; as Andrew Ritchie notes, the Hannibal Athletic Club of Washington, DC, staged a boycott of all league events and formed a parallel league of their own (25). Nonetheless, the exclusion proved difficult for African American racers, as even the widely celebrated record-holding male rider, Major Taylor, eventually left the United States for Europe, where he could race without the intense hostility he found at home. Idella Johnson, a racer from California's all-black Oakland Cycling Club, expresses her frustration in the *San Francisco Call* at being unable to race white women racers:

> I now hold the world's ladies' racing record and I intend to retain it. I do not wish to do so unless it belongs to me, and the only way to definitively decide the matter is for these ladies to . . . show what they can do. We hope to bring the white and colored cyclers together soon. ("Colored Riders Arrange a Meet," image 15)

Works Cited

Adams, Dan. "Ceremony Honors Cyclist Who Broke Barriers." *Boston Globe* 13 September 2013. Web. 20 August 2014.

Agnew, Lois et al. "Octalog III: The Politics of Historiography in 2010." *Rhetoric Review* 30.2 (2011): 115–17. Print.

Akrich, Madeline. "The De-scription of Technical Objects." *Shaping Technology/Building Society: Studies in Sociotechnical Change*. Ed. Wiebe Bijker and John Law. Cambridge, MA: MIT Press, 1994. 205–24. Print.

Applegarth, Risa. "Genre, Location, and Mary Austin's Ethos." *Rhetoric Society Quarterly* 41.1 (2011): 41–63. Print.

———. "Rhetorical Scarcity: Spatial and Economic Reflections on Genre Change." *College Composition and Communication* 63.2 (2012): 453–83. Print.

Ariel Cycle Manufacturing Company trade catalog, 1896. Indiana State Library Trade Catalog Collection. Web. 1 January 2015.

Bannon, Theresa. "Bicycling for Women." *Medical Record* 2 (1895): 142. Print.

Banta, Martha. *Imaging American Women: Idea and Ideals in Cultural History*. New York: Columbia University Press, 1987. Print.

Barad, Karen. "Posthuman Performativity: Toward an Understanding of How Matter Comes to Matter." *Signs* 28.3 (Spring 2003): 801–31. Print.

Barnes, Ida C. "Morbid Conditions Complicating the Menopause." *Woman's Medical Journal* 6 (1897): 341–44. *Internet Archive*. Web. 28 December 2013.

Barton, Ben, and Marthalee Barton. "Narration in Technical Communication." *Journal of Business and Technical Communication* 2.1 (1988): 36–48. Print.

Bates, [Arlo]. "On the Proper Economy of Truth." *Outing* 6.6 (1885): 695–98. *LA 84*. Web. 11 October 2011.

Battenberg, Effie. "Umbrella attachment for bicycles." Patent 560,077. 12 May 1896. Web.

Bell, Ida Trafford. *Bicycling for Women*. New York: Pope Manufacturing Company, 1890. Print.

———. "Bicycling for Women." *Harper's Bazaar* 14 July 1894: 27, 28. *ProQuest: American Periodicals Series Online*. Web. 23 July 2008.

"Belts for Wheelwomen." *St. Paul Daily Globe* 19 April 1896: 18. Library of Congress. *Chronicling America: Historic American Newspapers*. Web. 1 August 2013.

Bennitt, Alice A. "Bicycle canopy." Patent 574,235. 29 December 1896.

Works Cited

"A Bevy of Cycling Girls." *New York Evening World* 9 February 1889: 2. Library of Congress. *Chronicling America: Historic American Newspapers*. Web. 1 August 2013.

"Bicycle Bangs." *St. Paul Daily Globe* 10 May 1896: 14. Library of Congress. *Chronicling America: Historic American Newspapers*. Web. 1 August 2013.

"Bicycle Dress." *Harper's Bazaar* 14 April 1894: 27, 15. *ProQuest: American Periodicals Series Online*. Web. 23 July 2008.

"Bicycles during 1896." *Yakima (WA) Herald* 19 September 1895: image 4. Library of Congress. *Chronicling America: Historic American Newspapers*. Web. 1 November 2013.

"Bicycling and Bicycle Outfits." *Delineator*. April 1895. 579–80. Print.

Bijker, Wiebe E. *Of Bicycles, Bakelites, and Bulbs*. Cambridge, MA: MIT Press, 1995. Print.

Bisland, Mary. "The Making of a Woman's Bicycle." *Harper's Bazaar* 14 March 1896. *ProQuest: American Periodicals Series Online*. Web. 23 July 2008.

———. "Woman's Cycle." *Godey's Magazine* April 1896: 385–88. Print.

Bizzell, Patricia. "Frances Willard, Phoebe Palmer, and the Ethos of the Methodist Woman Preacher." *Rhetoric Society Quarterly* 36 (2006): 377–98. Print.

———. "Opportunities for Feminist Research in the History of Rhetoric." *Rhetoric Review* 11 (1992): 50–58. Print.

Bly, Nellie. "Champion of Her Sex." *New York Sunday World* 2 February 1896: 9–10. Print.

Bourdieu, Pierre. *Pascalian Meditations*. Stanford, CA: Stanford University Press, 2000. Print.

Bradley, Will. "Victor Bicycles." Overman Wheel Company. Poster. 1895.

Browne, Herbert Janvrin. "Athletics in Washington." *Outing* 17.1 (October 1890): 65–80. *LA 84*. Web. 11 October 2011.

Burke, Kenneth. *A Grammar of Motives*. Berkeley: University of California Press, 1969. Print.

———. *Permanence and Change: An Anatomy of Purpose*. 3rd ed. Berkeley: University of California Press, 1984. Print.

Butler, Judith. *Gender Trouble: Feminism and the Subversion of Identity*. New York: Routledge, 1999. Print.

Campbell, Karlyn Kohrs. "Agency: Promiscuous and Protean." *Communication and Critical/Cultural Studies* 2.1 (2005): 1–19. Print.

———. *Men Cannot Speak for Her*. New York: Praeger, 1989. Print.

Capital Bicycle Club records. Washingtoniana Collection of the District of Columbia Public Library, Washington, DC. Print.

"Chance for Genius: The Perfect Bicycle Costume Is Yet to Be Devised." *Los Angeles Herald* 24 May 1896. Library of Congress. *Chronicling America: Historic American Newspapers*. Web. 26 March 2013.

Chant, Laura Ormiston. "Woman as an Athlete: A Reply to Dr. Arabella Kenealy." *Nineteenth Century* 45 (1899): 745–54. Print.

Charland, Maurice. "Constitutive Rhetoric: The Case of the *Peuple Québécois.*" *Quarterly Journal of Speech* 73.2 (1987): 133–50. Print.

Christoph, Julie Nelson. "Reconceiving Ethos in Relation to the Personal: Strategies of Placement in Pioneer Women's Writing." *College English* 64.6 (2002): 660–79. Print.

Clarke, Edward H. *Sex in Education; or, A Fair Chance for Girls*. Boston: J. Osgood, 1873. *Project Gutenberg*. Web. 28 December 2013.

Clyde, Henry. *Pleasure-Cycling*. Boston: Little Brown, 1895. Print.

"Colored Riders Arrange a Meet." *San Francisco Call* 12 July 1896: image 15. Library of Congress. *Chronicling America: Historic American Newspapers*. Web. 20 September 2014.

"Color Line Drawn." *San Francisco Call* 10 July 1895: 2. Library of Congress. *Chronicling America: Historic American Newspapers*. Web. 20 September 2014.

Colt Bicycle Club records, 1890–96. Collection of the Connecticut Historical Society Library, Hartford. Print.

Columbia Ladies' Safety. Advertisement. *The Bicycling World and L.A.W. Bulletin* 10 January 1890: 225. *Internet Archive*. Web. 10 January 2015.

Comstock, Flora Lincoln. "Rosalind A-wheel." *Godey's Magazine* April 1896: 388–93. Print.

Condit, Celeste. *The Meanings of the Gene: Public Debates about Human Heredity*. Madison: University of Wisconsin Press, 1999. Print.

Connecticut Bicycle Club Pamphlet, 1890 (Organized October 20, 1879). Hartford, CT: Press of the Plimpton Manufacturing Company. Print. Hartford History Center, Hartford Public Library. 20 June 2010. Print.

Cooper, Marilyn. "Rhetorical Agency as Emergent and Enacted." College Composition and Communication 62.3 (2011): 420–49. Print.

Cooter, Roger, and Stephen Pumphrey. "Separate Spheres and Public Places: Reflections on the History of Science Popularization and Science in Popular Culture." *History of Science* 32.97 (1994): 237–67. *Astrophysics Data System*. Web. 1 Nov. 2009.

Cowan, Ruth Schwartz. *A Social History of American Technology*. New York: Oxford University Press, 1997. Print.

Crowley, Sharon. *Toward a Civil Discourse: Rhetoric and Fundamentalism*. Pittsburgh, PA: University of Pittsburgh Press, 2006. Print.

Dacre, Henry. "Daisy Bell." 1892. *Levy Sheet Music Collection*. Johns Hopkins University. Web. 26 December 2013.

Davidson, Lillias Campbell. *Handbook for Lady Cyclists*. London: Hay Nesbit, 1896. Microform. New York Public Library Preservation Laboratory. Reel 1.

de Certeau, Michel. *The Practice of Everyday Life*. Berkeley: University of California Press, 1984. Print.

Denison, Grace E. "How We Ride Our Wheels." *Outing* 19.1 (1891): 52–54. *LA 84*. Web. 22 December 2013.

———. "Through Erin Awheel." *Outing* 22.1 (1893): 28–34. *LA 84*. Web. 22 December 2013.

———. “Through Erin Awheel II.” *Outing* 22.2 (1893): 136–40. *LA 84*. Web. 22 December 2013.

———. “Through Erin Awheel III.” *Outing* 22.3 (1893): 236–40. *LA 84*. Web. 22 December 2013.

———.“Through Erin Awheel IV.” *Outing* 22.4 (1893): 311–15. *LA 84*. Web. 22 December 2013.

———. “Through Erin Awheel Concluded.” *Outing* 22. 6 (1893): 445–47. *LA 84*. Web. 22 December 2013.

Dickinson, Robert L. “Bicycling for Women from the Standpoint of the Gynecologist.” *American Journal of Obstetrics and Diseases of Women and Children* 21 (1895): 24–37. Print.

Dieterich, Fred G. *The Inventor’s Universal Educator: An Educational Guide for Inventors, Patentees, Manufacturers, and Mechanics and All Others Connected Directly or Indirectly with Patents*. Washington, DC: F. G. Dieterich, 1899. Web. 11 October 2013.

District Cycle Company Bicycle School. Advertisement. *Evening Post* 1895: 7. Library of Congress. *Chronicling America: Historic American Newspapers*. Web. 15 August 2013.

Dodge, Pryor. *The Bicycle*. Paris: Flammarion, 1996. Print.

Durack, Katherine. “Gender, Technology, and the History of Technical Communication.” *Technical Communication Quarterly* 6 (Summer 1997): 249–60. Print.

Eagle Bicycle trade catalog, 1890. Collection of Hagley Museum, Wilmington, DE. Print. 23 June 2008.

Eclipse Bicycle Company trade catalog, 1895. Collection of Hagley Museum. Wilmington, DE. Print.

“The 1883 Meet Again.” *The Bicycling World* 16 February 1883: 176. *Internet Archive*. Web. 20 July 2015.

Engineer Girl. National Academy of Sciences, 2013. Web. 28 December 2013.

Enoch, Jessica. *Refiguring Rhetorical Education: Women Teaching African American, Native American, and Chicano/a Students, 1865–1911*. Carbondale: Southern Illinois University Press, 2008. Print.

Epperson, Bruce. “Failed Colossus: Strategic Error at the Pope Manufacturing Company, 1878–1900.” *Technology and Culture* 41.2 (2000): 300–20. Print.

Everett, Edith Townsend. “Bicycling for Women.” *Harper’s Bazaar* 17 June 1893: 485. *ProQuest: American Periodicals Series Online*. Web. 23 July 2008.

Fahnestock, Jeanne. “Accommodating Science: The Rhetorical Life of Scientific Facts.” *Written Communication* 3.3 (1986): 275–96. *Sage Journals Online*. Web. 1 November 2009.

“Fashions in Paris.” *Salt Lake Herald* 15 November 1896. Library of Congress. *Chronicling America: Historic American Newspapers*. Web. 30 July 2013.

“The Feminine Scorcher.” *Godey’s Magazine* April 1896: 446. Print.

Finnegan, Cara. “Recognizing Lincoln: Image Vernaculars in Nineteenth-Century Visual Culture.” *Rhetoric and Public Affairs* 8.1 (2005): 31–58. Print.

Follett, Helen. "Honeymoon on Wheels." *Outing* 29.1 (1896): 3–7. *LA 84*. Web. 22 December 2013.

Franz, Kathleen. *Tinkering: Consumers Reinvent the Early Automobile*. Philadelphia: University of Pennsylvania Press, 2005. Print.

Garvey, Ellen Gruber. *The Adman in the Parlor*. New York: Oxford University Press, 1996. Print.

———. "Reframing the Bicycle: Advertising-Supported Magazines and Scorching Women." *American Quarterly* 47.1 (March 1995): 66–101. Print.

Girl Develop It. Girl Develop It, 2013. Web. 28 December 2013.

Goddard, Stephen B. *Colonel Albert Pope and His American Dream Machines*. Jefferson, NC: McFarland, 2000. Print.

Gold, David. *Rhetoric at the Margins: Revising the History of Writing Instruction in American Colleges, 1873–1947*. Carbondale: Southern Illinois University Press, 2008. Print.

Gordon, Mary. "Bicycle Saddles for Ladies." *British Medical Journal* 24 March 1906: 1079. Print.

Gordon, Sarah A. "Any Desired Length: Negotiating Gender through Sports Clothing, 1870–1925." *Beauty and Business: Commerce, Gender, and Culture in Modern America*. Ed. Philip Scranton. New York: Routledge, 2001. 24–51. Print.

Graham, S. Scott. "Agency and the Rhetoric of Medicine: Biomedical Brain Scans and the Ontology of Fibromyalgia." *Technical Communication Quarterly* 18.4 (2009): 376–404. Print.

Gray, Sally Helvenston, and Mihaela C. Peteu. "'Invention, the Angel of the Nineteenth Century': Patents for Women's Cycling Attire in the 1890s." *Dress* 32 (2005): 27–42. Print.

Gray, Sarah. "Bicycle Saddles for Ladies." *British Medical Journal* 12 April 1906: 1139. Print.

"Great Bicycle Feat." *Sacramento Daily Record Union* 1 December 1897: 6. Library of Congress. *Chronicling America: Historic American Newspapers*. Web. 28 December 2013.

"Great Increase." *New York Times* 10 September 1899: 27. *ProQuest Historical Newspapers*. Web. 28 December 2013.

Guertin, Florence. "The Wheel of Time." *Outing* 26.5 (1895): 347–54. *LA 84*. Web. 22 December 2013.

Gunby, Olive. "Women Inventors." *Scientific American Supplement* 51.13 (1901): 21241–42. Print.

Hall, Lucy. *Bicycling and Health for Women*. Chicopee Falls, MA: Overman Wheel Company, 1890. Print.

Hall, Ruth. "Only a Girl." *Outing* 10.4 (1885): 297. *LA 84*. Web. 14 August 2014.

Haller, John S., and Robin M. Haller. *The Physician and Sexuality in Victorian America*. New York: W. W. Norton, 1974. Print.

Harman, Graham. *The Prince of Networks*. Melbourne, Australia: re.press, 2009. Web. 14 September 2012.

"Hartford Wheel Club." Hartford History Center, Hartford Public Library. Hartford, CT. Print.

"Hattie Is a Winner." *Pittsburg (PA) Dispatch* 6 January 1889. Library of Congress. *Chronicling America: Historic American Newspapers*. Web. 30 December 2013.

"Heard about Town." *New York Times* 21 October 1900: 26. *ProQuest Historical Newspapers*. Web. 23 December 2013.

Heineke, Grace T. "Dress-guard for bicycles." Patent 620,651. 7 March 1899.

Henderson, Mary Foote. "Bicycle saddle." Patent 572,163. 1 December 1896.

"Here and There." *The Bicycling World and L.A.W. Bulletin* 28 June 1889: 251. *Internet Archive*. Web. 10 January 2015.

"Here and There." *The Bicycling World and L.A.W. Bulletin* 5 July 1889: 263. *Internet Archive*. Web. 10 January 2015.

"Here and There: Los Angeles." *The Bicycling World and L.A.W. Bulletin* 14 March 1890: 442. *Internet Archive*. Web. 20 July 2015.

Herlihy, David V. *Bicycle: The History*. New Haven, CT: Yale University Press, 2004. Print.

———. *The Lost Cyclist: The Epic Tale of an American Adventurer and His Mysterious Disappearance*. New York: Houghton Mifflin Harcourt, 2010. Print.

Herman, Ella. "The Bicycle Race." 1895. Library of Congress Historic Sheet Music Collection, 1800–1920. Web. 26 December 2013.

Herndl, Carl G., and Adela C. Licona. "Shifting Agency: Agency, Kairos, and the Possibilities for Social Action." *Communicative Practices in Workplaces and the Professions*. Ed. Mark Zachry and Charlotte Thraills. Amityville, NY: Baywood, 2007. 133–53. Print.

Herrick, Christine Terhune. "Habits and Faces." *Minneapolis Journal* 4 June 1904: 2. Library of Congress. *Chronicling America: Historic American Newspapers*. Web. 1 November 2013.

Hicks, Mary. "Umbrella attachment for bicycles." Patent 572,298. 1 December 1896.

Hobbs, Catherine. *Nineteenth-Century Women Learn to Write*. Charlottesville: University of Virginia Press, 1995. Print.

Hopkins, Mary Sargent. "The Bicycle for Women." *Harper's Bazaar* 19 August 1893: 26, 33. *ProQuest: American Periodicals Series Online*. Web. 23 July 2008.

———. "Bicycling for Girls: A Word to Mothers." *New England Kitchen: A Monthly Journal of Domestic Science* 2 (1895): 142–43. *Google Books*. Web. 28 December 2013.

———. "How the Bicycle Won Its Way among Women." *Harper's Bazaar* 14 March 1896: 244. *ProQuest: American Periodicals Series Online*. Web. 23 July 2008.

———. "The Outdoor Woman: The American Woman in Action." *Frank Leslie's Popular Monthly* 48.3 (1899): 313–16. *ProQuest: American Periodicals Series Online*. Web. 23 July 2008.

———. "Out-of-Doors M.D." *Good Housekeeping* 28 (1899): 127–30. *Google Books*. Web. 30 December 2013.

———. "Woman's Wheeling Dress." *New York Times* 23 December 1894: 21. *ProQuest Historical Newspapers*. Web. 23 December 2013.

Howe, Julia Ward. *Sex and Education: A Reply to Dr. E. H. Clarke's Sex in Education.* Boston: Roberts Brothers, 1874. *Internet Archive.* Web. 23 July 2015.

"How to Choose a Wheel: Advice for Women Who Want to Ride Bicycles." *New York Times* 19 May 1897: 3. *ProQuest Historical Newspapers.* Web. 23 December 2013.

Hubert, Philip G. "The Bicycle: The Wheel of Today." *Scribner's Magazine* 17 (July 1895): 692–702. Print.

Huntington, Charles. *The Cyclist's Road Book of Connecticut.* Hartford, CT: Brown and Gross, 1890. Print.

Jack, Jordynn. "Acts of Institution: Embodying Feminist Rhetorical Methodologies in Space and Time." *Rhetoric Review* 28.3 (2009): 285–303. Print.

Jackson, Edna C. "A Fin de Cycle Incident." *Outing* 28.3 (June 1896): 192–98. Print.

Jacobi, Mary Putnam. *The Question of Rest for Women during Menstruation.* New York: G. P. Putnam's Sons, 1877. *Internet Archive.* Web. 21 July 2015.

Johnson, Robert R. *User-Centered Technology: A Rhetorical Theory for Computers and Other Mundane Artifacts.* Albany: State University of New York Press, 1998. Print.

Johnson-Eilola, Johndan. "Relocating the Value of Work: Technical Communication in a Post-Industrial Age." *Central Works in Technical Communication.* Ed. Johndan Johnson-Eilola and Stuart Selber. New York: Oxford University Press, 2004. 175–92. Print.

Kelly, Casey. "Women's Rhetorical Agency in the American West: The New Penelope." *Women's Studies in Communication* 32.2 (2009): 203–31. Print.

Kenealy, Arabella. "Woman as an Athlete." *Nineteenth Century* 45 (April 1899): 636–45. Web. *Google Books.* 28 December 2013.

Khan, Zorina. "Not for Ornament: Patenting Activity by Nineteenth-Century Women Inventors." *Journal of Interdisciplinary History* 31.2 (2000): 159–95. Print.

Kimball, Miles. "Cars, Culture, and Tactical Technical Communication." *Technical Communication Quarterly* 15.1 (2006): 57–86. Print.

Kodak. Advertisement. *The Bicycling World and L.A.W. Bulletin* 3 May 1889: 15. *Internet Archive.* Web. 20 July 2015.

Koerber, Amy. "Rhetorical Agency, Resistance, and the Disciplinary Rhetorics of Breastfeeding." *Technical Communication Quarterly* 15:1 (2006): 87–101. Print.

———. "Toward a Rhetoric of Technology" *Journal of Business and Technical Communication* 14.58 (2000): 58–73. Print.

"Misses Cycling Trousers." *Delineator.* September 1895. 313. Print.

"Ladies Ride Neck and Neck." *St. Paul Daily Globe* 11 April 1899: 5. *ProQuest Historical Newspapers.* Web. 23 December 2013.

Latour, Bruno. *Reassembling the Social: An Introduction to Actor-Network Theory.* Oxford, UK: Oxford University Press, 2005. Print.

Lawson, Margaret Hobbs. "Bicycle-garment." Patent 491,057. 31 January 1893.

Lefevre, Karen Burke. *Invention as a Social Act.* Carbondale: Southern Illinois University Press, 1987. Print.

Le Long, Margaret. "Alone and Awheel: From Chicago to San Francisco." *Outing* 31.6 (1898): 592–96. *LA 84*. Web. 22 December 2013.

———. "From Chicago to San Francisco Awheel." *Outing* 31.5 (1898): 492–97. *LA 84*. Web. 22 December 2013.

"Limit to Women's Bicycle Rides." *Evening Star* 9 September 1895: 8. Library of Congress. *Chronicling America: Historic American Newspapers*. Web. 23 December 2013.

Lippincott, Gail. "Rhetorical Chemistry: Negotiating Gendered Audiences in Nineteenth-Century Nutrition Studies." *Journal of Business and Technical Communication* 17:1 (2003): 10–49. Print.

Longo, Bernadette. *Spurious Coin: A History of Science, Management, and Technical Writing*. Albany: State University of New York Press, 2000. Print.

Lutes, Jean Marie. "Beyond the Bounds of the Book: Periodical Studies and Women Writers of the Late 19th and Early 20th Centuries." *Legacy: A Journal of American Women Writers* 27.2 (2010): 336–56. Print.

———. "Into the Madhouse with Nellie Bly: Girl Stunt Reporting in Late Nineteenth-Century America." *American Quarterly* 54.2 (2002): 217–53. Print.

M. B. "The Pleasures of Bicycling." *Outing* 16.1. (1890): 78. *LA 84*. Web. 11 October 2011.

Macdonald, Anne L. *Feminine Ingenuity: Women and Invention in America*. New York: Ballantine Books, 1992. Print.

Macy, Sue. *Wheels of Change: How Women Rode the Bicycle to Freedom*. Washington, DC: National Geographic Society, 2011. Print.

Maik, Thomas, ed. *Fiction by Nineteenth-Century Women Writers: A New England Sampler*. Oxford: Garland Reference Library of the Humanities, 1999. Print.

Majestic Rattan Saddles. Advertisement. *Godey's Magazine* April 1896. Print.

Marks, Patricia. *Bicycles, Bangs, and Bloomers: The New Woman in the Popular Press*. Lexington: University Press of Kentucky, 1990. Print.

Martha. "We Girls Awheel through Germany." *Outing* 20.4 (1892): 298–302. *LA 84*. Web. 22 December 2013.

Martin, Bertha Ellis. "Skirt." Patent 608,469. 2 August 1898.

Mathieu, Paula, and Diana George. "Not Going It Alone: Public Writing, Independent Media, and the Circulation of Homeless Advocacy." *College Composition and Communication* 61.1 (September 2009): 130–49. Print.

Mattingly, Carol. *Appropriate[ing] Dress: Women's Rhetorical Style in Nineteenth-Century America*. Carbondale: Southern Illinois University Press, 2002. Print.

———. *Well-Tempered Women: Nineteenth-Century Temperance Rhetoric*. Carbondale: Southern Illinois University Press, 1998. Print.

McCartney, Elizabeth. "Bicycle garment." Patent 566,004. 18 August 1896.

McClure, S. S. *My Autobiography*. New York: Frederick Unger, 1963. Print.

Mead, Leon. "Women as Inventors." *Chautauquan* 18.4 (1894): 464–67. Print.

Measuring Worth Inflation Calculator. *Measuring Worth*, 2015. Web. 25 July 2015.

Merington, Marguerite. "Woman and the Bicycle." *Scribner's Magazine* 17 (July 1895): 702–4. Print.

Meyers, Charles Lee. "The Jersey City Athletic Club." *Outing* 13.5 (1889): 445–51. Web. *LA 84*. 13 August 2014.

Middletown Wheel Club program. Collection of the Connecticut Historical Society, Hartford. 3 June 2010. Print.

Miller, Caroline E. "Skirt-guard." Patent 600,010. 1 March 1898.

"Miss Gast Stopped." *New York Tribune* 20 October 1900: 5. *Chronicling America: Historic American Newspapers*. Web. 23 July 2015.

"Miss Gast's Cycle Riding" *New York Times* 19 October 1900: 9. *ProQuest: American Periodicals Series Online*. Web. 23 July 2015.

"Miss Lissette in America." *Washington Times* 24 August 1898: 6. *Chronicling America: Historic American Newspapers*. Web. 24 September 2014.

"A Monument to Bloomers." *Los Angeles Herald* 14 July 1895: image 18. Library of Congress. *Chronicling America: Historic American Newspapers*. Web. 18 December 2013.

Moque, Alice Lee. "A Bohemian Couple a-Wheeling through Middle England." *Outing* 29.5 (1897): 460–66. *LA 84*. Web 11 December 2013.

———. "A Bohemian Couple Wheeling thro' Western England." *Outing* 29.3 (1896): 186–91. *LA 84*. Web. 11 December 2013.

Mott, Frank Luther. *A History of American Magazines*. Cambridge, MA: Harvard University Press, 1968. Print.

"Mrs. Lindsay Has 500 Miles." *New York Times* 17 October 1899: 8. *ProQuest Historical Newspapers*. Web. 28 December 2013.

"Mrs. Lindsay's 800 Miles." *New York Times* 19 October 1899: 9. *ProQuest Historical Newspapers*. Web. 28 December 2013.

Myers, Greg. "Discourse Studies of Scientific Popularizations: Questioning the Boundaries." *Discourse Studies* 5.3 (2003): 265–79. *Sage Journals Online*. Web. 1 November 2009.

Naly, Sarah L., and Mary Scott Jones. "Bicycle seat." Patent 499,244. 13 June 1893.

Nash, Francis. "A Plea for the New Woman and the Bicycle." *American Journal of Obstetrics and Diseases of Women and Children* 32 (1896): 556–60. Print.

"The Natty Bicycle Girl." *New York Times* 17 September 1898: 6. *ProQuest: American Periodicals Series Online*. Web. 23 July 2008.

Neeson, Victor. *Dr. Neeson's Book on Wheeling*. New York: New Amsterdam Book Company, 1899. Print.

"Nelson and Baldwin Lead." *New York Sun* 9 January 1896: 4. Library of Congress. *Chronicling America: Historic American Newspapers*. Web. 23 December 2013.

"A New Bicycle Skirt." *New York Times*. 15 October 1893: 18. Print.

"New Saddle Needed: The Present Article Not Suited to Female Riders." *Sporting Life* 26.4 (October 1895): 16. *LA 84*. Web. 19 December 2013. Print.

Newell Saddle Poise. Advertisement. Author's personal collection. Print.

"News and Comments." *The Bicycling World and L.A.W. Bulletin* 5 October 1888: 441. *Internet Archive*. Web. 1 December 2014.

"News and Comments." *The Bicycling World and L.A.W. Bulletin* 26 October 1888: 497. *Internet Archive*. Web. 1 December 2014.

"News and Comments." *The Bicycling World and L.A.W. Bulletin* 10 May 1889: 36. *Internet Archive*. Web. 1 December 2014.

"News and Comments." *The Bicycling World and L.A.W. Bulletin* 10 May 1889: 352. *Internet Archive*. Web. 1 December 2014.

The New Woman: Annie "Londonderry" Kopchovsky. Dir. Gillian Klempner Willman. Spokeswoman Productions, 2013. Web.

"New Woman on a Tour." *Princeton Union* 23 May 1895. Library of Congress. *Chronicling America: Historic American Newspapers*. Web. 17 November 2013.

N. P. Curtice Company Bicycle School. Advertisement. *Lincoln Courier* 11 May 1895: 9. Library of Congress. *Chronicling America: Historic American Newspapers*. Web. 15 August 2013.

Oakley, Frances. "Scientific Saddles." *Harper's Bazaar* 14 March 1896: 29, 11. *ProQuest: American Periodicals Series Online*. Web. 23 July 2008.

Ohmann, Richard. "Where Did Mass Culture Come From? The Case of Magazines." *Berkshire Review* 16 (1981): 85–101. Print.

"The Original Seven." *Evening Star* 18 June 1881: image 2. Library of Congress. *Chronicling America: Historic American Newspapers*. Web. 13 August 2014.

Oudshoorn, Nelly. *How Users Matter: The Co-construction of Users and Technologies*. Cambridge, MA: MIT Press, 2003. Print.

"Our Monthly Record." *Outing* 4.6 (1884): 475. *LA 84*. Web. 20 July 2015.

"The Outdoor Woman." *Harper's Bazaar* 28 September 1895: 786–87. Cornell HEARTH Home Economics Archive. Web. 5 August 2015.

Overman Wheel Company trade catalogs, 1889 and 1890. Chicopee Falls, MA: Overman Wheel Company, 1889–90. Print.

Peck, Mattie. "Bicycle and walking costume." Patent 546,496. 17 September 1895.

Pickering, Andrew. *The Mangle of Practice: Time, Agency, and Science*. Chicago: University of Chicago Press, 1995. Print.

Pope Bicycle and Tricycle. Advertisement. 1885. Web. 23 December 2013.

Pope Columbia Bicycle with Racing Records. Advertisement. Web. 23 December 2013.

Pope Manufacturing Company. *The Bicycle in Relation to Health*. Boston: Pope Manufacturing Company, 1894. Print.

Pope Manufacturing Company Riding Lead. Advertisement. *The Bicycling World and L.A.W. Bulletin* 28 June 1889: 262. Web. *Internet Archive*. 10 January 2015.

Pope Manufacturing Company trade catalog, 1896. Collection of Hagley Museum, Wilmington, DE. Print. 23 June 2008.

Porter, Luther Henry. *Cycling for Health and Pleasure*. New York: Dodd, Mead, 1896. Print.

Pratt, Charles. *The American Bicycler: A Manual for the Observer, the Learner, and the Expert*. Boston: Houghton, Osgood, 1879. Print.

Prendergast, James. "The Bicycle for Women." *American Journal of Obstetrics and Diseases of Women and Children* 34 (1896): 247–53. Print.

Presbrey, Frank. *The History and Development of Advertising.* Garden City, NY: Doubleday, Doran, 1929. Print.

Press Claims Company. Advertisement. *Newark Daily Advocate* 8 July 1895: 3. Web. 23 July 2015.

Prior, Paul, Janine Solberg, Patrick Berry, Hannah Bellwoar, Bill Chewning, Karen Lunsford, Liz Rohan, Kevin Roozen, Mary Sheridan-Rabideau, Jody Shipka, Derek Van Ittersum, and Joyce Walker. "Re-situating and Re-mediating the Canons: A Cultural-Historical Remapping of Rhetorical Activity, a Collaborative Webtext." *Kairos* 11.3 (May 2007). Web. 10 August 2014.

Radway, Janice, and Carl Kaestle, eds. *Print in Motion: The Expansion of Publishing and Reading in the United States, 1880–1940.* Chapel Hill: University of North Carolina Press, 2009. Print.

Rave, Herman. "The Tell-Tale Mirror: A Bicycle Courtship." *Outing* 21.6 (1893): 487–89. *LA 84*. Web. 22 December 2013.

Reynolds, Nedra. "Ethos as Location: New Sites for Understanding Discursive Activity." *Rhetoric Review* 11.2 (1993): 325–38. Print.

Ritchie, Andrew. "The League of American Wheelmen, Major Taylor, and the 'Color Question' in the United States in the 1890s." *Ethnicity, Sport, Identity: Struggles for Status.* Ed. Andrew Ritchie and J. A. Mangan. Portland, OR: Frank Cass, 2004. 13–43. Print.

Rivers, Adeline. "How to Make a Bicycle Suit." *Richmond Times* 2 May 1897: image 9. Library of Congress. *Chronicling America: Historic American Newspapers.* Web. 1 November 2013.

Roosevelt, J. West. "A Doctor's View of Bicycling." *Scribner's Magazine* 17 (July 1895): 708–13. Print.

Rosenberg, Charles E. *The Therapeutic Revolution: Essays in the Social History of American Medicine.* Philadelphia: University of Pennsylvania Press, 1979. Print.

Rosey, George. "Rosey's Scorcher March and Two-Step." Lester S. Levy Sheet Music Collection, Johns Hopkins University, Baltimore. Web. 26 December 2013.

Rotundo, Anthony. *American Manhood: Transformations in Masculinity from the Revolution to the Modern Era.* New York: Basic Books, 1993. Print.

Roys-Gavitt, E. M. "Acute Miliary Tuberculosis." *Woman's Medical Journal* 6 (1897): 323–25. *Internet Archive.* Web. 28 December 2013.

Royster, Jacqueline Jones. *Traces of a Stream: Literacy and Social Change among African American Women.* Pittsburgh: University of Pittsburgh Press, 2000. Print.

Royster, Jacqueline Jones, and Gesa Kirsch. *Feminist Rhetorical Practices: New Horizons for Rhetoric, Composition, and Literacy Studies.* Carbondale: Southern Illinois University Press, 2012. Print.

Sager Manufacturing Company. Advertisement. *Godey's Magazine* April 1896. Print.

"Scenes at a Bicycle School." *New York Tribune* 3 February 1895: 21. Library of Congress. *Chronicling America: Historic American Newspapers*. Web. 15 August 2013.

Scharff, Virginia. *Taking the Wheel: Women and the Coming of the Motor Age*. Albuquerque: University of New Mexico Press, 1992. Print.

Schneirov, Matthew. *The Dream of a New Social Order: Popular Magazines in America, 1893–1914*. New York: Columbia University Press, 1994. Print.

Scott, J. Blake. "Extending Rhetorical Cultural Analysis: Transformations of Home HIV Testing." *College English* 65.4 (2003): 349–67. Print.

Seigel, Marika. "Instructions for Systemic Change." *College Composition and Communication* 61.2 (2009): 76–99. Print.

Selber, Stuart. *Multiliteracies for a Digital Age*. Carbondale: Southern Illinois University Press, 2004. Print.

Setnik, Linda. *Victorian Costume for Ladies, 1860–1900*. Atglen, PA: Schiffer Publishing, 2000. Print.

"Shall She Wear Bloomers?" *New York Sun* 1 September 1895: 5. Library of Congress. *Chronicling America: Historic American Newspapers*. Web. 18 December 2013.

Shelley, Caroline. "A Friend in Need." *Outing* 28.3 (1896): 163–72. *LA 84*. Web. 11 October 2011.

"She Won and Fainted: Miss Roos, a Long Branch Belle, Insensible for Hours." *New York Times* 29 July 1896: 2. *ProQuest Historical Newspapers*. Web. 29 December 2013.

Simonds, William Edgar. *Practical Hints on the Sale of Patents*. Hartford: privately printed, 1871. Print.

Sittig, Lena. "Skirt protecting garment." Patent 532,601. 22 May 1894.

Skinner, Carolyn. "Incompatible Rhetorical Expectations: Julia W. Carpenter's Medical Society Papers, 1895–1899." *Technical Communication Quarterly* 21.4 (2012): 307–24. Print.

Smith, Minna Caroline. "The Ladies Tour to Kettle Cove." *Outing* 7.4. (1886): 431–36. *LA 84*. Web. 11 October 2011.

———. "The Tricycle for American Women." *Outing* 5.6. (1885): 423–25. *LA 84*. Web. 11 October 2011.

———. "Women as Cyclers." *Outing* 6.3. (1885): 317–21. *LA 84*. Web. 11 October 2011.

Smith, Robert A. *A Social History of the Bicycle*. New York: American Heritage Press, 1972. Print.

Spaulding trade catalog, 1895. Collection of Hagley Museum, Wilmington, DE. Print.

SPIN. Dir. Evalyn Parry. Thalian Hall, Wilmington, NC, 4 April 2013. Performance.

Spinuzzi, Clay. *Tracing Genres through Organizations: A Sociocultural Approach to Information Design*. Cambridge, MA: MIT Press, 2003. Print.

Starr, Paul. *The Creation of the Media: Political Origins of Modern Communications*. New York: Basic Books, 2006. Print.

Steele, Marion. "On the Ladies' Wheel." *The Bicycling World and L.A.W. Bulletin* 11 April 1890: 563. *Internet Archive*. Web. 12 August 2014.

Stevens, Frances. "Women as Inventors." *Frank Leslie's Popular Monthly* 32 (1891): 234–38. *Google Books*. Web. 29 December 2013.

"Still a Wheel's Length Apart." *New York Sun* 10 January 1896. Library of Congress. *Chronicling America: Historic American Newspapers*. Web. 23 December 2013.

"Still the Wheelwoman: A Talk for the Daily Increasing Army of Beginners." *New York Times* 25 August 1895: 21. *ProQuest Historical Newspapers*. Web. 23 December 2013.

Stormer, Nathan. "Articulation: A Working Paper on Rhetoric and Taxis." *Quarterly Journal of Speech* 90 (2004): 257–84. Print.

Tally Ho Bicycle Lantern. Advertisement. Collection of the Connecticut Historical Society, Hartford. Print.

"The Tam: A Hat." *San Francisco Call* 29 May 1898: 27. Library of Congress. *Chronicling America: Historic American Newspapers*. Web. 1 November 2013.

Tebeaux, Elizabeth. *The Emergence of a Tradition: Technical Writing in the English Renaissance, 1475–1640*. Amityville, NY: Baywood, 1997. Print.

Thanet, Octave. "The Stout Miss Hopkins's Bicycle." *Different Girls: Harper's Novelettes*. Ed. William Dean Howells and Henry Mills Alden. New York: Harper and Brothers Publishers, 1906. 159–95. Print.

Thayer, George. *Pedal and Path: Across the Continent Awheel and Afoot*. Hartford: Evening Post Association, 1887. Print.

Tobin, Gary Allan. "The Bicycle Boom of the 1890s: The Development of Private Transportation and the Birth of the Modern Tourist." *Journal of Popular Culture* 7.4 (1974): 838–49. Print.

Townsend, Charles W. "Bicycling for Women." *Boston Medical and Surgical Journal* 132.24 (1895): 593–95. Print.

"Tricycle Notes." *The Bicycling World* 5 October 1883: 289. *Internet Archive*. Web. 12 August 2014.

Twain, Mark. *The Jumping Frog and Other Stories*. White Plains, NY: Peter Pauper Press, 1985. Print.

Tyng, Emma Moffett. "Exercise for Women: Bicycle and Tricycle." *Harper's Bazaar* 9 August 1890: 614. *ProQuest: American Periodicals Series Online*. Web. 10 October 2009.

———. "Exercise for Women: Walking." *Harper's Bazaar* 12 July 1890: 546. *ProQuest: American Periodicals Series Online*. Web. 10 October 2009.

Underwood, Bert, and E. Underwood. "The New Woman—Wash Day." Stereograph. 1901. Web. 20 May 2013.

Vertinsky, Patricia. *The Eternally Wounded Woman: Women, Doctors, and Exercise in the Late Nineteenth Century*. New York: St. Martin's Press, 1990. Print.

Victor Bicycles. Advertisement. *Godey's Magazine* April 1896. Print.

Voorhis, Eliza. "Cycling skirt." Patent 584,909. 22 June 1897.

Wajcman, Judy. *Feminism Confronts Technology*. Cambridge, MA: Polity Press, 1991. Print.

———. *Technofeminism*. Malden, MA: Polity Press, 2004. Print.

Ward, Maria E. *The Common Sense of Bicycling: Bicycling for Ladies.* New York: Brentano's, 1896. Print.

Wells, Susan. *Out of the Dead House: Nineteenth Century Women Physicians and the Writing of Medicine.* Madison: University of Wisconsin Press, 2001. Print.

Westfield Athletic Club Minute Book, 1885–1892. Rutgers University Special Collections and University Archives, Rutgers, NJ. Print.

"What Shall the New Woman Wear, Skirts or Bloomers?" *Los Angeles Herald* 15 September 1895: 14. Library of Congress. *Chronicling America: Historic American Newspapers.* Web. 29 August 2014.

Willard, Frances. *A Wheel within a Wheel: How I Learned to Ride the Bicycle.* New York: F. H. Revell Company, 1895. Print.

Winograd, Terry, and Fernando Flores. *Understanding Computers and Cognition: A New Foundation for Design.* New York: Addison-Wesley, 1987. Print.

Winsor, Dorothy. "Using Writing to Structure Agency: An Examination of Engineers' Practice." *Technical Communication Quarterly* 15.4 (2006): 411–30. Print.

"With the Return of the Cycling Season." *Chicago Eagle* 9 April 1898: 2. Library of Congress. *Chronicling America: Historic American Newspapers.* Web. 26 December 2013.

"Woman on a Wheel." *Philipsburg Mail* 6 June 1895: image 1. Library of Congress. *Chronicling America: Historic American Newspapers.* Web. 26 December 2013.

"The Woman's Bicycle Race." *New York Sun* 6 January 1896: image 9. Library of Congress. *Chronicling America: Historic American Newspapers.* Web. 23 December 2013.

"Women as Inventors." *Kansas City Daily Journal* 22 May 1895. Library of Congress. *Chronicling America: Historic American Newspapers.* Web. 26 March 2013.

"Women on Wheels: They Are Likely Soon to Discard Skirts While on the Road." *Provo (UT) Evening Dispatch* 21 July 1894. Library of Congress. *Chronicling America: Historic American Newspapers.* Web. 26 March 2013.

Wood, John Seymour. "A Dangerous Sidepath: A Story of the Wheel." *Outing* 2.3 (1893): 209–14. *LA 84.* Web. 22 December 2013.

"The World Awheel." *Munsey's Magazine* (May 1896): 131–59. Print.

"You Can Ride a Tricycle." Overman Tricycle Advertisement. Hagley Museum, Wilmington, DE. Print.

Zheutlin, Peter. *Around the World on Two Wheels: Annie Londonderry's Extraordinary Ride.* New York: Citadel Press Books, 2007. Print.

Zuckerman, Mary Ellen. *A History of Popular Women's Magazines in the United States, 1792–1995.* Westport, CT: Greenwood Press, 1998. Print.

Index

Italicized page numbers indicate figures.

access to technology, 165, 171, 173
Acme Belle bicycle, 27
Acme Bicycle Company, 27
activity theory, 20
actor-network theory (ANT), xx
"Acute Miliary Tuberculosis" (Roys-Gavitt), 140
advertising, 75–76, 79, 112; agential orientation toward, 172–73; specific ads, *9*, *13*, *25*, *26*, *27*, *55*, *76*, *77*; supported by fiction, 79–80
aesthetics of bicycle, 28, 46
African Americans, 155–56, 181n2, 182n1 (chap. 4)
agency, xxv; material networks and, 3–4, 100; user, 41–42, 65–67. *See also* rhetorical agency; technofeminist rhetorical agency
age of invention, 38–42
"Alone" (Le Long), 97–98
American Bicycle Company, 167
American Bicycler, The (Pratt), 6
American Eagle ("reverse" Ordinary), 21–22
American Journal of Obstetrics and Diseases of Women and Children, 53, 139
American Medical Association, 137
anecdotes, representative, 88
ANT (actor-network theory), xx
Anthony, Susan B., 168
anti-bloomer clubs, 42–43
Applegarth, Risa, 72, 138
Ariel Cycle Manufacturing Company, 28
Armaindo, Louise, 152
Associated Cycling Clubs of New York, 157–58, 159
autonomy, 18, 103, 128

Baldwin, Helen (racer), 154–55
Bannon, Dr. Theresa, 53
Banta, Martha, 35
Barad, Karen, 151
Barnes, Dr. Ida C., 140
Barton, Ben, 106
Barton, Marthalee, 106
Bates, Arlo, 19
Battenberg, Effie, 62
Bell, Ida Trafford, 111–13, 119, 122, 179–80n6
Bennitt, Alice A., 62–63
"bent up" handlebars, 26–27
bicycle. *See* Ordinary bicycle (high-wheeled bicycle); Safety bicycle
bicycle bang, 41
bicycle belt, 41
bicycle clubs, xxii, xxiii, 6–7, 29, 169, 180n2; Safety-based, 23; women's, xxiv, 170; women tricyclists gain access to, 14–15, 169
bicycle craze of 1890s, 28–32; legacy of, 167–68
bicycle face, 60–62

bicycle girl, xxiv, 68–70, 169; advertising, 75–76, *76*, *77*; as commentator, 87–93; courtship, representations of, 68–70; in fiction, 78, 79–87, 169; rise of, 99–100; women's constructions of, 72–73
Bicycle in Relation to Health, The (Zakrzewski), 141
"Bicycle Race, The" (Herman), 69
Bicycling and Health for Women (Hall), 141
bicycling culture, 8, 11–12, 168; objects and accoutrements, 29–30
"Bicycling for Girls: A Word to Mothers" (Hopkins), 148
Bicycling for Women (Bell), 111–13, 119, 121
Bicycling World and L.A.W. Bulletin, The, 17, 18, 23, 29; on women's riding technique, 31, 32
Bijker, Wiebe, 7, 8, 20, 180n7
Bisland, Mary, 91
bloomer balls, 43, 69
bloomers, 28, 35, 42–43, 45
Blumen, Elsa von, 152
Bly, Nellie, 179n1
bodily economy: commonplaces about women's fragility, xxiv–xxv, 132–36, 138, 143, 146–50, 155, 158–59, 162–65, 169; older metaphor, 142–43; renewable, 142–49; as system versus body parts, 141, 143
"Bohemian Couple Wheeling thro' Western England, A" (Moque), 93–94, 95
Boston Medical and Surgical Journal, 139
Bourdieu, Pierre, 6
Bradley, Will, 75, *76*
British Medical Journal, 59
Burke, Kenneth, 72, 88, 150–51
Bush, Irene (rider), 159
Butler, Judith, 150
Butterick Pattern Company, 44, 50
cameras, 29
Capital Bicycle Club (Washington, DC), 7, 8, 10, 180n2; Anniversary Literary Exercises, 15, 22; courtship activities, 15; rules for social engagements, 30
Cassell's Magazine, 17–18
Century Road Club of America (Chicago, IL), 157
century runs, 155–59, 166
channels of distribution, 170
Chant, Laura Ormiston, 133
Charland, Maurice, 103
CHAT (cultural-historical activity theory), xx
Chautauquan, 39–40
choice, rhetoric of, 45–46, 49
Christoph, Julie Nelson, 72, 87
Clarke, Dr. Edward H., 132, 133, 134, 139–40, 141
clothing (bicycle dress), xxi, 34, 37, 42–52, *51*, 111, 120; artifacts, 50–51; bicycle and walking costume, 46–48; bifurcated garments, 46, *47*; bloomers, 28, 35, 42–43, 45, 48, *49*; convertible garments, 48–49, *49*; dress guards, 25, *25*, 43; duplex skirt, 48–49, 65, 67; knickerbocker, 45; pattern catalogs, 49; racers and, 154; saddle cushions, 58; skirt-protecting garment, 48–49. *See also* design problems
clubhouses, 4, 14–15
Clyde, Henry, 107–8, 111–12, 114–15
Coleman, Ada, 42
collected rhetorical activities, 170–71
Colt Bicycle Club (Connecticut), 30
Columbia bicycle, 8, *9*
Columbia Ladies' Safety, 24–25, 28
commentators, women as, 87–93. *See also* medical commentators
commonplaces about women and bicycle, xx, 90, 93, 98; design problems and, 36–37; health improvement, 11; limited bodily economy, xxiv–xxv,

132–36, 138, 143, 146–50, 155, 158–59, 162–65, 169; medical practitioners constrained to, 138–39; saddles, 37, 52–53; separate "natures," 14, 28
Common Sense of Bicycling, The: Bicycling for Ladies (Ward), 121–26, 129, 130
company of other women, 121–23
competition: century runs, 155–59; racers, xxv, 150–56, 182n1 (chap. 4); women tricyclists, 18–19
Comstock, Flora Lincoln, 84–85, 91
Condit, Celeste, 136
consumers/users, 77–78
Cooper, Marilyn, xviii, 67
Cooter, Roger, 143
cosmetics, 60
counternarratives, 56–58, 61, 92–93, 102; written instruction, 114, 121, 127. *See also* medical commentators
courtship, bicycle, 12, 68–70, 93; bicycle clubs and, 14–15; in fiction, 79–87
Coville, Dr. Luzerne, 141
Cowan, Ruth Schwartz, 34
criticism and ridicule, 31–32, 42, 69–71; commentators on, 88–89; negative representations of women learning to ride, 104–6
crossbar models, 25–26, *26*
cultural-historical activity theory (CHAT), xx
cultural scripts, 150
cultural studies, xviii–xx, 175
culture of bicycling, xxii
Cyclists' Road Book of Connecticut, 29–30

Dacre, Harry, 68–69, 70
"Daisy Bell" (Dacre), 68–69, 70
Damascus Gentlemen's Model A, *26*
Damascus Ladies' Model D, *25*
Damascus trade catalog, 27, *27*
"Dangerous Sidepath, A: A Story of the Wheel" (Wood) 80
dangers of the bicycle, 7, 8, 21–22
Davidson, Lillias Campbell, 104, 126–28
decadent athleticism, 150–51
de Certeau, Michel, 36–37, 50, 102
Delineator, 44, 50
delivery systems, 175
Demorest's, 44
Denison, Grace E., 88–89, 90, 96–97, 145
deportment, rhetoric of, xxiv, 102
design problems, 36–38; alteration and adjustment, 46–48; collaborative approach, 45, 66; contemporary understandings, 7–8; face protection, 60–65; function and fashion, 45, 46–47; rhetoric of choice, 45–46, 49; saddles, 52–59, *55*, *56*. *See also* clothing (bicycle dress)
diamond frame bicycle, 25, *26*, 27, 34, 44, 58
Dickinson, Dr. Robert, 53–54
Dieterich, Fred G., 38, 39
District Cycle Company Bicycle School, 105
domestic duties, 70–71, *71*, 90–91
double tricycles, 15
dress guards, 25, *25*, 43
Dr. Neeson's Book on Wheeling (Neeson), 109–11, 112, 113
drop bars, 27
drop frame, 25–26, 33–34

Eclipse Bicycle catalog, 26–27
Eclipse Racer, 27
Eclipse Special, 27
education, 132
embodied acts, xvi, xxiii, 66–67, 130–31
embodied medical authority, women's: century runs, reporting on, 155–59; perspective by incongruity, 150–51, 155; six-day races, 153–57; women as embodied practitioners, 135–36. *See also* medical commentators

endurance riders, xxv, 150–51; Margaret Gast, 160–63, *161*
entertainment model, 74
ethos, 72, 73, 129, 169
Everett, Edith Townsend, 45, 145–46
"Exercise for Women: Tricycle and Bicycle" (Tyng), 143–44
"Exercise for Women: Walking" (Tyng), 144–45
exhibition riders, 2
experts, women as, 57, 95–98, 104, 114–15, 171; direct instruction, 120–21, 126

face protection, 35–36, 37, 60–65; gauze net, 62, 64; parasols/umbrellas, 60, 62–63, 65
Fahnestock, Jeanne, 142
Feminist Rhetorical Practices (Royster and Kirsch), xxii
fiction, 78, 79–87, 169; by men, 79–80; woman-authored, 80–87
"Fin de Cycle Incident, A" (Jackson), 85–87
Finnegan, Cara, 35
fit between user and technology, 36, 41
Follett, Helen, 94–95
Ford, Henry, 167
Foy, Lavinia, 40
Frank Leslie's Popular Monthly, 147
"Friend in Need, A" (Shelley), 81–82, 83, 89

Garvey, Ellen Gruber, 71, 76, 78, 79
Gast, Margaret, 160–63, *161*
gender order: denaturalization of, 136, 143, 150, 169; materialized, xxi, 3–4, 12, 16, 25, 29, 34; positive impact on, 118–19; undermined by bicycle craze, 29, 32
gender scripts, 5, 13–14, 169; blurred, 23–24, 25; challenges to, 17; handlebar options, 25–26, *27*; manufacturers and, 22–23; women tricyclists deviate from, 19–20
gender socialization, xxi
George, Diana, 174–75
Gibson, Charles Dana, 75
Gibson Girl, 75
Godey's Magazine, 61, 62, 75; bicycling issue, 84, 91
Gordon, Dr. Mary, 59
Gordon, Sarah, 44, 50
Graham, S. Scott, xvi
Grammar of Motives, A (Burke), 88
Gray, Dr. Sarah, 59
group identity, 103, 116, 128, 129, 130, 169
Guertin, Florence, 82–84
Gunby, Olive, 40

habitus, 5–6
Hall, Dr. Lucy, 141, 142, 179–80n6
Hall, Ruth, 1–2, 6, 16
Handbook for Lady Cyclists (Davidson), 126–28
handlebar options, 25–26, *27*
Harper's Bazaar, 45, 56, 143–45
Hartford Ladies Bicycle Club (Connecticut), 130
Heineke, Grace T., 43
Henderson, Mary Foote, 57–58
Herlihy, David, 28–29
Herman, Ella, 69
Herndl, Carl, xvi, 3
Herrick, Christine Terhune, 60
Hicks, Mary, 62–63, *63*
historically contingent rhetorical resources, 35, 166, 173, 174
History and Development of Advertising, The (Presbrey), 76
honeymoon narratives, 30, 93–95
"Honeymoon on Wheels" (Follett), 94–95
Hopkins, Mary Sargent ("Merrie Wheeler"), 146–49
hotels, 30
house magazines, 84, 87

"How to Choose a Wheel: Advice for Women Who Want to Ride Bicycles," 130
"How We Ride Our Wheels" (Denison), 88–89, 90, 96, 145
Hummel, Tillie (rider), 158–59, 164

ideological/institutional structures, xvi–xvii
image vernaculars, 35
immigrant women, 152
incongruity, perspective by, 150–51, 155, 162–63, 165
indoor bicycle schools, 105
inner tubes, 21
Internet, 171–72
interpretive flexibility, 20
invention of bicycle, women's involvement in, 33–67; accoutrements and tools, 34–35; context of use, xx, 37; feminization of inventors, 65–66; fit between user and technology, 36, 41; patents, 34–35; small innovations, 37, 39–40; successful women, 40–41; tactical and strategic behavior, 36–38. *See also* clothing (bicycle dress); design problems
Inventor's Universal Educator, The (Dieterich), 38

Jackson, Edna C., 85–87
Jacobi, Dr. Mary Putnam, 133
Jersey City Athletic Club, 14–15
Johnson, Robert R., xx, 171
Johnson-Eilola, Johndan, xix
Jones, Mary Scott, 55, *56*, 58

Kaestle, Carl, 78
Kelly, Casey, 73
Kenealy, Dr. Arabella, 61, 133–34, 136, 141
Khan, Zorina, 38, 40
Kimball, Miles, xix, 102
Kirsch, Gesa, xxii
knickerbocker, 45
know-how, arts of, 171
Knox, Kittie (racer), 155–56, 182n1 (chap. 4)
Koerber, Amy, xvii, 37
Kopchovsky, Annie "Londonderry," xi–xvi, 28, 175, 179n2

Ladies' Eclipse bicycle, 25
Ladies' Tricycle Club of New York City, 12
Latour, Bruno, xxi
Lawson, Henry, 181n5
Lawson, Margaret Hobbs, 46, *47*, 58
League of American Wheelmen, 4, 6, 12, 167; African Americans barred, 155–56; Safety bicycles at parade, 23; women barred, 156–57
Lefevre, Karen Burke, 72
Le Long, Margaret, 97–98
Licona, Adela, xvi, 3
life, bicycling as metaphor for, 116–17
Lindsay, Jane (rider), 159–60
Londonderry, Annie, xi–xvi, 28, 175, 179n2
Longo, Bernadette, xviii, 102–3
low-mount bicycles, 21
Lutes, Jean Marie, 78

Macdonald, Anne L., 181–82n2
Madison Square Garden, 155
magazines, popular, xxiv, 69–100, 169; bicycle girl, rise of, 99–100; bicycle issues, 76, 84, 89–90; commentators, 87–93; entertainment model, 74; fiction, 78, 79–87; irreverent attitude, 71, 74–75; rise of, 73–78; travel narratives, 77, 93–99
maintenance, 117–18, 120, 123–25, *125*; tire repair, 127
"Making of a Woman's Bicycle, The" (Bisland), 91–92
mannishness, 35, 36, 42

manufacturers, 167; during bicycle craze of 1890s, 29; gender scripts and, 22–23; medical commentators, 141; reluctance to promote Safety, 23–24. *See also* Overman Wheel Company; Pope Manufacturing Company
Marks, Patricia, 69
Martin, Bertha Ellis, 58
masculinity, 180n7, 181n3; falling, approval of, 5, 8, 22; male sense of superiority, 118–19; Ordinary bicycle associated with, 2–3, 7; threatened by bicycling woman, 70
material associations, 72
material-discursive practices, 151
material-rhetorical networks, xvi–xvii, xxi–xxii, 3–4, 42, 66, 166, 168
Mathieu, Paula, 174–75
Mattingly, Carol, 116, 181n1
McCartney, Elizabeth, 58
McClure, S. S., 77–78, 182n1 (chap. 2)
Mead, Leon, 39–40
medical commentators, xxiv–xxv, 53, 59, 169; bicycle and rise of scientific medicine, 136–42; bicycle as medical technology, 139–40; embodied arguments, women's, 149–63; on limited energy of women, 132–35; manufacturing company pamphlets, 141; mixed endorsements, 134; modern women, focus on, 144–45; public effect on, 136; reader as capable, 143–49; on reproductive function of women, 132–34; women commentators on renewable bodily economy, 142–49. *See also* embodied medical authority, women's
medical journals, 138–39
medical practitioners: clinical terminology, 139–40; limitations on opinions, 138–40, 149, 163; professional conferences, 137–38; rise of scientific medicine, 136–42; scarcity, rhetorical, 138, 142, 163–64
Merington, Marguerite, 89–91, 92
"Merrie Wheeler" (Mary Sargent Hopkins), 146–49
Miller, Caroline E., 43
mixed groups, 30–31
modern concepts: as desirable, xiii, 7–8, 11, 75; maladies, 5, 11, 60, 136–37. *See also* advertising; courtship, bicycle
Moque, Alice Lee, 93–94, 95
morals, 35–37, 42, 59–61, 147, 158–59; in popular magazine articles, 70–71, 73–75
"Morbid Conditions Complicating Menopause" (Barnes), 140
Munsey, Frank, 74
Munsey's Magazine, 33, 35, 37, 65, 74
Myers, Greg, 136

Naly, Sarah L., 55, 56, 58
Nash, Dr. Francis, 134, 136–37
"Natty Bicycle Girl, The," 70
nature, appreciation of, 75, 147; in fiction, 80, 81, 84, 87, 89, 92; in travel narratives, 96
Neeson, Dr. Victor, 109–11, 112, 113
Nelson, Frankie (racer), 154–55
neurasthenia, 5, 11
Newell Manufacturing Company, 54
New England Kitchen, 148
New Ideas, 39
"New Saddle Needed: The Present Article Not Suited to Female Riders," 52
newspapers, 73–74
New Woman on Tour, The (Kopchovsky), xi–xvi
"New Woman—Wash Day, The," 70–71, *71*
New York Times, 101; on endurance riders, 163, 160–62; "How to Choose a Wheel," 130; "Still the Wheelwoman," 119–21
N. P. Curtice Company Bicycle School, 105

Oakley, Dr. Frances, 56–57
objects and accoutrements, 29–30
Ohmann, Richard, 74
older riders, 10, 21, 101, 108
"Only a Girl" (Hall), 1–2
Ordinary bicycle (high-wheeled bicycle), xx, xxiii, 169, 179n3, 180n1; incompatibility with tricycle, 16–20; as masculine object, 2–3, 7; small and stable network, 4–9; vibration-cushioning height, 21
Oudshoorn, Nelly, 5, 17, 20
"Outdoor Woman, The: The American Woman in Action" (Hopkins), 147–48
Outing, 1–2, 10, 12, 76–78, 182n1 (chap. 2); article on women at bicycle clubs, 14–15; "How We Ride Our Wheels," 88–89; "The Ladies Tour to Kettle Cove," 19; travel narratives, 94–96; on two-seated tricycle, 17–18; "Women as Cyclers," 17
"Out-of-Doors M.D." (Hopkins), 146–47
outsider rhetorical resources, 173
Overman, A. H., 167
Overman Wheel Company, 11–12, 75, 76, *77*, 167; health pamphlets, 141
Owen, H. S., 7, 15

parasols/umbrellas, 60, 62–63, 65
patents, xxiii, 33–35; application procedures, 38–39. *See also* clothing (bicycle dress); design problems; saddles
payment plans, 29
Peck, Mattie, 46–48
performative regimes, 4
personification of bicycle, 117–18
Pinch, Trevor, 7, 8, 180n7
"Plea for the New Woman and the Bicycle, A" (Nash), 134, 136–37
Pleasure-Cycling (Clyde), 107–8, 111–12, 114–15
poetic imagery, 89
politicization of bicycle, 103, 129
Pope, Albert, 6, 107, 167, 181n5
Pope Manufacturing Company, 8, 9, 91; advertisements, 12, *13*, 13–14, 24; Columbia Ladies' Safety, 24–25; manuals, 111
posture, 26–27, 54, 58
Practical Hints on the Sale of Patents (Simonds), 38
practical riding, 22
Pratt, Charles, 6
Prendergast, Dr. James, 53, 139
Presbrey, Frank, 75
present-at-hand relationship, 20
Press Claims Company, 38, 40
print culture, 78, 100, 170
Prior, Paul, xxi
public nature of riding, 32, 59, 66, 70, 162, 164, 166
Pumfrey, Stephen, 143

Québécois, 103
Question of Rest during Menstruation, The (Jacobi), 133

racers, xxv, 150–56, 182n1 (chap. 4). *See also* endurance riders
racing bars, 26
Radway, Janice, 78
railroad era, 7
Rave, Herman, 79–80
Reich, Robert, xix
repair stations, 30
repetition, 170
representative anecdotes, 88
responsibility, sense of, 173–74
Reynolds, Nedra, 72
rhetorical agency, xvi–xviii, 66–67, 89, 172
rhetorical scarcity, 138, 142
riding lessons, 32, 108–9; indoor bicycle schools, 101–2, 105–6, 122; ownership of learning process, 119–20
Rivers, Adeline, 64

Riverside Cycling Club (Boston, MA), 155
roads, 4–5, 7, 95, 167
Roos, Miss (racer), 152–53
Roosevelt, Dr. J. West, 134
"Rosalind A-wheel" (Comstock), 84–85, 91
Rosey, George, 69
Rotundo, Anthony, 5
Rouse, Hazard, and Company, 29
Roys-Gavitt, Dr. E. M., 140
Royster, Jacqueline Jones, xxii

saddles, 37, 52–59, *55*, *56*; attachment design, 57–58; counternarrative, 56–58; immorality and, 53–54
Safety bicycle, xviii, xx–xxi, xxiii, 3, 8, 169, 179n3, 181n5; emergence of, 21–28
Sager Manufacturing Company, 54, *55*
Sager saddle, 54, *55*
scarcity, rhetorical, 138, 142, 163–64
"Scenes at a Bicycle School," 105
Scientific American, 40
"Scorcher March and Two-Step" (Rosey), 69
scorching, 26, 53, 89
SCOT (social construction of technology), 180n7
Scribner's Magazine, 89–90, 91, 134
secondhand machines, 29
Seigel, Marika, 104, 114–15
self-sufficiency, 121, 123–26, 129, 164
separate spheres, 2, 69, 168
Sex in Education; or, A Fair Chance for Girls (Clarke), 132, 133, 134
sexuality: facial expression and, 60–61; saddle and, 53–54, *55*, 58, 59
Shelley, Caroline, 81–82, *83*, 89
Simonds, William Edgar, 38
Sittig, Lena, 48–49, 65, 67, 173, 181–82n2
six-day races, 153–57, 166
Skinner, Carolyn, 137–38
Smith, Charlotte, 31
Smith, Minna Caroline, 2–3, 10, 17, 19–20
Smith, W. E., 32
sociable (two-seated tricycle), 17–18, 22
social change, 32, 72, 165, 170, 172–73
social construction of technology (SCOT), 180n7
solitary riding, 84, 119–20
songs, 68–69
speed discrepancy, 17
Sporting Life, 52
stakeholders, 36
Staples, Kittie (racer), 154
Starr, Paul, 74
Staten Island Bicycle Club, 121
Steele, Marion, 17, 31
Sterling men's bicycle, 28
"Still the Wheelwoman: A Talk for the Daily Increasing Army of Beginners," 101–2, 119–20
St. Louis Wheel Company, 29
Stormer, Nathan, 4, 166
"Stout Miss Hopkins's Bicycle, The" (Thanet), 104, 109
strategic behavior, 36–38, 67
stunt reporting, 179n1
stunts and challenges, 7
surveys, medical, 139
system-disrupting strategies, 104, 114–15

tactical behavior, 36–38, 50–52, 67, 102
tam-o'-shanter cap, 64
tandem bicycles, 4, 68–69
Taylor, Major (racer), 182n1 (chap. 4)
technical communication, xviii–xx, xxv, 130–31; historically situated practice, 102–3; narrativity of, 106–7
technofeminist rhetorical agency, 167–75; agential orientation, 172–73; responsibility, sense of, 173–74; writing as constitutive of technical object, 172, 174
technological scripting, 23–24
technological systems, 34, 37, 67

technology, xxii, xxv, 168; regulation by, 20; technological scripting, 23–24
technology user role, 103
"Tell-Tale Mirror, The: A Bicycle Courtship" (Rave), 79–80
Thanet, Octave, 104, 109
"then and now" shift, 91–92
tires, 21, 127
Titania bicycle, 28
tour books, 29–30
touring bars, 26
Townsend, Dr. Charles W., 139
transportation, bicycles as, 46, 127–28
travel narratives, 77, 93–99, 169; contrast, 94–95; like-mindedness with husbands, 93–94; toughness of riders, 96–98
tricycle, xxii, 2–4, 169; advertising and gender, 11; competition, 18–19; deviation from gender script and, 19–20; double, 15; as genteel and health-bringing, 10–16; incompatibility with Ordinary, 16–20; patterns of use, 16; role in promoting Safety bicycle, 8–9; tours, 19; two-seated (sociable), 17–18, 22
"Tricycle for American Women, The" (Smith), 2–3, 10
Twain, Mark, 4–5, 12
Tyng, Emma Moffett, 143–45

urgency, rhetoric of, 53
user agency, 41–42, 65–67
US Patent and Trade Office, 38, 45–46

Victoria Ladies Safety, 24
Voorhis, Eliza, 48, *49*

Wajcman, Judy, xxii, 168
Ward, Maria E., xxiv, 104, 121–26, 129, 130, 173
weddings, 69
"We Girls Awheel through Germany" ("Martha"), 95–96
Well, Jeannette (racer), 152–53
"Wheel of Time, The" (Guertin), 82–84
Wheelman, The, 76–77
Wheel within a Wheel, A: How I Learned to Ride the Bicycle (Willard), 115–20
Wheelwoman, 146
"wheelwomen," public of, 103
Willard, Frances, xxiv, 19, 20, 104, 172; *A Wheel within a Wheel*, 115–20
Winsor, Dorothy, xvi–xvii
"Woman and the Bicycle" (Merington), 89–91, 92
"Woman as an Athlete" (Kenealy), 61
Woman's Christian Temperance Union, 116
"Woman's Cycle" (Bisland), 91–92
Woman's Medical Journal, 140
"Women as Cyclers" (Smith), 17
Wood, John Seymour, 80
Wordsworth, William, 90
working women, 34, 46, 67, 92, 127–28
"World Is Too Much with Us, The" (Wordsworth), 90
written instructions, xviii–xix, xxiv, 102–31, 169; change, instructions for, 129–31; direct strategies, 126–28; expertise of women, 121–28; implicit representations of women in male-authored, 106–14; male-authored, 103–4, 106–14; for Ordinary, 107; reader empowerment, 104; woman-authored, 103–4, 114–28

Yatman, Jane (rider), 159–60

Zakrzewski, Dr. Marie, 141
Zuckerman, Mary Ellen, 79

Sarah Hallenbeck is an assistant professor of English at the University of North Carolina Wilmington, where she teaches courses in rhetoric and composition and professional communication. Her previous work has appeared in *Rhetoric Review*, *Rhetoric Society Quarterly*, and *Technical Communication Quarterly*, among other journals.

Studies in Rhetorics and Feminisms

Studies in Rhetorics and Feminisms seeks to address the interdisciplinarity that rhetorics and feminisms represent. Rhetorical and feminist scholars want to connect rhetorical inquiry with contemporary academic and social concerns, exploring rhetoric's relevance to current issues of opportunity and diversity. This interdisciplinarity has already begun to transform the rhetorical tradition as we have known it (upper-class, agonistic, public, and male) into regendered, inclusionary rhetorics (democratic, dialogic, collaborative, cultural, and private). Our intellectual advancements depend on such ongoing transformation.

Rhetoric, whether ancient, contemporary, or futuristic, always inscribes the relation of language and power at a particular moment, indicating who may speak, who may listen, and what can be said. The only way we can displace the traditional rhetoric of masculine-only, public performance is to replace it with rhetorics that are recognized as being better suited to our present needs. We must understand more fully the rhetorics of the non-Western tradition, of women, of a variety of cultural and ethnic groups. Therefore, Studies in Rhetorics and Feminisms espouses a theoretical position of openness and expansion, a place for rhetorics to grow and thrive in a symbiotic relationship with all that feminisms have to offer, particularly when these two fields intersect with philosophical, sociological, religious, psychological, pedagogical, and literary issues.

The series seeks scholarly works that both examine and extend rhetoric, works that span the sexes, disciplines, cultures, ethnicities, and sociocultural practices as they intersect with the rhetorical tradition. After all, the recent resurgence of rhetorical studies has been not so much a discovery of new rhetorics as a recognition of existing rhetorical activities and practices, of our newfound ability and willingness to listen to previously untold stories.

The series editors seek both high-quality traditional and cutting-edge scholarly work that extends the significant relationship between rhetoric and feminism within various genres, cultural contexts, historical periods, methodologies, theoretical positions, and methods of delivery (e.g., film and hypertext to elocution and preaching).

Queries and submissions:
Professor Cheryl Glenn, Editor
E-mail: cjg6@psu.edu
Professor Shirley Wilson Logan, Editor
E-mail: slogan@umd.edu

Studies in Rhetorics and Feminisms
Department of English
142 South Burrowes Bldg.
Penn State University
University Park, PA 16802-6200

Other Books in the Studies in Rhetorics and Feminisms Series

A Feminist Legacy: The Rhetoric and Pedagogy of Gertrude Buck
Suzanne Bordelon

Regendering Delivery: The Fifth Canon and Antebellum Women Rhetors
Lindal Buchanan

Rhetorics of Motherhood
Lindal Buchanan

Conversational Rhetoric: The Rise and Fall of a Women's Tradition, 1600–1900
Jane Donawerth

Feminism beyond Modernism
Elizabeth A. Flynn

Women and Rhetoric between the Wars
Edited by Ann George, M. Elizabeth Weiser, and Janet Zepernick

Educating the New Southern Woman: Speech, Writing, and Race at the Public Women's Colleges, 1884–1945
David Gold and Catherine L. Hobbs

Women's Irony: Rewriting Feminist Rhetorical Histories
Tarez Samra Graban

The Rhetoric of Rebel Women: Civil War Diaries and Confederate Persuasion
Kimberly Harrison

Evolutionary Rhetoric: Sex, Science, and Free Love in Nineteenth-Century Feminism
Wendy Hayden

Liberating Voices: Writing at the Bryn Mawr Summer School for Women Workers
Karyn L. Hollis

Gender and Rhetorical Space in American Life, 1866–1910
Nan Johnson

Appropriate[ing] Dress: Women's Rhetorical Style in Nineteenth-Century America
Carol Mattingly

The Gendered Pulpit: Preaching in American Protestant Spaces
Roxanne Mountford

Writing Childbirth: Women's Rhetorical Agency in Labor and Online
Kim Hensley Owens

Rhetorical Listening: Identification, Gender, Whiteness
Krista Ratcliffe

Feminist Rhetorical Practices: New Horizons for Rhetoric, Composition, and Literacy Studies
Jacqueline J. Royster and Gesa E. Kirsch

Vote and Voice: Women's Organizations and Political Literacy, 1915–1930
Wendy B. Sharer

Women Physicians and Professional Ethos in Nineteenth-Century America
Carolyn Skinner

Praising Girls: The Rhetoric of Young Women, 1895–1930
Henrietta Rix Wood